Fieldwork in Social Work

Fieldwork in Social Work

Sanjoy Roy

RAWAT PUBLICATIONS
Jaipur • New Delhi • Bangalore • Guwahati • Kolkata

ISBN 978-81-316-0528-8

Reprinted, 2019

Published by
Prem Rawat for **Rawat Publications**
Satyam Apts, Sector 3, Jawahar Nagar, Jaipur 302 004 (India)
Phone: 0141 265 1748 / 7006 Fax: 0141 265 1748
E-mail: info@rawatbooks.com
Website: www.rawatbooks.com

New Delhi Office
4858/24, Ansari Road, Daryaganj, New Delhi 110 002
Phone: 011 2326 3290

Also at *Bangalore, Guwahati* and *Kolkata*

Typeset by Rawat Computers, Jaipur
Printed and bound in India.

To all the social work students,
practitioners and educators

Contents

Foreword

To become a truly effective and capable social worker, it is essential, whilst a student, to have direct, guided practical experience and fieldwork practice, of 'doing social work' with real people. Whilst at a global level the form and shape of social work varies from country to country, region to region, city to city, this requirement for direct practice remains a constant. Yet, the approach to providing this experience of practice is as varied as are the forms of social work practice. Whatever the context, to provide good social work field education, we must first understand how it is provided and the educational and philosophical principles that underscore delivery. Only then is it possible to move beyond understanding current provision to creative innovation and the achievement of excellence. This book, *Fieldwork in Social Work*, written by Sanjoy Roy, provides a detailed account of fieldwork education as it is currently found in India. This is a bold and informative account that takes us beyond description of the current state of Indian field education to consider possibilities and futures. Given the size of India's population and the challenges faced by a large proportion of the population, in their daily life, to deal with problems associated with poverty, the future agenda for social work, as a profession in India, is considerable. Those entering social work deserve the best possible education, and as a part of that the best possible field education; this book will assist social work students and educators to meet these challenges.

This book is an extremely valuable addition to the growing literature on the subject of fieldwork practice and provides a wealth of information as well as valuable insights for students, academicians, research scholars, practitioners and the new entrants to the discipline of social work. It deserves a wide audience both within India and also in the global social work community.

Steven M. Shardlow, Ph.D
Chair of Social Work, The University of Salford, UK

Preface

Professional training of social work education has drawn interest all over India today. In the beginning, the training in social work started in labour welfare and correctional administration and later on, it has covered many other fields of social work like family, child, youth, rural and urban community development, medical and psychiatric, industry, etc. Similarly, in the beginning, professional training was introduced as generic training but in due course, different specializations like urban and rural community development, family and child welfare, medical and psychiatric social work, personnel management and industrial relation, criminology and correctional administration, etc., developed. At present, different schools of social work are providing both the generic and specialized training in view of the present situations and the regional requirements in each state. But, it is unfortunate that after 74 years of existence of professional training of social work in India, neither generic nor specialized method earned professional recognition and could not generate professional values as is expected in the globalized arena of professional service.

Fieldwork being the core and backbone of social work education, unfortunately professionally trained persons or educators seem to have failed to imbibe it fully in order to reach the core of fieldwork training. Actually, sufficient and focused efforts have not been made by the concerned to develop it based on the emerging needs and requirements of the community as well as our society. Still, we are focusing on community organization (rather than community work) or group work (rather than group activities) depending on the foreign literature and scholars like Mary Richmond, Konopka, M.G. Ross, etc. Still, our concerned theoreticians and practitioners are not able to produce good amount of practical literature on fieldwork. There is no single textbook on fieldwork in India from where students could consult about its different dimensions. So, they are confused or rather unable to understand how to use the social work values, techniques, methods in a proper manner. As a result, they are unable to solve the emerging social problems effectively in this fast changing and globalized society.

Some researchers, however, took initiatives to study fieldwork in different universities and colleges, and they have also put forth valuable suggestions and recommendations for its improvement, but fruitful and realistic changes have not taken place yet.

Fieldwork blends theory with practice, combines philosophy with action, and integrates the understanding about people with methods of helping them. It is functional and technical in nature and fosters learning to students. It is an integrated approach, which goes concurrently with the classroom teaching process. It gives an opportunity to students to apply the classroom teaching in the field. The significance of fieldwork in social work is very much consequential because of its nature of dealing with social problems practically. Fieldwork becomes important when proper supervision is made and only then the quality comes. Students are helped through this process to work on a complex, intricate and composite social phenomenon. So, it is said that "theory without practice is empty and practice without theory is meaningless".

Fieldwork in most of the universities consists of two phases: (1) orientation and observation visit, and (2) concurrent fieldwork. Also, there are other methods of fieldwork practice such as supportive field instruction, skill development workshop, rural camp, education/study tour, research project, summer/winter placement, block placement, etc. Though, all these methods are not imparted systematically and scientifically because of lack of infrastructural facilities, non-availability of trained personnel, needed literature, proper funds, areas of fieldwork, etc. Now, social work needs to take care of the emerging areas, issues and problems such as human rights violations, disability, female infanticide, weakening family ties, disaster management, displacement, eco-tourism, civil society organizations, participatory research, prostitution and child abuse, land mafia and land distribution system, industrialization, urbanization, child marriage, dowry system and divorce, juvenile delinquency, NGO management, problems of working women, wildlife studies and waste management, drug addiction, old-age problems and support system, extinction of rare species, etc.

Also, the overwhelming responsibilities are kept in the thinking and imagination of the mind of the educators, professionals, practitioners and social work associations to develop techniques, methods and indigenous literature according to our own societal problems in the new emerging scenario.

This book is the outcome of my research study as well as experiences gained in teaching and as a fieldwork supervisor in departments of social work in different universities in India like Delhi School of Social Work, Delhi University, CSJM University, Kanpur and Assam University, Silchar. It has seven chapters in all.

Chapter One introduces the study mainly by focusing on the world-view of social work education, concept of fieldwork, social work practicum, manual for self-study of social work institutions by National Assessment and Accreditation Council, UGC relating to curricular aspects of fieldwork practicum, concept of development fieldwork, present status of fieldwork, professional associations of social work education and the milestones of social work journals in India and UGC committees on social work education.

Chapter Two deals with research methodology and review of literature in the historical perspectives of fieldwork and then review of articles and studies from different social work journals.

Chapter Three discusses social work and its emerging perspectives which includes definition of social work, international definition of social work, social work theories, objectives, social work practice, history and development of social work in UK, USA and India, philosophy of social work, values of social work, social work as a profession, principles and skills of social work.

Chapter Four examines domain of fieldwork in social work education in India, focusing on domain of social worker, methods of practice, paradigm of the profession, fieldwork practice, orientation programme, agency visit, fieldwork placement of the students, agency responses to social work practicum, cooperation with the agency by the department, supervision, individual conferences and group conferences, mid-term sharing, recording, fieldwork reports, evaluation, supportive fieldwork instructions, skill development workshop, camp and study tour, summer and winter placement and block fieldwork.

Chapter Five discusses of issues addressed, programmes and assignments undertaken by the students in the community as well as in the agency during fieldwork and its outcomes.

Chapter Six concerns with the fieldwork and its emerging trends today, focusing on the existing pattern of fieldwork with new requirements of the present scenario for the social work professionals.

Chapter Seven is about social work in the 21st century, and conclusion pertaining to findings, suggestions and recommendations.

In preparing the book, I am grateful to a large number of people who generously helped me in all aspects. First of all, I sincerely and deeply acknowledge my indebtedness to A.N. Singh, Department of Social Work, University of Lucknow, for his kind and relentless guidance, encouragement, support and inspiration throughout the course of my research study in accomplishing it successfully.

I owe a deep sense of gratitude to my family who has been the source of inspiration and motivation to complete my study.

Thanks are due also to the various schools of social work in India for their permission for data collection and also providing valuable information from time to time for my research.

In no small measure, I am thankful to my colleagues and other eulogistic personalities in India especially Asok Sarkar, Department of Social Work, Visva Bharati; B.S. Gunjal, Reader, Department of Social Work, Karnataka State Women's University; S.Y. Siddegowa, Department of Social Work, University of Mysore; Sushma Batra, Department of Social Work, University of Delhi; Sanjai Bhatt, Department of Social Work, University of Delhi; S.V. Sudhakar, Vice Chancellor, B.R. Ambedkar University, Visakhapatnam; K.S. Mali Patil, Chairman, Department of Social Work, Gulbarga University; V. Venkathwralu, Department of Sociology and Social Work, Acharya Nagarjuna University; Prasanta Ghosh, Reader, Department of Social Work, Visva Bharati University and Ashvini Kumar Singh, Department of Social Work, Jamia Milia Islamia, for their invaluable assistance and help.

I am grateful to all my respondents without whose positive response and cooperation it would not have been possible for me to complete the hard task.

I am also thankful to Steven M. Shardlow, Chair of Social Work, The University of Salford, UK for writing a concise but inspiring foreword to my book, thus, making it a valuable manuscript.

In the end, last but not the least, I owe my gratitude to my parents, who in spite of all the taxing time, pressurized me to complete this work. Thanking them would be a bit harsh. In fact, without their constant inspiration, this work would have never seen the light of the day.

Sanjoy Roy

List of Tables and Figures

Tables

Figures

List of Abbreviations

ASIHSS	:	Assistance for Strengthening Infrastructure in Humanities and Social Sciences
ASSWI	:	Association of Schools of Social Work in India
BHU	:	Banaras Hindu University
BSW	:	Bachelor of Social Work
CCA	:	Criminology and Correctional Administration
CCDCM	:	Certificate Course in Disaster and Crisis Management
CGC	:	Child Guidance Centre
CCLD	:	Certificate Course in Leadership Development
CSWB	:	Central Social Welfare Board
DRDA	:	District Rural Development Agency
FCW	:	Family and Child Welfare
FW	:	Fieldwork
FWS	:	Fieldwork Supervisor
GC	:	Group Conference
HIV/AIDS	:	Human Immunodeficiency Virus/Acquired Immunodeficiency Syndrome
IATSW	:	Indian Association of Trained Social Workers
IC	:	Individual Conference
IRPM	:	Industrial Relation and Personal Management
MA	:	Master of Arts

M.Phil	:	Master of Philosophy
MSW	:	Master of Social Work
NAAC	:	National Assessment and Accreditation Council
NAPSWI	:	National Association of Professional Social Workers in India
NGO	:	Non-Government Organization
NRHM	:	National Rural Health Mission
NSS	:	National Service Scheme
OD	:	Operational Definition
PASW	:	Professional Association of Social Work
PGDHR	:	Post Graduate Diploma in Human Rights
PhD	:	Doctorate of Philosophy
PMRY	:	Prime Minister Rozgar Yojna
PRA	:	Participatory Rural Appraisal
PM	:	Practice Model
RCH	:	Reproductive and Child Health
SFI	:	Supportive Field Instruction Programme
SHG	:	Self Help Group
SW	:	Social Work
SWE	:	Social Work Education
TISS	:	Tata Institute of Social Sciences
TORC	:	Training, Orientation and Research Centre
TSSW	:	Trained Setter of Social Work
TSW	:	Trained Social Worker
UGC	:	University Grants Commission
UNDP	:	United Nations Development Programme
UNICEF	:	United Nations International Children's Emergency Fund
URCD	:	Urban and Rural Community Development
VCTC	:	Voluntary Counselling and Testing Centre
YMCA	:	Young Men's Christian Association
YWCA	:	Young Women's Christian Association

1 Introduction

"Education is not for knowing more but for behaving differently", John Ruskin said this in the general context of education, but this applies more to helping professions, particularly the social work profession.

Social work is a practice profession, hence, the context includes the vital component of practice learning opportunities. Practical training in the field forms an integral part of the total training programme. An educational programme is incomplete without guided practical learning. "Learning by doing" is the principle from which has developed the body of knowledge, specialized skills and the philosophy of professional work. Practical experience in social work teaching is offered through the method of fieldwork.

The social work practice is closely associated with the social, political, economic and cultural fabric of communities. Fieldwork carries different connotations in social sciences and in social work. In social sciences, it refers to observations of people in situations whereas, in social work it is concerned with changing people, situations or both and it is carried out in and through social welfare agencies and communities where the students learn skills and test out knowledge according to an educational plan. Fieldwork implies both training and education for the different levels of students.

World-view of Social Work Education and Training

Basically, the world in terms of social work education is divided into two parts: northern and southern. While the northern part consists of USA, UK, and other European countries, the southern part consists of

Asian, South-East Asian and Middle East countries, i.e., Third World countries. It was the social crisis in Western Europe and North America in the 18th and 19th centuries, which led to the creation of social work as an institution as well as a profession. Social work, thus, emerged as a response to this crisis, which is also referred to as 'Industrial Revolution'. Rapid industrialization and urbanization transformed the lives of all people – rich and poor alike. Social problems that had been dispersed and largely invisible in the countryside, such as poverty and overcrowding, poor housing, ill-health and disease, alcohol and drug abuse, prostitution, unsupervised children, etc., were also commonplace in the new towns and cities. Working class freedom and social deprivation spelt danger to the middle-class city dwellers who clamoured for something to be done to contain the threat from the 'dangerous classes'. A vast array of state social welfare initiatives have their origins in the 19th century. Schemes for public sanitation, education, policing, prisons, juvenile correction, public workhouses and mental asylums accompanied legislations governing working conditions and factory inspection as well as new mechanisms for recording population change. At the same time, the 19th century saw the creation and development of a wide spectrum of social work activity financed and run by philanthropic agencies, but working alongside statutory agencies such as courts, hospitals and workhouses. The Second World War had stricken much destruction, and peace and harmony in the Third World countries was in question. As a result, the UN came to the rescue and sent social work consultants from West to Third World countries to provide all kinds of support. They met different ministries, public and private sector functionaries and NGOs working in these countries. They concluded after having complete observation, that Third World countries need 'Trained Social Worker' (TSW) to control and prevent the ongoing situation. So, immediately two systems were developed for training: one was to call experts from western countries and another was to send persons from Third World countries to the western countries for training. So, the theories, knowledge and models of the West were developed and started applying in the Third World countries. But, the socio-economic and cultural milieu and indigenous aspects of Third World countries do not fit those of the West. As a result, intellectual movements started throughout the Asian, South-East Asian and Middle East countries against western models. Professionals then started for indigenization of profession, which means developing own theories, models and knowledge based on local professional standards to solve their own problems. Movement also started in the Middle East, especially in Tanzania, South Arabia, Morocco, Sudan, Tunisia and Egypt. Egypt was the pioneer country as 'Trained Setter of Social Work' (TSSW) among Arabian countries. The movement even reached Japan, South Africa, Botswana, etc. The Middle East countries also started Islamization (means use of Islamic value and theology through social work for the betterment of the society) of social sciences. As social work is the part of social sciences, it should therefore be given priority for development.

The new existing pattern of social work education in India as a profession is also influenced by the western pattern/model, as more than six decades ago, when the country had a different scenario of social, economic and political life, the profession grew in that atmosphere following the design of Western and European countries. No doubt, today's world is different and social problems are not alike. As stated earlier, the social work practice is closely associated with the social, political, economic and cultural fabric of communities/societies. Of this, social realities of this country are different. There is no uniformity in social systems and social structures. And to face all these realities and problems, the social work profession has to entirely evolve its own framework, particularly of practice or fieldwork. But on which aspect or approach it should work in India is very crucial, as much of its knowledge is 'borrowed knowledge'. But, at the same time, when the country is attacked by the flawless social problems like in other developed countries, to understand and apply that very knowledge is also important with some modifications according to the social culture and resources.

Emphasizing the importance of the social work profession, Friedlander (1964) stated the following criteria, which are needed in the clinical practice of social work as in any other profession like medicine/teaching, etc. To him, this profession has a core of ethics and values and based on following criteria:

1. Special competence acquired through intellectual training, which develops skills and requires the use of independent, responsible judgment, not merely mechanical skills.

2. Distinct techniques capable of communication through orderly and specialized educational discipline, with application of knowledge and skills based upon academic learning.
3. Practitioners who are conscious of common bonds and organized as a professional association for the promotion of high standards and of common interests.
4. The professional association has concern for the development of standards of service for the profession as a whole as expressed by a code of ethics, provision for specialized education, and the use of specialized knowledge and skills in order to apply them in public interest.
5. A professional person has a sense of personal responsibility and accountability to others in the same field for the kind of standards he sets for himself.[1]

Truly and sensibly, work experience is an integral part of any profession or curriculum. No professional education can be considered complete unless it is closely related with the learning in the field through practice. Social work as a profession is directly associated with the people.

It is widely accepted that "action speaks louder than words". As social work directly deals with persons in difficulties, action-oriented approach is needed with working knowledge and practical understanding of the profession. To put working knowledge efficiently and adequately in the field practice, the social work has to understand the theoretical skills of the social work which are the ingredients of professional self. This would help the social worker to utilize and integrate the theory into practice so that he/she can establish his/her operational practice on the basis of knowledge, attitude and skills learnt in the theory. It is also true that now very concise, effective practice will help the profession to accept the challenges resulting from the New Economic Policy and LPG (liberalization, privatization and globalization). According to Karger (1994), "As the effect of the global economy have led to increased social dislocation, especially in the secondary labour market, social workers are finding it difficult to reach clients, while at the same time having lesser resources. Hence, the challenge for social worker has been two-pronged: to develop new cost-effective interventions, capable of reaching difficult and multi-problem clients, and resisting politically and professionally, the attrition of human services".[2]

The concurrent fieldwork practice or training is an important part of social work curriculum in India accepting and internalizing the emerging areas and problems and has organized in such a way that the student learns the theory and its application simultaneously. This helps the student to assimilate prerequisite theory and the consistent application of its practice. It also deepens the critical faculties of the student and his/her practical competence in offering social work help. The student is enabled to develop his/her understanding about the client, his/her problem and process to solve it. Concurrent fieldwork also helps the student to know about the statue, structure, functions, programmes and process of the agency, where he/she is placed to learn and provide help.

The student learns and recognizes the necessity of mastering technical skills and attitudes to achieve the broader goals of social work with the perspective of the course content covered in the classroom. This learning by doing with the feedback of theory, though makes the student to put more concentrated efforts into practice, it sometimes creates confusion, as there are no specific guidelines or course outlines in fieldwork. But all schools have framed guidelines of this practice based on the aims of imparting social work education, which according to R.R. Singh (1985) are:

1. to impart professional training to suitable candidates in social work;
2. to develop and disseminate knowledge in regard to welfare problems and services with a view to bringing about improvement in and expansions of these services;
3. to promote close collaboration among different disciplines for a better understanding of human problems; and
4. to ensure better integration between scientific knowledge and practice in the field of social welfare.

It is a fact that even after seven decades of the creation of the first school of social work with paving a way to open more than 200 schools at present, the western model of fieldwork practice did not work here. Actually, our country does have different kinds of problems in the society like illiteracy, obsolete traditions, caste and class-ridden social milieu, poverty, malnutrition, diseases, etc. The students of social work find difficulties if they apply the western model of fieldwork, in its rigid form, in the agency or community dealing with the problems of individuals, groups and communities in local conditions.

According to the UGC Second Review Committee, in India, focus is more on the practice-setting than on methods. Our curricula are derived from the residual/remedial/rehabilitative model of practice as they are largely borrowed from the West, mainly the USA. Illustrative of this situation is that a majority of our curricula show emphasis on social and individual problems of pathology rather than problems of the individual and society in the context of poverty and development. Similarly, the curricula are more urban than rural, derived as they are from a western technologically-oriented society. They are largely adopted at the master's degree level when the need of the country is large number of low level workers.[3]

Concept of Fieldwork

Fieldwork, as is generally understood, is a way to translate knowledge through certain skills and techniques into action. Fieldwork is probably as old as history itself. Probably a primitive learner, a caveman had also to learn how to hunt in fieldwork situation. 'Learning by doing' has thus been the source of human acquisition, which finds a ready support in the ideologies of Rousseau and Pestolozzi. The concept of fieldwork, given by M.N. Srinivas (1979), is quite comprehensive and clear, according to which it is an educationally planned and professionally guided programme of interaction of a student with the real situation experienced through welfare, institutional, multi-organizations and people-based system in order to help him, perceive and understand appropriate existing human conditions and work to bring about designed improvement and change in them.

The term 'fieldwork' may be stretched to describe both experience and also advanced training in the use of knowledge, attitude, understanding the situation and refinement of skills. *The Dictionary of Sociology and Related Sciences* defines fieldwork as "social survey or process of collecting primary data from a population distributed geographically". In sociological context it is quite true but fieldwork in social work education is quite different.

Fieldwork is any kind of practical experience in a social organization or agency and community if this experience has been deliberately arranged for the education of students who are undertaking courses partly or wholly designed for those who intend to become social workers.

Social work, being goal-oriented professional education, aims at helping students to acquire deep knowledge of the theory and the technical skills for achieving social work objectives. When we used to talk of fieldwork in social work, we basically mean 'supervised fieldwork' that implies a method by which a social worker, in the beginning, learns how to translate his/her knowledge into practice. This beginning stage later on becomes a habit of the learner as soon as he/she acquires skills and techniques in the work situation. Fieldwork in social work education is a guided interaction process between a student and the actual and practical life situation in which social work as a profession has an abiding and deep concern, and which needed to be remedied, improved or changed for a fuller and complete development of human-environmental potential.

"Fieldwork in social work is carried out through social welfare agencies and communities, where the student learns skills and tests out knowledge according to an educational plan. The whole programme is student and field specific. Fieldwork training is supervised practice of social work under the guidance of a trained social work educator, or field personnel. It has been defined as an educationally sponsored attachment of social work students to an institution, agency or a section of community, in which they are helped to extend their knowledge and understanding, and experience the impact of human needs. Such an experience is deliberately arranged on a whole or part-time basis."[4]

Fieldwork, thus, implies both training and education. The distinction between the two is that while training is repetitive and skill-oriented, education is more broad-based, and it is imparted with a perspective. It consists of knowledge of different situations and is a creative, innovative and a dynamic process. It fosters development of intellectual and emotional processes and attitude.

Fieldwork training started as field instruction with apprenticeship in social agencies. The tasks given then were similar to the craftsman's task and there was a dichotomy between administrative and non-administrative skills.

Fieldwork training could be well-considered learning through doing. Dewey's idea of learning through doing has had a primary influence in the concept of fieldwork. Fieldwork is an integrating factor and acts as a balancing force between the theory and practice. It has a great significance in the training programme of social work education. It blends theory with practice, facilitates fusion of thinking with doing, combines philosophy with action, and integrates understanding about people and methods of helping them. Its techniques draw heavily on scientific knowledge about people and social phenomena. It is functional in nature and technical in process. It involves an educational process that fosters learning in students. It is an integrated approach that goes concurrently with the classroom instructions.

Fieldwork programme provides opportunities to the learner to apply his/her theoretical knowledge taught in the classroom appropriately in different practical situations. It could serve as a kind of social laboratory where the students are taught to test their theoretical knowledge and skills against practical situations of social living.

M.S. Gore (1981) has stated that "if the practical experience is to be an integral part of the educational programme, then there must be clarity connecting what the student is to learn in it. The setting up of objectives for classroom teaching has long been accepted as a basic step in curriculum building. Equal attention must now be given to a classification of the objectives and the content of the practical experience for the student at various stages in his training. In other words, we must spell out for the students, agency and the school the knowledge and the skill which students will be expected to acquire in the field".

The assumption that social work students receive sufficient training to achieve minimal levels of competence is dubious at best. Data continue to accumulate regarding the ineffectiveness of social work practice and other traditional forms of interpersonal helping. Currently, the data that document the acquisition of various interpersonal skills through social work is far from established (Siddiqui, 1987). The quest for achieving the desired 'professional competence' should inevitably commence from arriving at an operational definition of social work. This requires identifying the task of social work and its boundaries of practice.

The report on "Curriculum Development" submitted to the University Grants Commission by the Tata Institute of Social Sciences (1988) has also mentioned undernutrition, malnutrition, ill-health, deteriorating ecological environment, inaccessibility to opportunities, social conflict, poverty, bad housing, etc., as major problems, which ought to engage the attention of professional social workers in India. The report pleads for change in retarding institutional structures, and stresses the need to develop knowledge and skills which enhance the potential of people for their own development. In this connection, the report lists out developmental, promotive, remedial and rehabilitative tasks for professional social workers. The report recommends that fieldwork practicum in the schools of social work should provide opportunities to develop and enhance variety of skills, including analysis of social realities and participation through social intervention.[5]

Thus, problems of poverty, food supply, nutrition, population growth and environmental degradation in developing countries call for a commitment to a need-oriented, self-reliant, environmentally-sound and peaceful socio-economic process and harnessing of energy to meet the basic needs of target groups.[6]

Now, the question arises as to whether these old and new realities are adequately reflected in the curricula of the schools of social work, and methods of teaching including their fieldwork programmes. If not, how can they be incorporated and educational experiences could be provided to students in these areas of social concern? These questions transcend the boundaries of the generic and specialization programme in social work and call for the adoption of an integrated approach on the part of educators, in order to adequately respond to the complex social realities, discharging their social as well as professional obligations.

All the schools of social work use institutions and communities for providing fieldwork experiences to students both at the undergraduate and postgraduate levels. Open community placements, with or without any agency-based programmes (and with micro-action groups), were started by a few schools in the mid-1960s. These were followed by others in the eighties. The range of fieldwork placements has varied from a unit, institution, area, target group, social or environmental policy issue to micro-action groups and legislative work. All these varieties of placements however have not been utilized by most of the schools of social work. While the courses have included social development aspects to an extent, the pattern of fieldwork has remained traditional, and in some cases confined merely to sporadic visits. Even, the traditional approach has not been followed rationally and systematically in terms of the selection of suitable cases or situations, exploration and partialization of problems, appreciation of dynamics, and initiation of action on the basis of proper assessment, followed by the evaluation of its impact as well as of the educational experience in this process. This has happened because any useful reported activity in the area of placement has been regarded as fieldwork by some without any regards for its orientation, approach, and application of knowledge and skills. It is also worthy of note that while the contents of fieldwork or assignments have been worked out, reading lists have not been provided. They are neither insisted upon nor supplied at different stages of field learning. It has perhaps been assumed that students will automatically apply theoretical knowledge imparted in the classroom. *The Report of Social Work Education in India* (1988) has provided some reading lists, but more need to be done in this regard and it has been suggested that the first-year postgraduate students would gain experiences by working with the victims of circumstances (i.e., migrant workers, street children, etc.) and the second-year students would work with victims of the self (i.e., drug addicts, cases of family discord, etc.). This model assumes that the second year work assignments would be more complex than the first year. Since the theory courses would not always conform to the demands of the field, and there would always arise the necessity for teaching by the supervisor, the option of community or agency placement, work with the victims of self or the circumstances with a developmental focus (which includes curative, preventive and promotive aspects) and even the matters of ecology, policy, law, social welfare and alliance with micro-action groups, during the same year or alternately should be kept open by the schools. Field assignments in one or more areas mentioned above could be structured on the basis of progression in a student's learning, and also in response to an emergent problem or social initiative in the region where a school is located. Identification of assignment-related reading materials at different phases of fieldwork should however be made as much a requirement as they are for theory courses. This will make supervision more focused and meaningful, and provide more occasions for reflection (and reflective action) both by the supervisor and the supervisee.

In the beginning, schools that came into existence under the auspices of Christian missions were preceded by years of practical experience. Later, though the schools and colleges were set up by the predecessors but did not have direction or traditional practices.

Further, the sub-committee of Second Review Committee appointed to draw up course contents on fieldwork did not provide adequate guidelines. Mainly it left to the professional associations and schools of social work to give thought on it. However, the Review Committee on Social Work Education has emphasized on providing following aspects of students learning in fieldwork:

1. understand the relation of knowledge, value and skills;
2. understanding to develop self-awareness and self-discipline in professional relations;
3. ability to work knowingly and effectively with agency structure, function and philosophy;
4. knowledge of multiple positive factors in behaviours to acquire skills in use of professional knowledge;
5. system of effective use of community, state and national resources;
6. capacity of social work practice with professional compliance;
7. understanding the use of social action and capacity of leadership;
8. to become professional workers; and
9. compliance in systematic study, assessment and treatment in different fields of social intervention.

In fact, these guidelines did not provide adequate opportunities to train students within the available resources to make them competent workers for addressing emerging social issues. Therefore, the matter of fieldwork became an issue of more conferences and seminars held from time to time. But, we have not yet arrived at a clear-cut conclusion as to know whether we should impart our students training based on emerging specialized branches of knowledge or the knowledge based on generic fields of social work.

Because of this, due to day-to-day emerging demand in a new perspective of our intervention, some more schools of social work by and large have developed their own kind of fieldwork training programme based on the quality of educational resources and fieldwork opportunity available with them.

We know that the first fieldwork programme at the school of social work in India was evolved through pioneering and exploration and in response to the need as perceived by the professional elite of the time. For about two decades since then, the main pattern of fieldwork practice followed by the school was the learning of basic social work methods, i.e., care work, group work, community organization and in the area of child, women, old age, etc., the social work skills are applied.

Objectives of Fieldwork in Social Work Education

Today, fieldwork is recognized as a major and vital component in professional social work education because of its implications for professional practice.

Social work, being goal-oriented and intervention-oriented professional education, aims at helping social work trainees to acquire and internalize deep knowledge of the theory and techniques for achieving social work objectives. The social work trainee has to learn every practical aspect during his/her two years of postgraduate training programme. Further, they have to acquire an understanding of the principles, concepts, policies and processes, which constitute the profession of social work. Through the fieldwork programme social work trainee is prepared to be a competent professional social worker. The main objective of fieldwork in social work education is to provide the opportunities to the students to learn and practise the professional skills in the field that are taught in the class. A trainee social worker while in the field tries to interpret and diagnose the situation in the background of the knowledge and understanding and thus helps adjustment to the situations. Thus, fieldwork aims at developing the students' capacities and capabilities as a realistic worker. Direct contract and touch with the people helps students acquire knowledge about people and their problems by providing them with emotional maturity, power of judgment and stability in action.

The Second Review Committee on Social Work Education (1980) has mentioned the following objectives of fieldwork:

1. development of professional skills through learning to use knowledge for the study and analysis of problems and selection of appropriate means to solve them;
2. development of skills in problem-solving at the macro and micro levels;
3. integration of classroom learning with field practice;
4. development of skills required for professional practice at the particular level of training;
5. development of professional attitude, values and commitment; and
6. development of self-awareness and professional ideal.

The Delhi School of Social Work, University of Delhi organized a Faculty Development Workshop on Fieldwork in 1981. The major objectives of the workshop were:

1. to offer purposeful learning experience to the student through interaction with life situations under supervisory guidance for professional growth in terms of knowledge skills and attitude;
2. to foster attitudes in the student towards professional self-development, increasing self-awareness, appreciation of both capacities and limitations;
3. to develop in the student the required skills in helping the needy through organizational work, use of social work methods, that is, listening, participation, communication and so on; and
4. to enable the student to develop and deepen capacity to relate theory to practice, and to relate experience to theory.

The objectives of fieldwork training in social work education ultimately deepened upon the educational and service objectives of social work. These are related to the areas of knowledge, skills, attitudes, perspectives, and action within a dynamic theoretical framework. Thus, according to the workshops, the objectives of fieldwork training in social work education could be summarized as follows:

1. Acquisition of knowledge and understanding through educationally planned exposure to and experience in real-life situations

with reference to welfare and development needs, problems and resources at the macro and micro levels.

2. Acquisition of knowledge of process-oriented approach and selective use of integrated methods of social intervention to solve human problems, to effect changes in policy, and to undertake preventive, remedial and developmental tasks through institutional, multi-organizational and people-based systems.
3. Acquisition of professional action (practice) skills through field learning in problem-solving study, analysis, assessment, action reflection and organization of macro and micro levels.
4. Development of self-awareness, social and professional consciousness, leadership, values, commitment and a perspective to intervene in human situations of need as interdisciplinary group, and to develop skills of critical evaluation of own actions and systematic process.
5. Planning, organization and initiation of such action strategies through individuals, institutions and collectivities, which are designed to effect change in the existing conditions of the clientele group, or human populations, or in the method of service delivery.
6. Examination of the relationship of theory with practice and conceptualization of practical experience to build or modify social theory.

In a nutshell, main objectives of fieldwork are as follows:

(i) Develop professional skills through learning how to utilize the knowledge for the study of the relevant fact, the analysis of problem and selection of the appropriate means of problem-solving.
(ii) Develop skills for problem-solving in work at the micro level (individual, family, small group, community etc.) and change at the macro level in social institutions and processes.
(iii) Provide concurrent opportunity for the integration of classroom learning with the field practice and vice versa.
(iv) Develop skills required for professional practice at the particular level of training.
(v) Develop professional attitude involving impartiality, non-judgmental attitudes, objectively.
(vi) Develop professional values and commitments, such as respect for human dignity and worth, and the right to participation and self-determination compatible with the good of society.

(vii) Develop awareness of self and the ways in which psychological and cultural factors affect the perceptions and responses to others.

(viii) Develop the professional ideal.

Social work education at the master's degree level should be comprised of the classroom teaching having the core domain of social work profession: theory and practice, supportive domain of human growth, environment and socio-political bases, interdisciplinary domain and elective domain as suggested in the UGC Model Curriculum (UGC, 2001).

According to the Second Review Committee (1980), in India, there is more stress on the practice setting than on methods. In practical also, fieldwork helps students to assimilate theory and the consistent application of its practice. This way students are able to develop their understanding about the client, the problem and process to solve it. Concurrent fieldwork also helps students to know about the status, structure, functions, programmes, process of the agency where they are placed. The students learn and recognize the necessity of mastering technical skills and attitude to achieve the broader goals of social work with the perspective of the course content covered in the classroom. This learning by doing with the feedback of theory, though makes students to give more concentrated efforts into practice, but the content of fieldwork at different levels and in different fields should be determined in accordance with the goals of social work education and of fieldwork as identified by the schools.

Fieldwork Contents in Social Work Education

Social work is completely a practice profession. The educational programme is incomplete if guided practice learning/training inputs are not provided properly. The practice contents make up about 40 per cent of the total marks (though they vary from school to school). It is accepted that the career in this profession relates to a wide and complex range of human situations, calling for a versatile practice perspective and skill-based competencies. A student learner should have equal opportunity to practise and learn social work as profession, values and ethics theories and knowledge for understanding situations, problems and concerns of individuals, groups and communities, and to develop personal and professional competence through practice paradigm. Many social work institutions have yet to come out from "study diagnosis treatment module" and understand harsh realities of life and living.

Only in select institutions, students enjoy opportunity to practise beyond methods-based fieldwork learning, where they learn integrated approach to fieldwork practice. Therefore, we may provide opportunity to students to integrate supportive methods (social work research, social welfare administration, and social action) more in practice, and new correlates of social justice and human rights in practice context. R.R. Singh (1985) has aptly remarked that the unchanging pattern of fieldwork is another marked weakness of social work education in the country. Its pattern varies from one institution to another and no school seems to have tried to explicitly develop its content in relation to the goals of social work education and practice in the country. Quite a few schools have worked out contents semester-wise, method-wise and agency-wise or field-wise. He mentioned that most of the schools have not worked out contents of fieldwork and whatever the contents such schools follow are characterized by variations and ambiguities.

Contents of fieldwork are organized around theoretical and applied information resulting in knowledge, skills and values related to social work with individuals and families, groups, communities or in administration, and also bring about changes when required in the contents. New trend will appear at a time when all social workers will need to be able to view the full interventive repertoire of the profession and to understand how the various interventive actions are combined and used in practice, which means that all social workers will be aware of the full range of interventive measures encompassed by their profession, not as skills to be learned but as ways of offering help, influencing situations, and bringing about social change and take it with their own planning and action.[7]

But, as observed by Charles Guzzetta (1984), "Sometimes specific corners of the curriculum in many programmes give an appearance of innovation or major change. However, a view of the whole tapestry reveals the existence of a rather traditional and common pattern in graduate social work education in the United States."[8]

In India also, many seminars and workshops have been held from time to time on fieldwork contents where the professional social workers and educators have desired to make fieldwork more Indianized because the political, social, economic and cultural factors have now changed in our country and there is need that the students of social work should understand and apply the theoretical framework of social work in the context of Indian culture and situation. Ironically, the required changes are still awaited in the fieldwork as no significant change has been made in the contents of social work and very few schools have initiated new methods and strategies in the contents of both social work theory and fieldwork. The professional growth and development of the students is based on the learning contents for the fieldwork practice. The school has the responsibility of providing the required facilities to the students where they can understand the contents of social work and utilize them properly in the field practice.

In theory, where the models or phases of social work are taught in the classroom, all these need to be applied in the field agency. For this:

1. The school helps the student in understanding the nature of agency which is also referred to as educationally sponsored placement. The student is to understand the nature, aims and objectives, administrative structure, services, functioning and procedures of the agency where he/she is placed for the fieldwork term.
2. Through the effective contents, the student will be able to recognize individual's or group's needs in relation to the services of the agency and when these are met, he/she will be able to deny the request fairly comfortably. The student has to be trained to use termination skills where he/she would learn to deal with fighting, anger, taking shock, learning, sharing feelings with other members of the agency staff.
3. The fieldwork contents provide clear understanding to the student of his/her role in the agency where he/she would be able to work in cooperation with other members of the agency and learn importance of work discipline. He/she would also learns the sources of funding, methods of hiring personnel and becomes able to follow procedural routine, etc.
4. In the fieldwork, a student is provided an opportunity of using the philosophy of social work, which is based on the professional values, beliefs, ethics, etc. He/she also needs to incorporate the principles of self-determination, confidentiality, appropriate emotional involvement, and acceptance of different faiths in the fieldwork contents. The student thus becomes a professional worker with mature thinking, and his/her tolerance capacity also increases. He/she learns how to have realistic planning and can organize assigned work and increase his/her independence from supervisor. For the professional growth, the contents should help the student to develop his/her awareness and can work with limitations while adopting professional role skills in assertion.

5. As Barbara stated, "a social worker was regarded as someone employed at the 'consumer end' of a social service, who is in personal contact with those using it and who is able to appreciate them in their family and social background". There is need that fieldwork should emphasize the content of conviction in the principles of social work and the extent to which these are to be developed in the field practice.[9]

Social work practice was viewed as interventive activity in relation to these following dimensions which are interwoven with fieldwork contents:

1. *Problem*: The source of a dependent state being defined individually and/or socially.
2. *System*: The generalizing concept referring to a complex of components in mutual interaction, offering a way of organizing knowledge as well as a way of viewing the range of client system.
3. *Process*: The patterns of change over time, dynamics, growth, and resolution.
4. *Function/Purpose/Goals*: The direction and task of professional intervention.
5. *Value*: The professional commitment of man.
6. *Professional Role*: The properties of the social work position.
7. *Method*: Orderly, purposive, artful activity assessment, planning, implementation, and evaluation.
8. *Relationship*: The effective outcome of instrumental connections.
9. *Communication*: The fibre of interaction.[10]

According to the Second Review Committee, the specific knowledge drawn from the social and behavioural sciences and other professions, forms the knowledge base of the social work profession. In the utilization of the knowledge for practice, the student needs to develop intellectual skills which promote analysis of information and observed phenomena and the ability to synthesize, generalize and conceptualize. He/she also needs to develop attitudes expected of a model practitioner of his/her profession. Lastly, he/she must have skills which are usable for the type and level of jobs he/she is called upon to perform.[11]

The contents of fieldwork training vary at different levels in different fields. And for this, there is always a question whether the contents of the fieldwork training should be common for all? Or, should these be based on methods of social work? The contents of fieldwork training vary from agency to agency and also from one specialization to another. Thus, these require certain phases, which are common to both the fields and methods of social work. Actually, the contents of fieldwork training need a special programme at the level of agencies. As the contents of fieldwork training will be different from group work and also in the case of specialization, the contents of fieldwork have also to be different. The proceedings of the workshop for faculty development, organized by the Delhi School of Social Work in1981, have outlined the phases and the contents of fieldwork training in general. It has recommended four phases of fieldwork training and the contents therein. These are:

1. Orientation Phase
2. Placement Phase
3. Exploration-Assessment-Action Phase
4. Evaluation Phase

Phase 1: Orientation

This phase has two aspects: (a) introduction, and (b) visits.

The main contents of this phase are:

1. Introduction to the field, fieldwork curriculum and the agency/area.
2. General visits to social work settings – institutions and communities.
3. Recording and report writing on field visits.
4. A student taken for visits to institutions should be provided with certain guidelines in the following areas:
    - Historical background of the institution/area
    - Aims and objectives of the institution
    - Organization and structure of the institution
    - Financial position
    - Intake policy, procedure and service delivery
    - Programmes offered by the agency
    - Facilities provided by the agency and problem faced by it
5. In case the students were taken to a community, the broad outline/guideline that should be followed are:
    - Community history: a prospective-retrospective (evaluative) view
    - Composition of the community
    - Various facilities available to the people
    - Existing organization in the community
    - Problem faced by the community in general

Phase 2: Placement

The placement phase has also two aspects:

1. Introduction
    - Introduction by the school supervisor about fieldwork requirements and procedures
    - Introduction by the agency supervisor about the requirements of the agency/community
    - Introduction to the client system
2. Work Assignment
    - Definite work assignment
    - Definite target group
    - Work assignment that may evolve out of exploratory work by the student himself

Phase 3: Exploration-Assessment-Action

The contents under this phase are formulated as:

- Need-resource identification
- Programme development
- Assumption of social work roles and professional involvement
- Individual conferences
- Group conferences
- Fieldwork seminar
- Recording
- Ongoing assessment and perspective guidance

Phase 4: Evaluation

The evaluation of the students could be done at different levels:

- Student's self-evaluation
- Agency evaluation
- Evaluation by the supervisor at school
- Faculty evaluation

The content of the evaluation could be based on the following grounds:

- Summary records and other documents
- Personal qualities and professional skills, capability of relating theory to practice

Techniques Common to Social Work Practice

- Creating communication and helping skills
- Verbal communication skills

- Non-verbal communication skills
- Helping skills
- Understanding emotion and feeling
- Responding to deference communication
- Elements of professional behaviour
- Making ethical decision
- Cross-cultural helping
- Need identification skills
- Resource mobilization skills
- Programme planning and implementation skills
- Administrative skills
- Recording skills
- Skills of utilization of programme media

Social work initially focused on charity and welfare activities to help the needy people and it then shifted to development during the seventies. The major problems were mass poverty, inequality, oppression, etc.

So, the social work profession began to recognize the demands made on it and involved in interventional process. Besides these, the present trends of social work education in the field of environment, women and child specially mentally challenged, human rights and disadvantaged, vulnerable diseases like AIDS, TB, plague, etc., rural credit or rural marketing, etc., are more important and also in the age of LPG (liberalization, privatization, globalization), consumerism, marketization following the New Economic Policy, there is big scope for social work education. In the new phase of NGOs' domination in the field of development, social work education has to change its views in different angles or, in other words, there is need for a universal base of social work in India. Side by side the fieldwork practice and training has to be changed also.

Guidelines for Fieldwork Utilizing Social Work Methods

For any professional education, field learning or practical experience is the backbone for its existence and without it the profession becomes meaningless. As in social work profession, fieldwork provides students the feedback to learn about their intervention. How, when, where and why to use the various techniques of social work, and it makes the students to extend and widen their knowledge and understanding, and approach in dealing with societal issues and problems. Fieldwork provides an opportunity to utilize the theory taught in the classroom situation to work with the people and social systems and dynamics of the society where individuals, groups, communities and institutions are the main components. The social work structure lies upon six methods where first three are named as 'basic methods' and last three named as 'supportive methods' of social work. These are:

1. Social Case Work
2. Social Group Work
3. Community Organization
4. Social Action
5. Social Welfare Administration
6. Social Work Research

All these methods are to be used with their perspective to the techniques and skills while dealing with social problems.

Social Case Work

Pauline Young has given some guidelines for the case workers to deal with clients as:

1. Skill in investigation
2. Skill in case diagnosis and prognosis
3. Skill in planning treatment
4. Skill in administering case treatment
5. Skill in the mechanics of case work:
    (i) Skill in interviewing
    (ii) Observation skill
    (iii) Skill in the use of documents
    (iv) Skill in report writing
    (v) Skill in organizational work
6. Maintaining professional attitudes:
    (i) Team work ability
    (ii) Ability to grow and keep up to date
    (iii) Ability to maintain professional bearings
    (iv) Acquiring professional equipment

Then, the case worker has to deal with the case through four stages as: social study, diagnosis, treatment and evaluation with feedback.

Social Group Work

The social group work is concerned with providing and developing group experience amongst people in a group situation. The group worker should have complete knowledge of the sources and methods of finances, etc. Besides, as participant observer he/she should also get acquainted with the formal and informal group situations.

What skill should be used?

Traker has defined method and skill as under: Method means the purposeful use of insight and understanding based upon a body of knowledge and principles; whereas skill as the capacity to apply knowledge and understanding to a given situation. Method is the use of a process whereas skill is a capacity to use it.

The following elements come into play while dealing with group situation:

Individual	*Group*	*Situation*
Acceptability	Group feeling	Contingency factors of individuals
Motivation to individuals	Purposeful relationship	Utilization of resources
Sense of participation	Resource mobilization	Programme development and its proper implementation
		Evaluation and feedback

In a group situation, the group worker has to perform multifarious task.

Social Group Work Processes

The social group work has four processes:

(i) Group Study
(ii) Group Diagnosis
(iii) Group Treatment
(iv) Evaluation

Group Study: 'Study' involves critical analysis about ins and outs of the individual, group as a whole and the problem situation. Here 'individuals' form a group and then behavioural assessment of all the participating members should be made. This assessment will give a clear idea about the nature of individuals and the intensity of efforts they may put into effect. 'Group as a whole' is the cohesive unit of individual parts synchronizing in a manner to produce what is desirable. On the other hand, 'evaluation' is a crucial task before a group worker in the execution of his/her programmes into action. The strengths and limitations should be found out to make plans successfully. Also, effective utilization and resource mobilization could be another part of scrutiny. Lastly, a rational and objective enquiry is made about the prevailing situation and problematic areas after getting proper understanding of the group aspect.

Group Diagnosis: In this phase, problem of conflict or clash arises and certain group behaviours expressed in the conflicting situation like:

- Members become impatient and intolerant with one another.
- Many objections are raised before ideas are expressed.
- Members start favoritism and refuse to compromise.
- Members disagree to plans or suggestions for the group.
- Suggestions and comments are made with great deal of vehemence.
- Members attack one another on a personal level in subtle ways.
- Members insist that the group does not have the know-how or experience to get anywhere.
- Members feel that group cannot go ahead being too big or too small.
- Members disagree with leader's suggestions.
- Members start to make allegations on one another of not understanding the real points or issues.
- Members bear distorted views of other member's contributions.

On the basis of the conflicting situations in the group, some of the probable diagnosis could be made by the social group worker like:

- Initially, the members in the group find it difficult to connect and relate themselves with the group expectations.
- The tasks put before the group may be incomplete with the aspirations of group members.
- Every individual looks for his/her own identity and status in the group.
- All members are usually concerned about their own views and opinions and many times fail to amalgamate with other members.
- Support to the other group or outside group is provided having conflicting interests and motives.
- Members see the reflection of their views and ideas in other groups.
- The group clashes being expressed are constructive and members work meticulously to find solution of the problems.
- Members able to relate themselves with the group goals and start supporting and contributing to achieve group goals.
- Sometimes group goals may be insignificant to the members and confusion starts over group goals and processes and to attain those results in disinterest in the group activities.

- Problem-solving procedure seems to be improper and inadequate.
- Lack of clarity in the strategies causes reluctance in the members to take responsibilities.
- Disinterest and apathy in others result from the conflicts between few dominating members of the group.
- Lack of confidence and group cohesiveness may be very less.
- Difficulty level of the decisions may be very high.
- Fear and reluctance by the group to goals is shown in spite of their significance being realized.
- Members are not sure about their level of competence required for accomplishing group goals.
- Ambiguity about the approach is reflected.
- Fear of failure and consequences of the decisions cause inaction and taking of new responsibilities by the group members.

Group Treatment: Here, the group worker with his/her empathy, warmth and objectivity in relationship to the group, can make the group members feel comfortable and cooperative in nature. Empathy, unlike sympathy, gives group worker an opportunity to understand the individual member's sentiments. The warmth and genuineness of the group worker is not influenced by subjective factors and the interaction grows between group members and the group worker. Then, the members rely on each other and gain each other's confidence. During this process, sharing helps to disclose repressed feelings both of a group and a worker, group members express their covert behaviour with the assistance of a group worker and come to realize their unconscious and hidden motives. Group worker provides a helping hand in the form of psycho-social approaches and techniques like:

1. Cognitive Restructuring
2. Group Therapy
3. Encounter Therapy
4. Psychodrama
5. Focused Group Discussion

Whenever problematic areas are identified, the individuals are able to realize their internal maladjustments, misconceptions and incompatible habits that result in failure to cope up with new challenging tasks.

Evaluation: By evaluation, we mean appraisal or judgment of the worth and effectiveness of all the processes of social group work designed to meet the group goals. Evaluation may be centred around individual growth, programme contents, or worker's performances and is essential because it enables the group worker to discover to what extent the group has achieved its objectives and goals. Evaluation also helps to see the strengths and weaknesses and enables to explore the new ideas to develop the situation. A well-balanced evaluation helps to formulate new objectives and it could be an extension of the learning process.

Community Organization

Community organization became an important concept in the social work profession after the publication of Lane Committee Report in 1939, which identified community organization as a method of social work. The report stated that:

> the general aim of community organization is to bring about and maintain a progressively more effective adjustment between social welfare resources and social welfare needs. This implies that community organization is concerned with (a) the discovery and definition of needs; (b) the elimination and prevention of disabilities, as far as possible; and (c) the articulation of resources and needs, and the constant readjustment of resources in order to better meet changing needs.

The phrase 'community organization' is made of two words, namely, community and organization. While community has been defined in terms of geographical area or boundaries, organization is a process through which it is made possible for people of community to work out problems involved in coordinating social services that are provided by all types of agencies furthering the goals of economic and social development.

Steps in a Community Organization Process

The process of community organization initiates from the identification of community needs and their problems and finally reaches the desired and effective solutions. The process involves analysis of problem state, felt needs, their priorities, resources identification and community efforts in achieving what they have actually aimed for. Lindeman has suggested 10–Step Community Organization Process as under:

1. Consciousness of needs
2. Spreading of consciousness of needs
3. Projection of needs
4. Emotional impulse to meet needs

5. Presentations of solutions
6. Conflict between solutions
7. Investigation process
8. Open discussions on issues
9. Integration of solutions
10. Compromise on the basis of tentative progressive solutions

So, every social worker or community organizer has to go through the process dealing with any community issues or problems and they also maintain the models of community organization such as Locality Development Model, Social Planning Model, and Social Action Model (given by Rotham).

Roles of a Community Organization Worker

During the community work, a community organization worker performs many roles in dealing with community problems in the fieldwork practice.

1. As an enabler:
   - (a) Helps people to understand needs, problems and resources at their command.
   - (b) Arouses and focuses discontent with the existing situation.
   - (c) Assists in creation of organization.
   - (d) Fosters cooperative and collaborative relations.
   - (e) Promotes consensus on the areas and courses of action.
   - (f) Helps develop the capacity of the people.
2. As an expert:
   Provides expert advice and guidance to people on social problems in their community when the situation so demands. M.G. Ross correctly maintained that "as an expert, he provides research data, technical experience, research material, advice on methods".
3. As a guide:
   Helps the community in establishing and finding means of achieving its goals. His/her main role is to bring community people in contact with needed resources of the community for which they need to work, but they do not know it.
4. As an advocate:
   Does the advocacy of his/her clients against injustices being done to them in providing benefits and services to which they are entitled from various organizations and welfare institutions established to save the community people.

5. As a social therapist:
   Deals with those deep lying and often unconscious forces that are constantly and often in hidden form threatening to disrupt the community organization process.
6. As an activist:
   Tries to solve the community problems through mobilization of community people against government or service providing agencies. As Panitch has expressed that the activist role is a legitimate stance for a social worker, especially the community organizer. The passivity and objectivity of the service professions is after all something of a myth.

Learning Goals of Fieldwork with Communities

1. To provide opportunities for the students to understand the communities – rural, urban, tribal, etc.
2. To imbibe the skills required for practice in open communities such as skills in interacting with people, conflict management, resource mobilizatiob, etc..
3. To undersand the unique needs of the different communities.
4. To understand the importance of people's participation in implementation process.

Social Action

Social action helps creating among the people or in the community an awareness regarding their own problems and mobilizing people's resources for concerned action.

Social action is all about attempting to sort out mass social problems at any level or of any kind. It may stretch from grass-roots level to regional and even up to national level. At the very beginning, an agency or an institution, through its leadership and specialized professional workers (such as social worker), may provide a concrete forum to represent the grass-roots grievances and then mobilize public opinion to facilitate necessary alterations in the system and its policies for the welfare of the people. Through social action, social worker or social action worker brings about improvement in mass conditions, influences institutions, policies and practices, and redistributes power and resources to the people. When corruption, favouritism, nepotism, discourtesy, neglect of duty, discrimination, delay in work, maladministration, and inadequate redressal of machinery have become the common practices today, there is need for new approach that could be less generic and more public, less descriptive and more prescriptive, less institutional-oriented and more client-oriented, and less neutral and more normative.

Objectives of Social Action as a Practice

1. To provide a consensual social point of view in the implementation of social policies;
2. To put various facts and information and explain their actual meaning to the people;
3. To suggest ways and means to resolve social problems;
4. Integration of social means;
5. To create awareness and social consciousness regarding social problems, various government schemes and plans, etc.;
6. To get permission for various plans from policy makers;
7. To make efforts in the context of programmes executed by government;
8. To recognize social work as a profession; and
9. To encourage the government to develop social welfare activities.

For this vast foundation of scope of activities, social action in the present context envisages characteristic features like:

- Change orientation
- Goal orientation
- Progressive planning
- Innovativeness
- Flexibility in approach
- High degree of motivation
- Client orientation
- People's participation
- Effective integration of efforts
- Coping ability to serve its purpose

Processes and Approaches Dealt with by Social Worker in Social Action

1. Developing awareness among the people about their core issues through:
   (a) Providing social education
   (b) Doing research
   (c) Using multi-media, etc.
2. Organization or working for organizing community through:
   (a) Cooperation
   (b) Organizing
3. Making strategies through:
   (a) Arbitration

   (b) Negotiation
   (c) Mild coercion
   (d) Persuasion
4. Action through:
   (a) Joint action
   (b) Violation of legal norms

Sarvodaya and Antyodaya as Approaches to Social Action

Sarvodaya, first used by Gandhiji, means "the rise of all". According to Vinoba Bhave, a disciple of Gandhiji, the motto of Sarvodaya is a far higher state: 'Live and Let Others Live'; it is life for the sake of others. But, Sarvodaya, in term of social action approach, aims at fulfilling of necessities, education, decentralization of power, regional self-dependency, freedom from exploitation, administration based on public policy, self-discipline, and proper means of earning and complete development of an individual in particular, and society in general. Thus, the spirit of 'Sarvebhavantu Sukhina, Sarve Santu Niramaya' is imbibed in the Sarvodaya approach of social action. All focuses on development of all without any discrimination, whereas 'Antyodaya' as an approach to social action aims at "poorest among the poor". So, both the approaches work for the development of the poor and disadvantaged groups and needy people of the society.

Both the approaches find place in the present stage of social problems related to poverty, rural development, unorganized labour, effects of liberalization, globalization and privatization (LPG). Social workers can utilize both the approaches in their fieldwork dealing with above problems.

Essential Strategies for Social Action

Now, a question comes to our mind that who will start or in what circumstances social action should start. This would happen due to:

(a) arising demanding situation,
(b) malfunctioning of specific social institutions,
(c) wrong or anti-people policies framed by the representatives of the people,
(d) inability of social agencies to deliver the services in a desirable manner, or
(e) core social issues and problems prompting for social attention.

Whenever such situations arise, the need of an 'actor' is a natural requirement to perform on behalf of the people in an opportune moment. This actor may be a leader, a group of people, association or a welfare agency or a social worker, who defines the problematic situation, manages and utilizes all the community resources to their optimum to settle their priorities.

The 'action' part of the actor includes coordination of total work, planning strategies and tactics, deciding proper approaches and models and lastly implementing the plan of action after capitalizing on strength and minimizing the weaknesses and limitations. The ultimate attainment is the 'end results' or goals deliberately determined by the people concerned. So, the essential elements of the process circle around:

Problem situation→Actor→Means→Actions→End results.

Role of Social Worker in Social Action

Clarke has assigned the following roles to a social worker to bring about desirable changes through social action:

1. Social work practitioners have the responsibility of keeping their constituency informed of conditions, creating the awareness about problems they handled so that the agency which is composed of supporters, staff and clients can share thoughts and opinions in achieving social change.
2. Social work professional as a citizen has a constitutional right to participate in any form of legal social action.
3. In a democratic society like ours, all reforms are eventually bound up with political action and hence if we are to be realistic about social change we cannot evade association with political action groups.
4. Support specific programmes because they believe in them, not because they have professional expertise of them.
5. Social work professional may participate at any level – be it primary or secondary.

Social workers also use Public Interest Litigation (PIL) and Lok Adalats as instruments of social action.

Social Welfare Administration

Social welfare administration, as a method of social work, offers the wider knowledge and skills required for effective rendering of services for the people. It is a process of transferring social policy into social action. As a science, it consists of a systematic body of knowledge, the validity of which has been tested and the use of which makes it possible to render the services in a more direct and effective manner. Social welfare administration also recognizes the principle of 'POSDCoRBEF', i.e., planning, organizing, staffing, directing, coordinating, reporting, budgeting, evaluation and feedback.

Administrative Processes and Practices

Social workers in social welfare administration follow some basic administrative techniques such as:

1. Planning
2. Organization
3. Communication
4. Decision-making
5. Coordination
6. Delegation
7. Supervision
8. Budgeting
9. Financial control
10. Reporting
11. Evaluation
12. Feedback

Social Work Research

Social work research is the method of social work. According to Friedlander (1964), social work research is the systematic, critical investigation of questions in the social welfare field with the purpose of yielding answers to problems of social work, and of extending and generalizing social work knowledge and concepts.

According to Ripple, social work research begins with practical problems, and its objective is to produce knowledge that can be put to use in planning or carrying on social work programmes.

Macdonald states that research in social work may be taken to encompass those questions which are encountered in social work practice or in planning or administering social work services, which are solvable through research, and which are appropriate for investigation under social work auspices.

Objectives of Social Work Research

Fletcher has mentioned the following objectives of social work research:

1. To improve and enlarge the techniques of diagnosis and treatment as they are used in social work practice;
2. To develop the efficiency and define the functions of social work agency as the medium through which social work is practised;
3. To appraise and measure the community needs for social work service; and

4. To add to the general knowledge of the etiology of social pathology so that social action can be directed towards the prevention of problems that might later require social work treatment.

Social Work Research Process

The social work research process includes following stages:

1. Problem Identification
2. Hypothesis Formulation
3. Research Design
4. Procedure for Sampling
5. Collection of Data
6. Processing of Data, Data Analysis and Interpretation
7. Hypothesis Testing
8. Research Report

Every social worker has to go through these stages whenever they undertake a social work research based on social problems.

Social Work Knowledge Practicum

In a profession like social work, it is not possible to separate theory from practice or concept from action. In fact, practice is the process of using knowledge and applying theory in order to bring about specific types of change. A practice uninformed by theory tends to become repetitive and sterile, whereas theory uninformed by the realities of practice tends to be merely interesting and usually irrelevant. The many theories, models and perspectives discussed in the social work literature can all be considered 'conceptual frameworks'. A 'conceptual framework' is composed of a coherent set of concepts, beliefs, values, propositions, assumptions, hypotheses and principles. Such a framework can be thought of as an outline of ideas that help one to understand people, how people function, and how people change. These frameworks are important because they have utility. For example, they provide a structure for analysing complex and often highly emotional human problems and situation; they organize information, beliefs and assumptions into a meaningful whole; they provide a rationale for action and decision-making; they promote a systematic, orderly and predictable approach to work with people; and they facilitate communication among professionals.

In their practice, social workers use a variety of theories, models and perspectives. Although these terms have somewhat different meanings, they are often lumped together and simply termed theory.

However, it is helpful to make some distinctions as to the types and usage of terms used to describe these conceptual frameworks. Howe (1987) explains that, broadly speaking, there are 'theories of social work' and 'theories for social work'.[12] The theories of social work focus on the profession and explain its purpose, domain and character within a society. They also explain what the profession is all about, who it is for, and why it functions as it does. By contrast, the theories for social work focus on clients and helping activities. They explain human behaviour, the social environment, how changes occur, and how change can be facilitated by the social worker in order to benefit clients.

In their work with clients, social workers make use of orienting theories and practice frameworks. Mailick (1990) explains that orienting theories describe and explain behaviour and how and why certain problems develop. They provide important background knowledge and are usually borrowed from other disciplines, such as biology, psychology, sociology, economics, cultural anthropology, and the like. Examples include the various theories related to human development, personality, family systems, socialization, organizational functioning, and political power, as well as theories related to specific types of problems such as poverty, family violence, mental illness, teen pregnancy, crime, and racial discrimination. Orienting theories, by themselves, provide little guidance, on how to bring about change. For such guidance one must look to a second category called 'practice frameworks'. They are of three types: practice perspectives, practice theories, and practice models.

The most overarching type of practice framework is a 'practice perspective'. A practice perspective can be described as a conceptual lens, through which one views human behaviour and social structures and which, simultaneously, guide the selection of intervention strategies. Like a camera lens, a practice perspective serves to focus on or magnify a particular feature while placing other features in the background. Two perspectives, the general systems perspective and the ecosystems perspective, are commonly used in social work for assessing the relationships between people and their environment. Others, such as the generalist, feminist and ethnic-sensitive practice perspectives, focus more on the philosophy and processes to be followed in working towards change.

The second type of framework is a 'practice theory', which offers both an explanation of certain behaviours or situations and broad guidelines about how those behaviours or situations can be changed.

A practice theory serves as a road map for an intervention that will bring about a certain type of change. Most practice theories are rooted in one or more orienting theories. An example is the psychological approach that is based primarily on psychodynamic theory and ego psychology. Another is behavioural therapy that is based on theories of learning.

The third type of practice framework is a 'practice model'. A practice model is a set of concepts and principles used to guide certain interventions. However, in contrast to a practice theory, a practice model is not tied to a particular explanation of behaviour. For example, crisis intervention is viewed as a practice model, rather than a practice theory, because the action steps of these interventions are not tied to any one explanation of crisis situations. For the same reason, the task-centred approach is termed a practice model rather than a practice theory. Most often, a practice model develops out of actual experience or experimentation rather than evolving from a particular theory of behaviour. Now fieldwork approach is changing its conventional outlook into developmental outlook in connection with the present societal understandings and conditions.

Fieldwork Practicum

According to UGC's National Assessment and Accreditation Council (NAAC), fieldwork practicum is a closely supervised educational internship in a social work setting that provides planned opportunities to apply theory taught in classrooms to field situations, which, in turn, enhances classroom teaching.

Objectives

1. Fieldwork practicum specifically aims at the following:
    - Observation and understanding of the interaction between human behaviour and the social, economic and political systems, and systemic marginalization of vulnerable groups at the micro levels.
    - Development of critical self-awareness about one's attributes, values and sensitivities with reference to the ideology of social justice and human rights and ethical requirements of social work profession, through experience.
    - Learning and practice of social work methods and skills for prevention and amelioration of social problems at micro, meso and macro levels, administration of non-profit organizations and documentations, and monitoring and evaluation of one's social work intervention.

2. Objectives of fieldwork practicum are coordinated with the overall knowledge, attitude and skills objectives appropriate to the level of the programme and the theories taught in classrooms.
3. Fieldwork objectives are differentially worked out for each semester term.
4. Fieldwork manual, covering the aims and objectives, components, role of faculty, advisors, fieldwork supervisors and field contacts, format for process and summary recordings, administrative rules, code of conduct, ethics, manuals, credits, assessment criteria and procedure and so on, is distributed to all the students and fieldwork supervisors at the beginning of the year. It is reviewed every five years.

Components

Fieldwork practicum comprises of the following components:

- Life skill workshops
- Organizational visits
- Concurrent fieldwork
- Block fieldwork
- Social work skill workshops
- Rural/tribal camp/study tour

1. Workshops are conducted for development of life skills, such as self-awareness and self-esteem, positive, creative and critical thinking, enhancing positive emotions and minimizing negative emotions, assertive and sensitive interpersonal communication and synergy in social interaction and relationships.
2. Workshops to develop social work skills are organized by fieldwork supervisors in coordination with the social work methods' teachers.
3. Manuals are developed for skill training.
4. Organizational visits, followed by discussion, acquaint students to the social work scenario.
5. Rural/tribal camps are organized to expose students to the problems and issues of the marginalized ruralites.
6. Study tours of innovative projects are organized in rural/urban areas.
7. Concurrent/block fieldwork during the programme provides opportunities, for process-oriented, sustained interventions with specific groups, according to the level of the programme.
8. Holistic approach to practice, practice-based research and researched fieldwork is emphasized.

Selection of Fieldwork Settings for Concurrent/Block Fieldwork

1. Criteria for selection of fieldwork settings for concurrent/block fieldwork include the following:
   - A variety of learning opportunities are available to practise all the methods of social work as far as possible.
   - Opportunities are available to work with social issues of rural/urban poor and other vulnerable groups.
   - Sçope is available for students' creativity and initiatives.
   - Range of diverse settings made available including institutional/open/government/non-government agencies.
2. More unstructured and challenging settings are tried out, with a social issue being the entry point for interventions, especially in areas where structured fieldwork agencies are not adequate.
3. Students are involved in intervention during emergency situations like riots, cyclone and earthquake and specific time-bound, issue-based campaigns.
4. Fieldwork placements are selected on the basis of the objectives at each levels and students' needs.
5. Students are allowed to select their fieldwork setting in the final year.
6. Periodic review is carried out of the 'practicum worthiness' of the current settings and identification of new agencies.

Selection and Preparation of Fieldwork Supervisors

1. Fieldwork supervisors are professional social workers with a BSW degree and a minimum of three years of field experience, or an MSW degree with a minimum of two years of field experience.
2. Orientation and reading material is made available to new fieldwork supervisors.
3. Faculty members are required to undergo periodic refresher course in fieldwork supervision.
4. Field supervisors' meetings are regularly held for discussion on issues and innovations in supervision of fieldwork.

Roles of Fieldwork Supervisor

1. Orientating students to the agency/community, help them to identify objectives and client groups.
2. Make students realize the opportunities available for them to learn practice skills.
3. Hold individual conferences of at least 30 minutes' duration per student, per week.

4. Check students' recordings on a weekly basis, make written comments on them and discuss the same in the individual conferences.
5. Hold at least one group conference in a month wherein each student is given the opportunity to make at least one presentation in a year.
6. Make regular visits to the fieldwork settings for discussion on the students' plans and progress.
7. Faculty fieldwork supervisors are actively involved in the fieldwork setting.
8. Field supervisors are reimbursed commuting expenses by fieldwork agencies.
9. Written/audio/video recordings of students' fieldwork are used for classroom teaching.
10. Helping students to acquire good work habits among students.
11. Continuous appraisal of students throughout the fieldwork and working towards augmenting their professional growth in a structured manner.

Developmental Fieldwork

Developmental fieldwork has emerged as a new concept shifting from conventional model of fieldwork in social work education today. It is need-oriented rather than problem-oriented. The emphasis is given more on the non-established and unstructured field situation wherein the trainee is provided with number of opportunities for the practice of developmental fieldwork. Open community placements, with or without any agency-based programmes, were started by a few schools of social work in the mid-sixties. Others followed the suit in the eighties. This placement has been known as 'open community placement' in India whereas in other countries, they were called 'innovative community settings'. The idea is to give to the students an exposure of mass problems, such as poverty, illiteracy, poor health and housing, etc. Thus, the students were expected to try and grapple with the social milieu, which was seen as the root cause of many of these social problems. Even UGC has provided funds to some schools so that they can develop more programmes and projects to perform community-based development-oriented field placements.[13]

The main focus of development fieldwork is to identifying possibilities for field training, establishing the objectives, designing the learning tasks, the content of instruction and developing an evaluation criteria for assessment of the student performance; to provide the educators with an opportunity for increasing their own practice knowledge and skills; and to document case studies of action projects, testing alternative strategies and techniques for working with people and models of field investigation. The students may be involved in the work areas like working with weaker sections, consumer protection, national integration, prohibition of dowry, organizing poor and the exploited, slum clearance and improvement, environment protection, welfare of labour in unorganized sector, population control, improvement in standard of living of vulnerable sections, protection available to them under various laws and facilities under various schemes, awareness regarding the newly emerged health problems such as AIDS, environmental degradation, terrorism, communalism, corruption and such other social problems emerged from time to time in our society.

Professional Associations of Social Work in India

Professional associations or bodies play a significant and important role for the growth of any profession and advancement of its practice. India has a long history of social work education as compared to other South Asian countries and professional associations formed much later to play proactive roles. The professional associations in India are yet to get permanent affiliations and membership in the International Federation of Social Workers (IFSW). Unfortunately, in India, there is a lack of professional associations or organizations in social work in terms of quality.

The idea of establishing professional associations was first mooted by J.M. Kumarappa, the first Indian Director of TISS, in 1961, at the annual meeting of the Indian Conference of Social Work (now known as the Indian Council of Social Welfare, established in 1947). With this, the ASSWI (Association of Schools of Social Work in India) was initiated the same year. During the period from 1975 to 1984, ASSWI published five books, based on seminars that it had organized on different aspects of social work education and practice.[14]

Apart from the alumni associations of different schools of social work, we had a professional association called Indian Association of Trained Social Workers (IATSW) in Delhi with chapters in different states and cities. The IATSW published a quarterly journal, organized seminars and conferences to discuss important national issues concerning the profession and set up innovative good demonstration projects. After about ten years the work of the association declined and now the central body is nearly dead.[15]

In the initial stage, we had several professional associations in India like Labour Welfare Officers' Association, Probation Officers'

Association, and Association of Alumni of Schools of Social Work in India and so on. Some regional level associations also came into being like Bombay Association of Trained Social Workers (BATSW), Karnataka Association of Professional Social Workers (KAPSW), Professional Social Workers Forum, Chennai (PSWFC), Maharashtra Association of Social Work Educators (MATSWE), etc. Maharashtra has a good number of schools of social work. At present, three professional associations are working in the country at national level, i.e., Associations of Schools of Social Work in India (ASSWI), established in 1959 at Baroda; Indian Society of Professional Social Work (ISPSW), 1988 and formerly known as Indian Society of Psychiatric Social Work established in 1970 by R.K. Upadhyaya and his staff in the Department of Psychiatric Social Work, Central Institute of Psychiatry, Ranchi; and NAPSWI (National Association of Professional Social Workers in India), which has come into being from 9 September, 2005 and got legal status as a society under the Society Registration Act of 1860. These associations are aimed at motivating the professional social workers to debate, discuss and develop conceptual frameworks and feasible indigenous interventions of social work for practice, promoting the social work profession across the country for improving the quality of services in the social welfare and development sector.

With the establishment of Indian Council of Social Work one can hope that legacy and legitimacy of professional social work could be materialized. This council was jointly set up by Associations of Trained Social Workers, Association of Schools of Social Work, UGC, and the Ministries of Welfare and Human Resource Development. It may undertake periodic reviews of working of social work training institutions; assist and guide in the development of curriculum and fieldwork practice; grant accreditation/recognition for undergraduate, graduate and postgraduate courses; help in development of training methods; work out and enforce minimum standards of teaching, fieldwork, etc.; help in the production of indigenous literature and case records on social work and to act as a storehouse for exchange of information about indigenous social work literature; arrange interaction between training institutions, UGC, government departments, voluntary organizations; and organize orientation and refresher courses for educators and practitioners and seminars and workshops on social work.

Publications of Professional Associations in Social Work in India

- *The Indian Journal of Social Work* was started by TISS in 1940.

- The first book on social work, called *Students and Social Work*, was published by TISS in 1949.
- The journal, *International Social Work* was started by the International Conference of Social Work and International Association of Schools of Social Work, with a base in Bombay in 1958.
- The Lucknow University *Journal of Social Work* was started by the Department of Social Work of Lucknow University, now called *Contemporary Social Work*, in 1962.
- Indian Association of Trained Social Workers (IATSW) started publishing a journal called *Social Work Forum* in 1963.
- The first edition of *Encyclopedia of Social Work in India* was published by Planning Commission in 1968.
- A journal called *Perspectives in Social Work* was launched by the College of Social Work of the Nirmala Niketan Institute in 1984.
- The second edition of *Encyclopedia of Social Work in India* was published by the Ministry of Welfare in 1987.
- *National Journal of Professional Social Work* was started by the Indian Society of Professional Social Work in 2000.[16]

UGC Review Committees and Social Work Education

The UGC has a panel on social work education on the same lines as has been done for the other disciplines.

The First Review Committee

The first review committee for social work education in India was appointed by the UGC in 1965. This committee was in favour of specialization.

The Second Review Committee

The second review committee was appointed in 1980 and it observed that the prevailing situation of social work in India did not favour social work specializations. The scope of the review covers the critical review of the existing programmes of social work education, including courses, fieldwork and research; to suggest the changes that may be introduced with a view to making these programmes more meaningful and relevant; and to suggest ways and means of effecting these changes, etc. The fieldwork was identified as another major area requiring changes. The committee believed that the University Grants Commission (UGC) and the Association of Schools of Social Work in India will have to pay considerable attention to objectives, design, contents and methodology of fieldwork.

An analysis of the developmental focus in the student's field experience, in each setting, is required. The strategies of interaction for social change need to be strengthened through field practice. The student needs to be prepared for the role of change agent rather than just performing the traditional remedial and rehabilitative functions. Adequate fieldwork opportunities should be made available. This should first be ascertained before situating a new institution in a specific location. Students should spend at least 15 hours on fieldwork every week; in case the student takes up research project he/she should be given 12 hours of fieldwork. Block fieldwork may be continued where a specific learning gain is attached to it and it is feasible. The rationale of having block fieldwork at the end of the two years need to be reviewed. The student might probably see this as a period of disengagement, rather than re-engagement, as it comes towards the end of his/her learning. It is also difficult for the institution to help the student integrate this new learning that may take place, especially when block fieldwork requires the student to stay in a location too far away from the institution. Hence, it may be necessary to experiment with block fieldwork in the middle of the academic year. It is necessary to accord high priority for the review of fieldwork in each institution, especially in relation to integrating the developmental emphasis. There is considerable need to define tasks and contents in the field learning and to make evaluation related to such contents. The same mechanism suggested for the frequent review of syllabi may also be utilized for fieldwork, since classroom courses and fieldwork should be well integrated.

Notes

1. Walter Friedlander, *Introduction of Social Welfare,* 2nd edition, 1964, pp. 541–42.
2. Howard Jacob Karger, 'The Future of Social Work in Changing Economy, Preparing for the Year 2000', 27th IASSW, Amsterdam, 1994, p. 9.
3. Second Review Committee, A Review of Social Work Education in India: Retrospect and Prospect, New Delhi, UGC, February 1978, p. 298.
4. J.E. Hegerty, *The Training of Social Welfare.*
5. Tata Institute of Social Sciences, *Social Work Education in India: A Report,* Mimeographed, 1988, p. 28.
6. Paul Kurian, "Rational Energy Strategies", *Economic and Political Weekly,* Vol. XXV, No. 2 (January 6, 1990), p. 35.

7. Harriet M. Bartlett, *The Common Base of Social Work Practice: Integrating Social Work Methods*, 1970.
8. Charles Guzzetta, *MSW Education, The Present State*, Hunter College of the City University of New York School of Social Work, New York, 1984.
9. Vimla Nadkarni, TISS (Unpublished Paper, Bombay).
10. Barbara N. Rodgers, *A New Portrait of Social Work*, p. 25.
11. Report of Second Review Committee, p. 46.
12. Bradford, W. Sheafor, Charles R. Horejsi and Gloria A. Horejsi, *Techniques and Guidelines for Social Work Practice* (4th edition) pp. 50–52.
13. B.T. Lawani and I.S. Subedar, *Social Work Perspectives*, 2006, pp. 53–54.
14. Murli Desai, *Ideologies and Social Work: Historical and Contemporary Analysis*, 2002, pp. 140–141.
15. K.K. Jacob, *Social Work Education: Retrospect and Prospect*, 1994, p. 60.
16. Murli Desai, *Ideologies and Social Work: Historical and Contemporary Analysis*, 2002, p. 148.

2 Research Methodology and Review of Literature

As stated in the preceding chapter, social work is a practice profession, hence the context includes the vital component of practice learning opportunities. Practical training in the field forms an integral part of the total training programme; an educational programme is incomplete without guided practical learning being satisfactorily provided. 'Learning by doing' is the principle from which has developed the body of knowledge, specialized skills and the philosophy of professional work. Practical experience in social work teaching is offered through the method of fieldwork.

In the beginning, schools came into existence under the auspices of Christian missions, preceded by years of practical experience. Later, though the schools and colleges were set up by the predecessors but they did not have direction or traditional practices. Further, the sub-committee of Second Review Committee appointed to draw up course contents on fieldwork did not provide adequate guidelines. Mainly, it left to the professional associations and schools of social work to give serious thought on it. However, the Review Committee on Social Work Education has emphasized to provide following aspects of students' learning in fieldwork:

(i) Understand the relation of knowledge, value and skills;
(ii) Understanding to develop self-awareness and self-discipline in professional relations;
(iii) Ability to work knowingly and effectively with agency structure, function and philosophy;

(iv) Knowledge of multiple positive factors in behaviours to acquire skills in use of professional knowledge;
(v) System of effective use of community, state, and national resources;
(vi) Capacity of social work practice with professional compliance;
(vii) Understanding the uses of social action and capacity of leadership;
(viii) To become professional workers; and
(ix) Compliance in systematic study, assessment and treatment in different fields of social intervention.

In fact, these guidelines did not provide adequate opportunities to train students within the available resources to make them competent workers for addressing emerging social issues. Therefore, the matter of fieldwork became further an issue of more conferences, meetings held from time to time. But we have not yet arrived at clear-cut conclusion, as to know whether we should impart our students training based on emerging specialized branches of knowledge or the knowledge based on generic fields of social work.

Because of this, some more (due to day-to-day emerging demand in a new perspective of our intervention) Indian schools of social work by and large have developed their own kind of fieldwork training programme based on this quality of educational resources and fieldwork opportunity available with them.

As we know, the fieldwork programme at the first school of social work in India evolved through pioneering and exploration and in response to the need as perceived by the professional elite of the time. For about two decades since 1956, the main pattern of fieldwork practice followed by the school was the learning of social work methods, i.e., care work, group work, community organization and in the area of child; women, old age, etc., where the social work skills are applied.

Today, fieldwork is recognized as a major component in professional education because of its implications for professional practice. Hence, it is necessary to examine the objectives of fieldwork. These are:

(i) Develop professional skills through learning how to utilize the knowledge for the study of the relevant fact, the analysis of the problem and selection of the appropriate means of problem solving;

(ii) The development of skills for problem solving in work at the micro level (individual, family, small group, community, etc.) and change at the macro level in social institutions and process;
(iii) Provide concurrent opportunity for the integration of classroom learning in field practice and vice versa;
(iv) Develop skills required for professional practice at the particular level of training;
(v) Develop professional attitude involving impartiality, non-judgmental attitudes, objectively;
(vi) Develop professional values and commitments such as respect for human dignity and worth, and the right to participation and self-determination compatible with the good of society;
(vii) Develop awareness of self and the ways in which psychological and cultural factors affects the perceptions and responses to others; and
(viii) Develop the professional ideal.

Social work education at the master's degree level should comprise the components of classroom teaching having the core domain of social work profession: theory and practice, supportive domain of human growth environment and socio-political bases, interdisciplinary domain and elective domain as suggested in the UGC Model Curriculum (UGC, 2001).

According to Second Review Committee (1980), social work in India has given more focus on the practice setting than on methods.

In practical also fieldwork helps the students to assimilate theory and the consistent application of its practice. The students are enabling to develop his/her understanding about the client, the problem and process to solve it. Concurrent fieldwork also helps the students to know about the status, the structure, functions, programmes, process of the agency where he/she is placed. The students learn and recognize the necessity of mastering technical skills and attitude to achieve the broader goals of social work with the perspective of the course content covered in the classroom. This learning by doing with the feedback of theory though makes the students give more concentrated efforts into practice. But the content of fieldwork of different levels and in different fields should be determined in accordance with the goals of social work education and of fieldwork as identified by the schools.

Techniques Common to All Social Work Practices

1. Creating communication and helping skills

2. Verbal communication skills
3. Non-verbal communication skills
4. Helping skills
5. Understanding emotion and feeling
6. Responding to deference communication
7. Elements of professional behaviour
8. Making ethical decision
9. Cross-cultural helping

Social work initially worked as charity and welfare activities to help the needy people and it then shifted to development during the seventies. The major problems were mass poverty, inequality and oppression.

So, the social work profession began to recognize the demands made on it and involved in interventional process. Besides these, the present trends of social work education in the field of environment, women and child, specially mentally challenged, human rights and disadvantaged, vulnerable diseases like AIDS, plague, etc., rural credit or rural marketing, communalism, terrorism, etc., are more important and also in the age LPG (liberalization, privatization, globalization), computerization, mercerization following New Economic Policy, there is big scope for social work education as its intervention. In the new phase of NGOs' domination in the field of development, social work education has to change its views in different angles, i.e., needs a universal base of social work in India. Incorporating to these situations, fieldwork practice and training also has to be changed.

Present Status of the Study

In the present scenario, fieldwork is an integral and compulsory part of social work education in India. Different schools of social work in the country follow and practice the fieldwork in various ways as per their suitability. So, when professionally social work is implemented, there is an effort to put theory into practice to achieve the goals. Fieldwork in social work education serves the purpose of training students in different areas, hence, we have several guiding factors for fieldwork for a student like:

- The institution
- Philosophy
- The structure of the course

- The subject of specializations
- The capacity of the students
- The goals and objectives of the fieldwork
- The role of the fieldwork director and supervisor, etc.

Even whatever be the setting of the fieldwork, i.e., rural or urban, open community (unstructured) or agency (structured) and before or after developmental area, the above guiding factors have the same role but in varied context.

In order to provide different areas of field exposure and working opportunities to the students as per the objectives of fieldwork, visit to welfare agencies, block work programme, rural camp and research project is necessary depending upon the kind of field opportunity and adequate number of teaching faculty available with the department. Some departments have not been able to introduce all the above kinds of opportunities to the students. By and large, schools of social work have prepared fieldwork manual which is used as useful guidelines by the students and the teaching faculty supervising student's fieldwork from time to time.

Some Research Questions

Following are some research questions that have been put before fieldwork programmes in response to promoting its usefulness for the 21st century:

1. Are our designed admission criteria appropriate to admit right kind of students to join career in social work?
2. Have we created the philosophical base for students' learning in fieldwork to produce trained and competent workers to be able to address emerging social issues?
3. Have we designed proper classroom instructions and fieldwork guidelines in accordance with the need of social work education and students learning for enabling them to learn the true art of social work practice?
4. Have the teachers in the schools got special orientation or refresher course in fieldwork?
5. Have we got adequate number of experienced and interested teaching faculty in our schools that really keep in touch with the field and create adequate models useful for students' learning and guidance in emerging perspective?

6. Have we got unanimity on the area of field exposure/knowledge that needs to be created in students, so that the designed kind of fieldwork opportunity can be identified for students' training?
7. Have we got proper and specialized agencies near our schools for real training and field exposure to the students?
8. Do we have fieldwork agency with trained and experienced personnel whose work and experiences in the fieldwork agency can provide guidance in accordance with the need of social work education?
9. Does the system of our school allow or encourage the teacher-cum-supervisors to frequently visit fieldwork agencies for enabling the placed students in their learning?
10. Do the students in all schools get adequate time for individual/group conferences to get their fieldwork programme properly guided?
11. Whether the teacher-cum-supervisors, while accepting other assignments in or outside the school, give priority to their primary responsibility of fieldwork guidance to the students?
12. Are we designing our fieldwork system and students learning in accordance with the need of student's future career and in accordance with the need of emerging fields of intentions?
13. Are we adapting existing pattern of concurrent fieldwork with new requirements of the present scenario?
14. Do the students as well as teachers try to imbibe different values and ethics of social work?
15. Do the students know the policies and programmes of agencies and their ethical responsibility?
16. Do the students involve in research work in fieldwork?

Rationality of the Study

The study aims at reviewing the trends in fieldwork practice/training in fifteen schools of social work in India. Emphasis has been given in understanding the aims and objectives of fieldwork practice and training of students characterized by the school of social work.

The study has further emphasized on the perspective of trainee, i.e., MSW final year students of the institutes regarding the objectives, goals, contents of fieldwork, supervision, assignments and its outcome. How it is related to their career and their practice in the near future? The existing system or market scenario has been changed for new professionals and new concepts have emerged like social ecology, good governance, health communication, development communication, management in health, management in social sectors, etc. The fieldwork should also deal with the changing pattern of the market so that emerging professionals would be able to adopt themselves to the flow pattern.

As fieldwork is an integral part of the social work curriculum, this study hopes to explore the kind of training that goes into the making of a social worker. It hopes to examine the different components that fieldwork is comprised of; and the findings of the study would hopefully be able to give directions for improvement and enrichment of the fieldwork training being imparted to the students. There is dearth of empirical study in fieldwork and fieldwork practice, and training has not been touched upon so seriously. Fieldwork supervision of the student-learner is done in the agency setting, whereas the agencies themselves are not well equipped for such a fraction.

Keeping a positive view in my mind, I have done this study based on fieldwork in different schools of social work in India.

Operational Definitions

Work

'Work' makes it obligatory for a profession to concentrate its attention mainly on practice which has to be done with people, particularly of weaker and vulnerable section in a society; and for this, every professional must be properly equipped with required knowledge and understanding of the people, their problems (particularly psycho-social) and situation in which they are located, as also with skills and techniques required for introducing the desired changes in people's personality structure as well as social structure.

Field

In social sciences, 'field' means community of human beings who will be studied for a certain purpose. Field is a patterned system of objective forces and a relational configuration endowed with a specific gravity which it imposes on all the objects and agents which enter in it.

In social work, field could be a situation which offers avenues for students' interaction with clients and clients' systems where social workers practice social work methods under supervisory guidance for the achievement of learning goals of professional social work. Such field may be an agency setting, multi-agency setting, community without any formal agency and community with single or multiple agency or citizen or groups.

Fieldwork

Operationally, fieldwork can be defined as practice of social work theory and methods in implementation of programmes or projects within the community or agency. It can be purposefully achieved through setting of objective or classifying goals for the intervention purpose. Purposeful fieldwork would be guided by the working philosophy of the institutions. Even supervisors have a great role to intervene in the activity of the supervisees to make their fieldwork more purposeful and objective-oriented.

So, an analysis of adoption of fieldwork means a study of several variables from the level of the institute, the agency and community setting to the capacity of the workers or students.

Social Work

Social work is a form of professional and social activity which encompasses a wide range of social strategies aiming to help, enable, support and empower the individual, group or people with whom social worker works.

Social work is a profession promoting social change, problem-solving in human relationships and the empowerment and liberation of people to enhance well-being, utilizing theories of human behaviour and social systems.

Social work is a helping and problem-solving profession to enhance and utilize their own resources to develop coping capacities.

Social work as helping individuals, groups and communities enhance or restore their capacities for social functioning, developing and creating societal conditions favourable to achieving goals.

Social work is a diverse, complex and multidimensional model of professional practice. It includes intervention in models that deal with individuals and households, with communities, and organizations, and shares the process of policy analysis, and social action and advocacy with many other groups in society.

Case Study

Case study is basically an empirical enquiry that investigates a contemporary phenomenon within its real life context, deeply and intensively.

Case study is also a diagnostic study oriented towards finding out what is happening and why it is happening and what can be done about it. Case study could be defined as that study usually characterized by thorough examination of specific social settings or particular aspects of social settings, including in varying details psychological descriptions of persons in those settings.

Case study is a method of analysing and exploring the life of a social unit of an individual, group, family, institution or a total community.

Case study is an intensive study of a case which may be an individual, a group, an institution, a system or a community, an organization, an event or entire community in their natural environment, and for a longer period of time. Case study can provide a richly detailed 'portrait' of a social phenomenon. It often answers to How? Why? Who? What? and When? However, the questions are focused on a contemporary phenomenon within a real life context.

Objectives of the Study

The general objective of the study is "to analyse the nature and content of fieldwork training in different schools of social work in India".

The specific objectives of this study are:

1. To find out the background and perception of the social work students and educators regarding the objectives, content of fieldwork and supervision at schools of social work;
2. To understand the nature of assignments undertaken by the students both at agency and community level emphasizing on the issue, programmes and nature of work, and its outcomes;
3. To explore the domain of fieldwork in schools of social work;
4. To explore new process and mechanisms of fieldwork; and
5. To explore and evaluate the emerging trends of fieldwork today.

Research Design

There are different dimensions of areas that have been explored under this study such as goals, contents of fieldwork training, supervision, assignments undertaken by the students, goals' assignments, issue addressed, programme and nature of work, client groups, new ways and means of fieldwork used by the students, exploring the emerging trends of fieldwork with new requirements of the present scenario of the market of globalization, etc. In order to carry out the present research, an 'Exploratory Research Design' has been adopted following the above objectives of the study.

Types of Data Required

To achieve the objectives we need the data from the students, teachers/educators, departments, senior professors and fieldwork coordinators.

The study has been conducted in four phases. In the first phase, secondary data related to fieldwork and its different issues and components have been gathered through extensive literature review. In the second phase, the list of the different social work schools was prepared and useful contact had been established with social work educators, fieldwork directors in different schools in India for the purpose of the present study. The fifteen schools of social work were selected by using purposive sampling to make an in-depth case study. In the third phase, the pilot study has been made for a week to test the tools of data collection. In the last phase, the respondents of different categories like MSW final year students, fieldwork directors in some schools, social work educators were focused through mailed questionnaires and personal interview with senior educators in different schools of social work in different universities and focused group discussion with students (FGD) were also taken care of, to collect detailed information for the study. Total of 300 (20 from each school) students and 90 (6 from each school approximately) social work educators were taken as respondents for this study.

The collected data have been analysed and interpreted by generating different themes and categories relevant to the topic and presented by descriptive writing.

Sampling Design

Universe

The study is based on fifteen schools of social work in different universities of India. It has covered four zones, i.e., North, South, East and West zones of India. Seven schools from North, five from South, two from East and one from West zone have been covered under my study.

It has used "random sampling" covering 20 MSW final year students, their perceptions on fieldwork training both in community or agency level and also the perceptions of the social work educators towards fieldwork training from the schools of social work. Also the study has used 'case study' method to get in-depth understanding about the fieldwork.

Sampling Size

Total 300 students and 90 social work educators were taken as respondents for this study from different schools of social work in India.

Sampling Unit

In this study, the sampling unit consists of both the male and female MSW final year students and educators from the schools of social work institutions in India.

Sampling Technique

Since the universe was undefined, both 'probability and non-probability sampling' techniques have been used by the researcher in this study. To achieve the first objective 'simple random sampling' has been used. To achieve the other objectives, the 'purposive sampling' technique (non-probability) has been used for collecting primary data and also secondary data will be supported for analysing of departmental profiles, and fieldwork manuals on the basis of purposive sampling.

Pilot Study

The researcher has taken sufficient care and efforts while framing the 'questionnaire schedule' for different categories of respondents. Before the finalization of the questionnaire, the researcher had conducted some interviews of some respondents from all the categories for the purpose of knowing and understanding whether questions set in the questionnaire schedule were meaningful, clear and properly fulfilling the objectives. After doing the pilot study, data was processed and results were also obtained and then few questions were reformulated, replaced and deleted for seeking the desired and expected responses from the respected respondents, and making the questionnaire meaningful from research point of view.

Methods and Techniques of Data Collection

The data was collected through both 'primary and secondary sources'. All the students of MSW final year of all the institutions were given 'questionnaire' to collect the data as primary sources. All the educators of the institutions had administered questionnaire to collect the primary data. Also, the researcher had 'discussions' with senior professors and fieldwork directors to get more in-depth understanding about the fieldwork and related issues. The researcher used Focused Group Discussions (FGDs) with both students' community and educators' community in some of the institutions/departments to get a concrete idea and additional idea and knowledge about fieldwork and other related issues as a primary source of data. The researcher also used 'Observation Method' for the present study to acquaint himself with the actual fieldwork training, supervision and evaluation practices in some of the schools of social work in India and field welfare agencies during my supervision time to time.

As a secondary source, books, journals, the fieldwork files, fieldwork manuals, departmental profile, have been consulted to get data.

Analysis and Interpretation

After collecting the data, the researcher has checked carefully and all the entries were edited properly. Then, the code book was prepared and master sheets were filled. The master sheets were processed through computer using Microsoft Excel and SPSS package and tables were prepared in which data was furnished in different tabular form. Then the proposed data was analysed and interpreted, and the results were obtained accordingly. Lastly, conclusions containing findings and suggestions were drawn on the basis of the observations, discussions and interpretation of the data.

Research Gaps and Limitations

Previous review of literature have mainly focused on philosophy, content, principles of fieldwork, objectives, techniques, supervision, fieldwork in agency setting have been touched upon but the domain of fieldwork, process and mechanisms and emerging trends were not taken into account. In this study, the researcher has tried to focus on those areas of research gaps especially the domain, fieldwork process, mechanisms and emerging trends in the present scenario.

During the whole research study, the researcher faced some problems relating to review of literature, collecting data and information from some of the schools. They are as follows:

1. Till now, very few studies (if any) have been done related to fieldwork in India and as a result, there was dearth of data and

materials available (only 4–5 books on fieldwork are available that can be relied upon). The researcher completely depended on his own study only.
2. Initially, some of the schools were unwilling to support and provide detailed information especially about the supervision, the students in the field by the department faculty, problems of fieldwork and availability of programmes and extension activities in the department, etc.
3. As far as the review of literature is concerned, there are very few articles and studies available. Only some articles and studies based on fieldwork and supervision in fieldwork are available in the *Indian Social Work Journal* and *British Social Work Journal*. But these were written in the era of 1970s and 1980s and there is a scarcity of new relevant articles and studies so far in India.

The Historical Perspective of Fieldwork

The professional social work education started in India in 1936 with the establishment of Sir Dorabji Tata Graduate School of Social Work, now known as Tata Institute of Social Sciences. The school came into existence after ten years of practical social work in a neighbourhood of Bombay (now Mumbai) which brought out the needs for professional training into bold relief. The intellectuals at that time were engaged in solving of social, cultural and political causes, though in number they were very few. Then, the next milestone to achieve was the establishment of a community centre at Nagapara in Bombay (now Mumbai), i.e., 'Nagapada Neighbourhood House' in 1926. There was an inspiration, idealism and a perspective of Clifford Manshardt, who was a Protestant Missionary, which provided sustenance to the early pioneers of the new profession. In the growth of any human effort, and also profession for that matter, if the inspiration becomes reutilized and ritualized, it breeds a sense of despondency. Therefore, for its nature, exploration and idealism are always necessary at different stages of growth. On the occasion of the opening of the school, dangers and uselessness of modern social work ideas imported from the West had been clearly pointed out, and the advice had been given that the real power of the new institution and of the emerging profession would lie in influencing the people who had lived and worked in the neighbourhood. The spirit of service, and deep and profound practice experience was emphasized on this occasion. The school, therefore, while aiming to uphold high academic standards also sought to be eminently practical and endeavoured to apply the best of modern social thinking to the solution of social problems. The field and the ferment of the time charted the course for the nascent profession. Even though the model of neighbourhood work, and later, social work education was western, it could not remain unaffected by such developments taking place in a traditional industrializing society as the Factory Act of 1891 (amended later on), The Workmen's Compensation Act 1923, Organization of Trade Unions, The Report of Royal Commission on Labour in India 1931, The Payment of Wages Act 1936, The Bombay Trade Dispute Act 1934, etc., and the demand for workers in the juvenile courts. These developments led to the institution of special courses in labour welfare and correctional administration then. The growth of the new institution thus was abundantly influenced by the pioneering, dynamic, and interdisciplinary approach to professional social work. The other schools which came into existence under the auspices of the Christian missions also were preceded by years of practical experience, but later on, this trend was reversed, and the university, colleges and departments were established without any tradition of practice. Although these institutions were modelled on the lines of their predecessor's inspiration and idealism in their cases were lacking. Routinised and stereotyped academic focus was predominant which did not prove helpful to explore the field and to pioneer new ventures depending upon the needs and problems of the areas and the challenge of the time.

Even after 74 years of existence, the individual schools and the professional associations are yet to define the goals of social work education and fieldwork in a society which is wedded to the ideals of socialism, secularism, social justice and democracy. The Second Review Committee Report also has not spelt out in clear and precise terms the goals of social work education although it has given description of its needs, functions and the direction that it should take. It also suggested for the constitution of a sub-committee to draw up the course content of fieldwork. The secondary importance is given to fieldwork by the committee is clear from the fact that while it found time to make recommendations on theory courses extensively, it disposed of fieldwork in a few pages leaving it to the professional associations and the schools to give serious thought to this important aspect. Initially, the main focus of fieldwork was primarily community-based and client-based but with the development of problems, areas fieldwork as well as social work has been scattered and very wide.

In spite of the growth of social work education and practice, the growth of social work literature produced in the country has been very much slow and not up to the satisfaction level. Siddiqui (1987) had pointed out that "the trend of interchange from practice to teaching and vice versa is rather weak in India as people tend to stick to either practice or teaching". This led to creation of a wide gulf between social work educators and practitioners. The practitioners possess valuable experience, but they lack the research and writing still necessary for producing literature. Educators, on the other hand, do not possess the grassroots experiences needed to modify their understanding of methods grounded in the literatures produced in the West. From the viewpoint of sustaining the claims of social work as a profession, it must be accepted that a differential knowledge base of social work derived from Indian experience and material has yet to be developed. The main reasons are the lack of research activity in professional schools, absence of involvement of the teaching faculty in social work practice, irrelevant role situations of the practitioners in the field, etc. So, social work has to move towards professionalism, it must have indigenous foundations incorporating dominant cultural philosophies on one hand, and projected goals which are being promoted on the other.

Review of Literature

It is known that field education is one of the core components of professional social work training programmes worldwide. Review of available literature appears to suggest that research and publications on field education are very few, with even less relating to field education in national, international and cross-cultural contexts. Ryan and Martyn's (1996) observations was that although students are the main actors in fieldwork, their inputs are very limited in field education research. Spencer and McDonald (1998) note that there were no articles written by students projecting the student perspective. Thus, remarkably, the voice of the student was absent from the literature. They further point out that what the students learn during the placement or concerning their process of learning was largely missing in the field education literature and suggest the importance of including students' perspectives in future research. Recognizing this gap, Patford (2000) has explored students' perceptions of key learning experiences and has analysed seven significant learning experiences (feeling at a loss and the need to gain knowledge and skills, academic learning; operating solo, organizational constraints, discomforting social interactions, regulating emotion, and reappraising his/her commitment to social work) and seven lessons learnt (the embodiment of social work principles/values in practice, self confidence and self-management, the impact of organizational structures and staff relationships on practice, the management of emotion; that life is fragile and unpredictable, the importance of process; personal suitability for particular social work roles in particular settings) during practice in the area of disabilities and reflected on the role of a social worker.

There is a great drawback of social work education in not having enough indigenous literature and everybody accuses each other, some accuse academicians and practitioners of not being able to produce requisite relevant literature for both the teaching and practice of it.

Kulkarni (1993) made a point that professional social work, as it has evolved in India, is a graft on the ancient heritage and not an independent transplant. So far as the production of indigenous literature on social issues and problems, welfare services, and other social work scene in India is concerned, the country has produced immense amount of literature on wide variety of social work subjects almost from 1947. Though social work in India has adopted and adapted a lot from western countries, but undoubtedly it has a soul and a body of its own.

Our social work literature has been surveyed by our professionals and educators at different intervals which include Dudlani, Pathak, *ASSWI*, *IJSW*, Desai, Jacob, etc. The very first initiative was taken by the University Grants Commission and Ministry of Education, Social Work Education and Indian Universities in 1965. G.C. Dudlani of MS University, Baroda, had done a survey of social work education in India in 1967 and concluded by saying that there is lack of literature for teaching and research, but he pointed out the ongoing efforts to produce literature as praiseworthy. *The Indian Journal of Social Work* (*IJSW*) had brought out a special issue titled "Thirty Years of Social Work in India" in 1967. Then, the University Grants Commission (UGC) appointed the First and Second Review Committee in 1965 and 1987 respectively where they found that the majority of social work institutions in India have a very small number of publications and teaching material. T.K. Nair has published a collection of papers organized by *ASSWI* in 1981, on "Four Decades of Social Work Practice and Education in India" at Madras School of Social Work. S. Pathak had reviewed *Fourty Years of Social Work Education in India* in 1987. K.K. Jacob (1994) edited papers presented in National Seminar on "Five Decades of Social Work Education in India: Retrospect and Prospect", jointly organized by Udaipur School of Social Work and *ASSWI* under the title *Social Work Education in India: Retrospect and Prospect.* On the auspicious occasion of the completion of diamond jubilee, 60 years on social work in India in 1997, Murli Desai had compiled all the contributions made by Indian social work educators under the title, *Literature on Social Work Profession in India 1936–96: A Classified Bibliography* divided into ten major groups. She also reported in her article on literature *On Social Work Profession in India1936–1996: An Overview* by Desai (1997) that a project on the review of the literature of different aspects of the profession was undertaken with the following objectives: (i) study year-wise trends in the type of literature developed; (ii) compare it with knowledge developed internationally to identify the component of indigenization in the Indian context; (iii) identify Indian literature and organize them into a body of knowledge; (iv) identify gaps in indigenous social literature and evolve directions for further knowledge development; and (v) draw consolidated implications for advancement of professionalism in current social work practice and education.

Jacob (2001) has conducted a survey of social work literature produced by social work educators. As a sponsored research study by Ministry of Social Justice and Empowerment, Jacob has mentioned that articles or books written by social work educators are more on specific fields of social work rather than on social work philosophy, methods or applications.

The important viewpoints of scholars like Kulkarni, Majumdar, Pathak, and Desai have already demonstrated the availability of indigenous literature of social work teaching and its practice. The pioneer educators of social work education like B. Mehta, M. Vasudevan Moorthy, M.S. Gore and G.R. Banerjee contributed considerably to the development of indigenous social work literature by frequently writing articles. Later on, organized campaign for indigenous literature in Asian countries was initiated by Farancas Ysas who was consultant to United Nations Social Welfare and Development Centre for Asia and Pacific (SWDCAP). A strong conviction was laid down by her saying that a profession like social work, which is based on human relationship, must have its literature truly reflecting values, culture, problems of the society in which it has to be taught and practised. Desai stated in 1984 that the profession needs to move away from too much dependence on the provision of services to organizing people to promote change; from institutional to non-institutional programmes; from remedial to those which seek to affect the very causes, which create poverty; from private concern to public issues; from research with a problem focused to one of the action oriented studies-testing ways and means to solve out multiple problems, building models and testing processes and approaches. The social work profession had made a shift, but not significant enough (Desai and Narayan, 1988). A review of literature by Pathak states that social work authors have made substantive and pioneering contribution to the emergence of developmental perspective in social welfare, both nationally and internationally. R.R. Singh argues against prosperity of sorts of some, and deprivation of multitude. He also favours austerity for posterity under a global social charter which would not only map the priority areas of social renewal, both material and moral but would also balance vital human concerns with those that are ecological in a just and evolving plural global social order. He also opined that there should be concern of professional fraternity in human service and others who are concerned with social development and international social work.

The demand of literature in regional languages on social work started with the expansion of undergraduate courses in different parts of our country. Few books are available now in Hindi, Gujarati, Marathi, Bengali, Kannada, Telugu, etc. The Uttar Pradesh Hindi Granth Academy has played a crucial role to bring out about two dozen books on social work methods and fields of social work which have been used by both graduate and undergraduate degree courses students in Hindi heartland. Professors Raja Ram Shastri, Surendra Singh, S.P. Srivastava, Iman Shastri and Kirpal Singh Soodan have provided enormous literature on social work and practice in regional languages. It is important of mention that despite many books originally written in English and translated into regional languages, there is hardly any book originally written in any regional language.

There are very few studies on fieldwork in India so far studied and efforts have been made in this part to review more national and international literature related to the area of present research study. The chapter has been divided into two parts. Part I reviews the existing literature pertaining to the 'Fieldwork Practice in Social Work Education' and Part II highlights the 'Supervision Social Work'.

I
Fieldwork Practice in Social Work Education

This section intends to systematically review and analyse articles and study from *Indian Journal of Social Work, British Journal of Social Work* and a book on the various aspects of "Fieldwork Practice in Social Work Education".

The article, "Fieldwork Training in Social Work" by Moti Ram Maurya (1962) expounds the philosophy of social work in the purview of fieldwork programmes. He says fieldwork programmes serve as a social library in social work. He added that the importance of field experience for an empirically evolved science like social work is evidently paramount and its practice arts are still evolving through the experiences of those who are working in it. Thus, we see that social work has two facets – theory and practice. The significant role of bringing these two aspects of social work together with a view to equipping students to help people realistically and constructively is performed by fieldwork. He further added that fieldwork fuses harmoniously and thus gives a real shape and form to the professional practice of social work that aims at attaining satisfying relationship between people. In either person-to-person or person-to-group practice both class and field instruction contribute to the student's learning to use himself as a professional person and to apply his increasing knowledge in a manageable union of experience. According to him, the fieldwork means both goal-oriented and student-centred in its approach to learning and also it is as know-how of social work focuses on the student's professional need and the competence required for his successful and effective work. Lastly, he explains some components of fieldwork situation such as the student, the supervisor and the social agency.

The article, "The Role of Fieldwork in Modern Social Work Education" by J.M. Kapoor (1961) has emphasized on the importance of fieldwork in social work and how students slowly progress towards professional competence. Containing some questions like who is a field worker? and what are the objectives of fieldwork training in social work education?, he explains that fieldwork training in professional education is consequential because of its nature of dealing with the problems practically. He added, it is evident that fieldwork varies in quality and quantity. The duration of time is one factor, amount of working another and it is not merely visiting an agency or observing what goes on. But training of fieldwork is always done under the able supervision of well-equipped faculty supervisor and also, sometimes, under the supervision of an agency supervisor. According to him, a supervisory process has the five-fold objectives such as to integrate two complementary companions, i.e., classroom teaching and fieldwork practice with a view to maintaining equilibrium between the academic level of the learner and his working capacities with his clients; to translate the theoretical knowledge into action; to provide the working situation to the learners in order to enable them to acquire competence and skills in tackling the problems scientifically; to explore the needs of students in professional learning; and to develop emotional maturity of the students. He also mentions 'supervised fieldwork' which means a method by which a social worker, in the beginning, learns how to translate his knowledge into practice. This beginning stage, later on, becomes a habit of the learner, as soon as he acquires skills and techniques in the working situation.

Reynolds Rosemary (1961), in her article, "The Relationship of Field Placement to Classroom Teaching" has elaborately described three basic principles of modern professional social work training: (1) complementary classroom and fieldwork; (2) actual work in social agency rather than merely an opportunity for observation; and (3) individualized supervision of a tutorial nature. She further described that fieldwork comprises three elements, i.e., plan, methods and goals and all the three methods can be tested according to the principles. In the first principle, she mentions that schools of social work use two types of fieldwork learning – the concurrent plan and the block plan. In schools using concurrent plan, a student usually spends two days a week in field and four days a week at school throughout his two years of professional training. In some of the schools, in India as well as abroad, the fieldwork days are increased from two to three owing to greater emphasis on fieldwork. In the second principle, it is said that the fieldwork placement provides realistic work situation to students for practical experience. During the whole work situations, a student is supervised directly or indirectly and certain safeguards are maintained with a view to overcome his difficulties which he faces often and to remove the pressure of work or forces internally or externally. In the absence of these safeguards, his field experience follows the general plan and pattern of work within the agency. In the third principle, she analyses that throughout the field placement the student is provided with constant supervision. Supervision of student is done for various reasons. The student of social work is expected to become a professional worker upon completion of his training.

The next article "Field Instruction in Social Work Education in India: Some Issues" by Devi Prasad and B. Vijayalakshmi (1997) has rightly narrated that field instructions is a crucial component of social work education and is recognized as an educational process to facilitate integrative and experiential learning. Though the pattern and organization of social work practicum have some universality, the micro-based practice model adopted in the Indian context has led to inappropriately designed field education programmes producing students unsuited to meet the developmental need of the Indian society. They further added that field practice comprises experiential learning where the field instructor and the student use the theoretical perspectives taught in the classroom as foundations for the development of practice skills of techniques in the field and the major role of the field instructor is to help the student to see connection, relationship, differences and similarities between concepts taught in the classroom and realities in the field. They mention fieldwork instruction in an international perspective and say irrespective of the dichotomies between micro and macro social work practice models of the region or nation, the field instruction programme seems to have greater consistency cross-nationally in terms of its educational values, pattern of field practicum and the profession's accountability for the quality of field learning of students.

M. Vasudeva Moorthy (1953), in his article, "Scientific Approach to Field Work", points out various aspects and tools of fieldwork. He says that in the social work training the term 'fieldwork' is used to signify that area of training in which a candidate acquires experience of actual social situations with reference to their control, functioning and administration. Fieldwork is distinct from classroom work or library work. He has given some objectives of fieldwork like: (1) first hand acquaintance of social and personal situations or problems of which he reads; (2) to indicate in him the ability to apply techniques developed in each social work area for the solution of the said situations; and (3) to give an experience of the use of routine procedures relating to recording and administration, this is incidental to the second. In his article, he tried to raise some questions like what should be the content of the fieldwork programme? Who should plan it? Where the programme should be worked? How can the items of the fieldwork programme be effectuated? What are the available criteria to judge whether a student has fulfilled the fieldwork requirements and how well he has fulfilled it? And finally, within what time should fieldwork be completed and how should this time be arranged, as a continuous block period or at regular or irregular intervals? Should it be gone through before or during or after the theoretical training programme? Further he tried to answer all these questions systematically. He introduced seven tools of fieldwork through which the programmes could be built such as: (1) visits and observation, (2) interview, (3) study of reports, records, books, class, pamphlets, etc., (4) actual participation in work situation, (5) recording, (6) reporting of these experiences in class seminars, and (7) participation in seminar and criticism of one's own work and others.

He also uses those tools in seven different situations such as:

1. Physical environment
2. The cultural environment (language, religion, traditions, history)

3. The social and political environment (mores, public opinion, government)
4. The economic environment which includes the work environment (income, nature of work, leisure)
5. The family environment (type of family, authority, affection)
6. The individual personality (personal attachments, interests, aspirations, hopes, fears)
7. The organization or agency (codes, forms, procedures)

He finally incorporates that person or persons responsible for teaching in the classroom should also plan the programme of the fieldwork through cooperation of agencies, problem of placement, training in theory, block period placement and candidate's evaluation. Side by side he has produced five factors towards the success of the fieldwork programme:

1. Equipment of the student;
2. Appearance of the field worker;
3. Approach that is adopted;
4. Acceptance of the programme and the field worker by the clientele and the agency; and
5. Guidance.

Fiona Jones, Ben C. Fletcher and Keith Ibbetson (1991), in their empirical study, *Stressors and Strains amongst Social Workers: Demands, Supports, Constraints, and Psychological Health* has described the work stressors and psychological strains experienced by social workers in Hertfordshire using a questionnaire, based on Payne's model of occupational stress, investigated the perceived demands, supports, and constraints of the work including threats and violence in addition to more subjective perception of pressure. Their research study aimed to establish the extent and nature of stress amongst social workers in the fieldwork and to pinpoint the specific features of the work which are associated with particularly poor levels of psychological health. It also tried to suggest possible courses of action to alleviate excessive pressure. Their research evaluated that while the social worker found their job satisfying, they perceived the work as very pressured and felt that the pressure adversely affected the service they provided. The psychological health measures indicated that levels of general anxiety were particularly high. The most highly stressed worker perceived their jobs as more demanding and less supportive and estimated that they took twice as much sick leave. Various recommendations are also made at alleviating strain by reducing demand and constrains and increasing support. They also focus on the comparison between 'high stress' and 'low stress' social workers in a field situation using some proposed services like: staff counselling service, mutual support within teams, Stress management training, staff appraisal, paid sabbaticals and unpaid leave.

The article, "Integrated Methods Approach: A Challenging Possibility in Field Work Instructions" by V.D. Mehta (1975) has referred three basic methods of social work, viz., case work, group work and community organization and its practice in the field. She observed that by and large it has been found that among all the methods, case work gets the strongest concentration in schools of social work where there is both generic and specific training and the students well informed about case work practice in the fields of family and child welfare, medical and psychiatric social work, correctional administration, etc., without the subsequent focus on other two. She also referred that unlike the USA, we have not adopted the system of method specialization in our school curricula and undoubtedly, the Indian social worker is much more of a generalist and has been a forerunner in this than this western counterpart, who considers himself as a case worker, group worker or community organizer. Adding to this, she mentions that while we have been called upon to use all the techniques, many of our educationists and practitioners have not theorized or grasped the content and mode of integration of methods and the various innovative ways in which we can implement social work programmes. She has given concentration on the basic theoretical framework for the integrated methods approach by saying that there can be no effective implementation of programmes in the field unless the students have a prior and sound conceptual understanding of the methods. She has also clarified the role of a supervisor and responsibility of the schools in dealing with students during their fieldwork. She lastly concluded by an observation that social work theory and practice, today more than even before are in a state of dynamism and flux because of new technologies and political movement and the current feature in the field of social work is to venture and pioneer. Very little was done in this direction during the 1940s and 1950s when social workers were more concerned with their professional identity and development, but today the profession is looking for ways to take the agency to the community and reach out to the alienated victims of technocracy.

R.R. Singh (2005), in his article, "Configuring Field Practice and Field Education in Social Work" has clearly mentioned some terms like field practice, field education, fieldwork and practical training used by social philosophers, educators and practitioners, and also explain those terms and its application in the context of professional training in social work. He also brings out the interrelationship and unity of theory and practice in social work.

Karen Healy (2005), in her book, *Social Work Theories in Context: Creating Frameworks for Practice* has clearly discussed the importance and relationship of theory with practice. She tried to identify the major ideas that form the foundation of social work practice for gaining knowledge of these ideas and increasing its relevance to social work's values and goals. She idealistically focused on social work ideas which cover a complex terrain including context, discourse and theories. By 'context' she tried to mean the interaction between the organization and the profession's formal base. The term 'discourse' explained by her was based on the influence on practice by bio-medicine, economics and the law, for example, seem to minimize the rich complexities inherent in the real life situations of social workers and their clients. In terms of social work 'theories', she argues that theories are critical to accurate assessments and effective delivery and that practitioners, along with academics, share responsibility for their development. She tried to mean theory as 'theories in situ' and ultimately it is at the level of these specific case theories that social workers make sense of the problems in broader aspect.

II
Supervision in Social Work

This section also intends to systematically review and analyse articles from *The Indian Journal of Social Work* on the various aspects of "Supervision in Social Work".

G.R. Banerjee (1975), in her article, "Professional Self and Supervision in Social Work", has rightly discussed the social work profession, demands on the self, i.e., professional self and personal self and supervision as an aid of development of professional self. She minutely observed that unlike a pure academic discipline, social work is a service-oriented discipline and a helping profession. She added that in discharging his professional duties, in most of the professions the practitioner has to give something based on his knowledge of the subject concerned. The profession attempts to enable the client to mobilize his resources towards the goal and great emphasis is laid on client participation, i.e., doing things 'with' the client rather than 'for' him, believing in self-determination of the client (individual, group or community) as well as in self-help which is a natural corollary. According to her, the most important tool at the disposal of the social worker is his own person – his own 'self'. She dictated that social work profession makes demands on the practitioner especially in four areas of 'knowing', 'feeling', 'doing', and 'being'. In all professions, the practitioner has to assimilate a body of knowledge to equip himself for practice. So a demand on the 'knowing' aspect of the self is unavoidable. She emphasized on the professional and personal self and she cited that when one talks of the professional self, one seems to mean the 'disciplined self'. In social work profession the disciplined self in all its knowing, feeling, doing and being aspects plays an important part. Referring to supervision as an aid to the development of the professional self, she highlighted that originally supervisor's role was seen as an administrative one. As schools of social work came to being broadly, the profession began to take form, and within it the role of the supervisor as a person particularly concerned with the development of professional methods and standards, and gradually teaching and helping aspects in supervision for staff development or education in social work assumed importance.

S.H. Pathak (1975), in his article, "Supervision in Social Work: Historical Development and Current Trends" has clearly mentioned the supervision, its development in USA as well as in India and the problems of supervision in social work. He dictated that it is a part of the administrative process having two main functions, i.e., administrative and teaching. He further added that in the early years of social work education (which began in USA during the last decades of the 19th century), it was almost a practical necessity for the schools to send students for fieldwork to the agencies and to have them supervised by the agency staff. The schools in those days did not have adequate financial resources either to start their own training centres or to employ the required number of teachers for supervision of students. Referring to the supervision in social work in India, he highlighted that very little has been written on this topic. He added that as early as 1830 there was a social welfare agency in existence in Calcutta (now Kolkata) and between in 1880 to 1910 the Christian missionaries and Indian social reformers had started several institutions for the orphans and the widows in different parts of the country. Social service league was founded in Bombay (now Mumbai) in 1911 and started programmes for the welfare of women and industrial workers and some form of supervision at least in its administrative aspect might have existed during this period. Lastly, he highlighted some problems of supervision like the social welfare agencies has compelled the schools of social work to provide supervision in field instruction mainly through their teachers. This has increased the workload of the teachers in many schools which are understaffed and affected adversely the quality of supervision, there are few schools which have not yet recognized the importance of supervised field instruction for professional practice and also there is the glaring discrepancy between the approach of the agency staff (mostly non-professional) and the approach of the school supervisors young, theoretically well versed but inexperienced in practice, which often creates confusion instead of clarity, and cynicism instead of commitment to the profession in the minds of the students.

The article, "Educational and Helping Aspects of Field Work Supervision" of Grace Mathew (1975) has clearly indicated some dimensions like motivation and learning, capacity for learning, learning and growth, and some obstacles to learning and its resistance. He mentions that fieldwork in social work is the learning-by-doing aspect of social work education and the supervisory process is the facilitating medium and the demand of learning and doing in fieldwork exert heavy pressure on the student-worker and this situation calls upon the fieldwork supervisor to play the double role of teacher-cum-helper. He also added that there are opportunities for learning and growth and the student-worker has two opportunities: (1) students need to get up-to-date knowledge regarding theory and practice, and (2) also have a variety of learning situations.

K.D. Gangrade (1975), in his article, "School of Social Work: Field Work Agency Liaison" has focused mainly on the relationship between school and agency from the experiences of organizing fieldwork at the Delhi School of Social Work. He highlighted on the adoption criteria to select agencies, its fieldwork programmes and relevant prerequisites. He showed the criteria to select agency like: (1) the agencies should have a programme of activities through which the student could obtain first-hand experience in the use of social work skills; (2) the student should be able to obtain, through observation and participation in its various programmes, an understanding of and insight into human problems, both social and individual; (3) the agency should be willing to give to the students access to all relevant records and reports, pertaining to his work; (4) the agency should be willing to designate some responsible person from its staff who would meet the student regularly, at least once a fortnight, to discuss the programme of the student and any problems or difficulties that the student might want to bring up; and (5) the agency should recognize the value of training and decide not to use the student as a substitute for its regular staff to assign him work that would have no educational content. Further, he added that the school provides observational visits, rural camp, concurrent fieldwork and block fieldwork programmes to the students. Again, he added that there are three types of agencies such as: (1) the first which has a sound programme and trained personnel staff, (2) the second category of agencies are those which are neither able to provide a trained worker nor are convinced of the usefulness of trained personnel, and (3) the third type of agency is developed by the school itself to pioneer and demonstrate the efficacy of a new service. Lastly, he has pointed out some prerequisite of the agency-school relationship such as correspondence, visits, staff meetings, quarterly meetings, institutes and seminars, special lectures, participation in study circles, other facilities and block fieldwork agencies.

In the previous studies, many dimensions of fieldwork like challenges, instructions, scientific approaches, supervision, professional training, evaluation in fieldwork, agency's liaison, etc., were discussed and focused. But as per as the area of fieldwork research is concerned, it has not been scientifically and systematically focused and less research has been done so far in India.

3 Social Work and Its Emerging Perspectives

Any profession in any society has to be socially relevant and must provide its services with all professional competence to the satisfaction of its clients. Social work originated as a philanthropic activity by few well-to-do individuals or groups but gradually grew as a profession in between these temporal and conflict processes of change in value-facts and means-ends interrelations. The perceptions, cognitive processes and whole approach towards life is in the continuous cycle of change. As challenges have increased in number, complexity and variety, the mechanisms for coping with these difficulties have also taken a paradigm shift. Now, we can see that a person is not labelled as a patient who is sick psychologically, but a client who is in need of a professional service with knowledge, skills and expertise in human affairs. A client in this sense of the term is prepared for the service rendered to him, and is very much aware of the results he is expecting to derive from such a professional relationship.

The evolution of any profession or discipline should be understood in the context of transient socio-economic and political conditions and its cumulative effects on an individual, groups or community or society as a whole. Before it takes as a discipline or professional shape, it has to go through certain phases that question its need and relevance, conceptual framework, scope, methods and techniques, application in day-to-day life situation and above all its qualification to a scientific nature. Here social work as a discipline is not an exception either. Social work has developed in essence and nature through temporal changes in its approach to the problems and their solutions, reaching to almost every aspects of life. So, the necessity of social work developed from the side-effect of the process of urbanization, industrialization and social insecurity, maladjustment within individuals, groups, etc. As a consequence, a problem-oriented and a systematized form of assistance known as the 'professional social work' came into being.

Even during the last decade, the policies of liberalization, privatization and globalization (LPG) and its effects have played a major role in some aspects such as: (1) the source of public service delivery system have tremendously increased through volunteerism, foreign assistance and development of non-governmental organizations; (2) the horizon of agencies and institutions offering such public welfare services have grown beyond expectations due to revolution in the field of information technology leading to global networking of social welfare organizations; (3) it has enhanced the status of an individual as a client who is not ready to compromise with the quality of services; (4) the customer satisfaction is the prime focus of all the public service delivery systems today; (5) international organizations have started working in the developing countries because of the increasing number of social problems which have tremendously increased for the effect of LPG. In the backdrop of such scenario, there is a need for professionalism in social work practice.

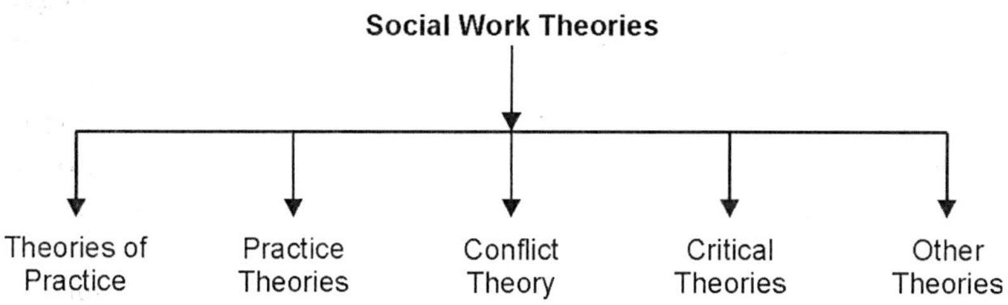

Theories of Practice: The concept and understanding drawn from other social sciences like Sociology, Psychology, Economics, Anthropology, and Political Science.

Practice Theories: They use directly to solve the problems using Social Work Methods like Case Work, Group Work, Community Organization, Social Action, Social Research and Social Administration.

Conflict Theory: This includes and believes in Radical Social Work.

Critical Theories: This includes Feminist Social Work, Anti-Oppressive Social Work (working with Dalits, Blacks in USA, etc.), Post-Modernist Social Work, Structural and Post-Structural Social Work.

Other Theories: There are many other theories which are useful for social work intervention such as Psycho-Analytic Theory, Psycho-Dynamic Theory, System Theory, Eco-System Theory, etc. These theories mainly focus on the individual and these are not change-oriented but adaptive.

Conflict and critical theories are basically change-oriented; their main focus is on structural change.

Definitions of Social Work

Alice (1926)

"Social work includes all voluntary attempts to extend benefits in response to needs which are concerned with social relationships and which avail themselves of scientific knowledge and methods".

Witmer (1942)

"The prime function of social work is to give assistance to individuals in regard to the difficulties they encounter in their use of an organized group service or in their performance as a member of an organized group".

Anderson (1943)

"Social work is a professional service rendered to people for the purpose of assisting them, as individuals or in groups, to attain satisfying relationships and standards of life in accordance with their particular wishes and capacities and in harmony with those of the community".

Clarke (1947)

"Social work is a form of professional service comprising a composite of knowledge and skills, parts of which are not distinctive of social work, which attempt on the one hand to help the individuals satisfy their needs in the social milieu, and on the other to remove as far as possible the barriers which obstruct people from achieving the best of which they are capable".

Friedlander (1951)

"Social work is that process which deals with directly and differentially with persons who have problems relating primarily to their social situation and which endeavours, individual to individual to understand what help is needed and to assist the individual to find and utilize the help indicated".

Friedlander (1955)

"Social work is a professional service, based on scientific knowledge and skill in human relations, which assist individuals, alone or in group, to obtain social and personal satisfaction and independence".

Konopka (1958)

"Social work is an entity representing three clearly distinguished but interrelated parts: a network of social services, carefully developed methods and processes and social policy expressed through social institutions and individuals. All three are based on a view of human being, their interrelationships, and ethical demands made on them".

Boehm (1959)

"Social work seeks to enhance the social functioning of the individuals, singly and in groups, by activities focused upon their social relationship which constitute the interaction between man and his environment. These activities can be grouped into three functions: restoration of impaired capacity, provision of individual and social resources, and prevention of social dysfunctions".

Stroup (1960)

"Social work is the art of bringing various resources bear on individual, group and community needs by the application of a scientific method of helping people to help themselves".

Pincus and Minahan (1978)

"Social work is concerned with the interaction between people and their social environment affects the ability of people to accomplish their life tasks, alleviate distress, and realize their aspirations and values".

Definitions of Social Work from Indian Perspective

Definition of social work profession from Indian perspective is influenced by the changing socio-economic as well as the politico-cultural set-up across India.

Kher (1947)

"The aim of social work, as generally understood, is to remove social injustice, to realize distress, to prevent sufferings and to assist the weaker members of society to rehabilitate themselves and their families and, in short, fight the five giant evils of (1) physical want, (2) disease, (3) ignorance, (4) squalor, and (5) idleness".

Conference of Social Work (1957)

"Social work is a welfare activity based on humanitarian philosophy, scientific knowledge and technical skills for helping individuals or groups or community, to live a rich and full life".

Ahmed (1969)

"Social work is a professional service based on knowledge of human relations and skill in relationships and concerned with problems of intra-personal and/or inter-personal adjustments resulting from unmet individual, group, or community need".

Moorthy and Rao (1970)

"Social work is help rendered to any person or group, who or which is suffering from any disability, mental, physical, emotional or moral. So that the individual or group so helped is enabled to help himself or itself".

International Definition of Social Work

In July 2001 in Copenhagen, both International Association of Schools of Social Work (IASSW) and International Federation of Social Workers (IFSW) reached agreement on adopting the following international definition of social work:

> The social work profession promotes social change, problem solving in human relationships and the empowerment and liberation of people to enhance well being. Utilizing theories of human behaviour and social system, social work intervenes at the points where people interact with their environments. Principles of human rights and social justice are fundamental to social work.

The above definition could be analysed and understood in terms of objectives, processes used therein and the principles followed to fulfil the desired purposes. Here social change, problem-solving and attainment of well-being are illustrated as the foci of social work profession. By social change is meant only such alterations as occur in social organizations, that is, the structure and function of society, which also require changes in the mindset, perceptions. Social change is a universal phenomenon that may be natural, spontaneous and unpredictable; while it could be deliberate and conscious efforts on the part of change agents to proceed towards their goals in a pre-planned manner.

Objectives of Social Work

Objectives are the purposive statements that imbibe in it the values and priorities of the concerned organization or a profession that are reflected in its planning and future course of action. Social work also focuses on its objectives with humanitarian philosophy and democratic values as its base. Objectives being the driving force of any institution or a profession are not formulated once in a while only, but objectives have the characteristic features of 'moldability' which provides a profession a much needed validity. In other words, it is modified in accordance with the demands of the people and society as a whole.

Social Commission, Economic and Social Council of the United Nations, states that social work

1. seeks to assist individuals, families and groups in relation to the various social and economic forces by which they are affected, and differs in this respect from certain allied activities, such as health, education and the like;
2. seeks to perform an integrating function for which no other provision is made in contemporary society; and
3. strives to maximize the resources available in the community by promoting the social well-being.

In the present scenario social work ought to perform following objectives:

1. *Self-sufficiency:* Encouraging material and social security as well as income generation activities through socio-economic as well as political organizations due to the increasing side effect of LPG (liberalization, privatization and globalization) policies so that it will ensure every individual and a family the means of satisfying basic physical wants. As a result, the dependency factor gets minimized and an individual or/and family is strengthened to carry on its livelihood.

2. *Social functioning:* Need to create a harmonious balance between individual's tasks and a coping behaviour. It has to solve the psycho-social problems and other related adjustmental problems in order to enhance the social functioning of a person so that he/she can utilize the available opportunities to its optimum level and live cordially with his/her social surroundings.
3. *Social harmony:* Social harmony is the need of the hour as various kinds of inter-group conflicts and prejudices persists in the society on the grounds of caste, religion, and regions. Social justice through fair and ordered relationships between groups should be aimed so that intra-group and inter-group relations are positively established.
4. *Social development:* The fundamental objective of development is to enlarge people's choices. In principle, these choices can be infinite and can change over time. People need greater access to knowledge, better nutrition and health services, more secure livelihood, security against all social vices and physical violence, satisfying leisure time, political and cultural freedom and sense of participation in developmental activities, freedom from terrorist activities, etc. The objectives of social work also intensifies economic growth and distributive justice and simultaneously create an enabling environment for people to enjoy long, healthy and creative life.

Other Contemporary Objectives of Social Work

1. To help people in dealing with their psychological and social problems;
2. To promote the realization of potentials which people have and quite often are not able to actualize because of non-availability of required opportunities and varied kinds of impediments, natural as well as man-made;
3. To care for the health – physical, mental, social and moral – to enable people to perform the roles and responsibilities assigned to them;
4. To create awareness among people of the rights which they have and duties which they are supposed to perform in various walks of life;
5. To empower people by enhancing their capacity to the optimum level to enable them to deal with their problems and difficulties at their own level in an effective manner;

6. To strengthen the existing social institutions conducive for promoting people's well-being;
7. To create new institutions required in the wake of fast changing situations for ensuring fulfilment of unmet needs of the people;
8. To introduce structural changes for equitable redistribution of resources available in society such that inequalities may be as far as possible reduced and equality of opportunities for weaker and vulnerable sections may be guaranteed;
9. To educate people regarding social evils which are against human dignity and are disapproved by existing laws and moral standards that prevail in a society;
10. To organize the oppressed and suppressed in society by conscientizing them and breaking their culture of silence and enabling them to raise their voice against the forces obstructing the realization of their potentials, depriving them of the rights which they are entitled to and perpetrating various kinds of atrocities against them; and
11. To conserve and develop environment by directing developmental efforts in such a manner that the need, and not greed, of everyone be satisfied and enough resources are left for the future generations to lead a minimum desirable standard of living.

Scope of Social Work in India

The scope of social work stems from the basic human needs and its course towards overall human development enriches every aspect of human life. The 'needs' are to be differentiated from 'wants' in the sense that they are inherent and intrinsic in nature, whereas 'wants' are extrinsic and are acquired through environment. All these needs act as driving forces for all human behaviour.

The principle aim was to solve the psycho-social problems which obstructs the individual and social advancement. In reality now the scope is expanding. It is now international and inter-racial.

When we think of the scope of social work in India, some questions come to our mind such as, what is the purpose of the various activities in social work and what exactly do we want to achieve? Who are capable of working as social workers? Who are the target groups? What should be the dimension and magnitude of help? If we get the answer of these questions, certainly we will understand the scope of social work in India at present. The emphasis given on various activities is very often situational. It also depends on the level of priority of planners rather than on the need of the society. In the beginning, social welfare in India covered services for the underprivileged sections, but now it has got broader areas and it becomes difficult to draw a boundary where social work intervention could be the ultimatum. Some of the common areas covered under welfare are as follows:

- Child development and child welfare
- Women development and women welfare
- Youth welfare and development and vocational guidance
- Welfare of weaker sections, especially Scheduled Castes and Scheduled Tribes
- Welfare of physically and mentally challenged, their care, training, and rehabilitations
- Welfare of socially handicapped like prostitutes and their children, leprosy patient and their children, prisoner's family, destitute and homeless peoples
- Social welfare for the rural community and urban poor and slums
- Welfare of labourers of mines, tea gardens, factories and unorganized sectors
- Welfare of criminal and delinquents and their related services
- Welfare activities of rural development programmes and anti-poverty programmes
- Housing programmes for both rural urban poor
- Welfare, treatment and rehabilitation of drug addicts and alcoholics
- Work on the social policies for issues like dowry death, custodial death, rape, inheritance and other women related issues.

Emerging areas should be covered like:

- Issue of Special Economic Zones (SEZs) and its effects
- Evaluation and implementation of 'Bharat Nirman' programme for rural development
- RTI Act regarding accountability of government and other administrative sections to common people
- Micro-finance and micro-credit as a tool of poverty alleviation, evaluation of NREGA scheme/programme
- Migration of unorganized labours
- Corruption and corrupted mind of the people
- Misuse of natural resources
- Environmental pollution, deforestation, global warming and its impact on social life

- Terrorism and communalism and its impact on society
- Violation of human rights
- Relief and rehabilitation on natural disaster and disaster management
- Displacement of people especially tribal
- Eco-tourism, livelihood management
- Gay and lesbianism
- Industrialization and its problems and impacts
- Poverty, homelessness and starvation death
- Increasing communalist feelings in people
- NGO management
- Problem of working women
- Wildlife studies and waste management
- Increasing drug addiction in call centres
- Issues related to extinction of rare species

The traditional concept of main three usual tasks assigned to the profession of social work such as restoration, development and change gives a shape to the vast canvas of social work. Werner's description will not only acquaint us with the boundary and scope of social work but will also serve as the common parameters of social work practice between India and western country like USA. Werner W. Boehm had discussed some functions in 1958 but still today any major deviation from them has not taken place. To him social work:

- Helps people enhance and more effectively utilize their own problem-solving and coping capacities;
- Establishes initial linkage between people and resource system;
- Modifies and builds new relationship between people and new resource system;
- Contributes to the development and modification of social policy;
- Dispenses material resources; and
- Serve as agent of social control.[1]

The above-mentioned functions by Werner of social work indicate the growing emphasis on environment rather than on individual behaviour and personality.

It is pertinent for social work students to understand that the scope of social work intervention can be limitless, but we have to operationalize the definition of social work and its intervention according to our resources and needs of the society.

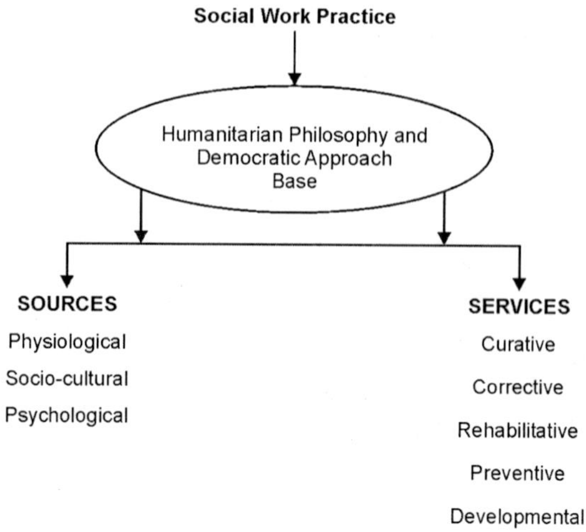

According to P.D. Mishra the functional areas of social work practice can be categorized as shown above in figure. Here 'curative' function provides services like medical services, health services, services relating to psycho-social and mental health, psychiatric services, child guidance, child welfare services, services for the handicapped and disabled and rehabilitative services. 'Corrective' social work has three broad base areas such as 'individual reform services' which include prison reform, probation, parole and other related services; 'services for strengthening and improving relationship' like family welfare services, school social work, industrial social work; and 'services for social reform' like employment services, prevention of prostitution, beggary, prohibition services and removal of untouchables.

On the other hand, 'preventive services' include life insurance, public assistance, social legislation, labour welfare, adult education and prevention of diseases. 'Developmental tasks' are socio-economic developmental activities, education and recreational services, urban and rural development programmes and the policies for integration.

History and Development of Social Work

Evolution of Social Work in England

Historical Understanding

England practically was the pioneer in developing social work in the world, which represent the several centuries of growth during which divergent views have been held at different times regarding the community responsibility for helping the needy and disabled people of the society. Luckily, these experiences have helped to shape the present state of social work.

Although social work in England developed as a philanthropic activity on the margins of statutory services, social work in 20th century became increasingly a professional activity, either carried out directly by the state, or by the voluntary sector on its behalf. Social work has been incorporated steadily into statutory mechanisms since its 'high tide' in the 1970s. Not only has the state won the right to intervene in the lives of individuals, it has effectively taken control over how this should be carried out, and by whom.

Here social work can be discussed through stages like:

Before 1200 AD

This period was considered as the primitive age when the concept of social work and social welfare had not existed. If, there was any problem, people believed that it was a curse from God and they had to face the consequences and there was no other way to escape from it.

1200–1500 AD

This era was called Christian period and had a wide effect all over England. Charity work was prevailing at that time, and in the church large number of missionaries, schools, parishes, dioceses, hospitals and social welfare agencies came into being for helping the needy.

1500–1600 AD

First time in this period, the monarchs started their intervention in charity work. The first constructive measure taken by the government for the relief work was the statute of Henry VIII in 1531. According to the statute, mayors and justices of the place should investigate applications of the aged and papers of those who were unable to work were maintained by the parish. They were to be registered and licensed and were allowed to be in an assigned areas. This law was the beginning of recognition of public responsibility for the poor and needy people. During this period, nationalization of church and charity institutions were done by the government.

1600–1800 AD

This period became important because of the introduction of Elizabethan Poor Law in 1601 and this was the first ever social legislation introduced in England. Under this law, many provisions for social welfare were made such as:

(i) *Residence:* It provides for rendering services to the poor people who were born and brought up in a particular area. Those who were immigrants were not supposed to get residence and at least three years staying in a place was necessary for getting the benefit of social services.

(ii) *Relatives:* If there is an earning member in a family of the destitutes then he or she is not eligible for any social services, because it was the duty of the relative to take care of them.

(iii) *Able-bodied Homes:* There were some people who though physically able, found begging an easy way of living; for them homes were made and small work was given to the people according to their ability to meet their needs. Children of destitutes were given shelter. During this period charity work was discouraged.

1800–1900 AD

During this period, some individual members started working for the welfare of the needy people, and many social scientists also gave their theories for the sustenance of welfare development in the society.

Adam Smith's Theory

This theory was against the government's intention of helping procedure, and it said that the government should minimize its involvement in any field for any purpose, as more help will lead to much dependency. So, this theory was in the favour of controlling of help to the people.

Malthusian Theory

Malthusian said that lot of free service will lead to desire for more children. So charity work should be stopped.

From all these accounts, a Royal Commission emerged in 1832 and it strongly recommended the amendment of Elizabethan Poor Law. Then new Poor Law came into existence in 1834. According to the new poor law, the able-bodied continued to work in able-bodied homes and better help for slum dwellers were provided. A Slum Public Health Act came into force and Factories Act came into being in 1833. Under this Act, minimum facilities should be provided to industrial workers in the factories. Towards the end of the 19th century, many charity organization movements started which was essentially related to professional social work. They started to provide training to their own social workers. In each city these organizations started extending their services to the children, women and destitutes of the society. Later on, they started a special kind of training for professional social workers. In this way here social work became professional and the first school of social work started in 1910.

Period 1900 to Second World War or Early 20th Century Development

By the 19th century a strong reaction had begun against the form and spirit of the Poor Law and new methods of public provision began to appear. So in this connection some measures could be very important to discuss:

(a) *Pensions for Poor Aged People:* Government introduced Old Age Pension Act in 1908 and under its arena, it was the responsibility of the government to help the poor who are over 70 years of age, with a substantial amount of pension.

(b) *Scheme of Social Insurance:* A scheme of statutory social insurance was followed in England in the year 1911. The National Insurance Act was introduced; compulsory insurance against unemployment for workers in certain industries and against sickness and medical costs for lower paid workers.

(c) *Payment of Benefits as a Right:* The National Insurance Act embodied a new provision, namely, the payment of benefits as a right in return for contributions, instead of being dependent on a test of need. Financial sufficiency was ensured by the inclusion of employers and the state itself as contributors, as well as the insured workman.

After Second World War

After Second World War, the scope and variety of provisions beyond the poor increased rapidly in England. Certain gaps and anomalies were found in the provisions at the beginning of the war and nearly every scheme was administered by a different authority. But, all workers were not covered under the insurance scheme and some were covered by one scheme but not by another. Even there was no special provision of protections for dependents of a large family.

The Beveridge Report

There were major changes that took place in June 1941 when a Committee, popularly named as William Beveridge Committee, was established under the Chairmanship of William Beveridge who was entrusted with the task of surveying the existing national scheme of insurance in allied services. His report was presented to the British Parliament in the year 1942 and since then it has been put into by various Acts of the parliament. The main recommendations were:

(i) A comprehensive plan for a unified system of social insurance and social assistance on national basis;
(ii) A new system to overcome the deficiencies found in existing arrangements;
(iii) Instead of a multiplicity of authorities, there should be one authority in the Ministry of Social Security;
(iv) The rates of benefits for different contingencies should be uniform;
(v) Instead of only one part of the population being insured, the whole population should be insured and protected and all within one group to pay one rate of contribution;
(vi) No means test for any insurance benefit taking account only of a person's savings and other resources. It is because management of one's income is an essential element of a citizen's freedom;
(vii) Standing behind the social insurance schemes, the report envisaged a scheme of national assistance for those who for one reason or the other did not satisfy the contribution of other conditions for benefit; and
(viii) Provision for industrial accident and disease should be made through a scheme to be administered by the Ministry of Social Security with regard to workman's compensation.

Implementation of Beveridge Plan

The British Government accepted the report and it was the basis on which the social security structure should be decided. After the War, most of the recommendations were embodied and laws were enacted such as:

- Family Allowances Schemes was introduced in 1946;
- National Health Service was created in 1948;
- National Insurance and Industrial Injuries Acts came into force in 1948; and

- The Poor Law came to an end with the passing of the National Assistance Act of 1948.

Present Social Services in England

The present social services were based on Beveridge Report in England. Since 1948 there have been some extensions and modifications, yet the basic structure of the schemes have not undergone any dynamic changes. The following services and protections were provided after the implementation of Beveridge report such as:

Family Allowance: The Family Allowance Act, 1945 is the legal basis of the family allowances provisions in England. They are provided according to the number of children and allowances are paid out of general taxation. It was intended to benefit the whole family at large.

National Insurance: The National Insurance Act, 1948 is the legal basis of the National Insurance Scheme in Britain. This Act has been amended several times since its operation and certain changes have been made in the years 1952, 1956 and 1959. Under this scheme, every person of working age regardless of his or her income or position in society is legally bound to take part in the scheme and in which regular contributions are paid towards the cost of benefits payable in particular contingencies. Contributions are paid on the basis of class contributor and the benefit available to that class. For this purpose, the insured population is divided into three classes: employed, self-employed and non-employed persons.

National Assistance: The National Assistance Act, 1948 is the legal basis of this assistance and it acts as a kind of safety not to cover those who fall through the other social security schemes. This has no contribution conditions and requires no qualification except financial hardship. It is assessed entirely on the personal basis.

There are many voluntary organizations that played a significant role in the field of social services in England such as:

1. National Council for Social Service
2. The Family Welfare Association
3. The National Old People's Welfare Committee
4. The Standing Conference of National Voluntary Youth Organization
5. The Catholic Child Welfare Council
6. The British Red Cross Society
7. The British Federation of Social Workers

Evolution of Social Work in USA

Social welfare services have existed in USA since the establishment of the original thirteen colonies on the eastern seaboard in the 17th and 18th century. The Elizabethan Poor Law served as the basic pattern for extending financial assistance to the disabled, temporarily unemployed and needy.

Social work in USA could be categorized into phases.

Before 1800 AD

First alms house was established in Massachusetts in 1662 for the disabled and as a workhouse for the able-bodied paupers. After the settlement of New Amsterdam came about several 'sick entroosters' – minor ecclesiastical functionaries whose duties were to visit sick persons in their own homes. The first 'overseas of the poor' was appointed in 1691 in the city of Boston. Associations for the function of charitable aid or mutual benefit were also formed on the basis of national origins and church affiliations. Scots Charitable Society was the first such association which was established in 1657 in Boston and another was the Society of Friends in Pennsylvania. Another development was the broadening of the base of responsibility from the town to the province in Massachusetts for a special category of the poor. The rapid growth of manufacturing industries after the civil war intensified the complexities of social need. People came in large numbers to the urban areas and faced the wrath of poor wages, poor housing, unemployment, etc., but on the other hand a wealthy class of industrialists emerged who contributed voluntary to charity work.

In USA, social work was discovered as a result of 1776 war of independence. At that time, USA was ruled by British. During this time, churches were the main agencies for social work services to the needy. Able-bodied homes were established for the able beggars of the country.

1800–1900 AD

Many voluntary associations emerged during this time, but they were not sincere towards their functioning because exploitation and duplication were common there. At the end of 18th century, different charity organizations emerged throughout the country. Those organizations used to raise funds jointly and distributed it among different agencies. They were also involved in doing survey in the field of social welfare.

Then training programme started for the members engaged in social work activities in 1898. During this time, the first school of social work was established at New York in 1898 with the purpose of imparting training to the members who were engaged in the field of welfare services. It was called New York School of Social Work.

Even the settlement movement led to the establishment of settlement houses like 'Neighbourhood Guild' in the New York City in 1880; J. Adams Hull House in Chicago and Mary Greenrich House in New York City. By the last decades of the 19th century, several new social agencies were established to help the immigrants from Southern and Eastern Europe like Hebrew Sheltering and Immigrants Aid Society. More significant developments took place such as:

- Gradual recognition of the social needs of the people with particular handicaps. Child Labour Legislation was enacted.
- Greater responsibilities to the states when local units could not provide adequate relief to these special groups. First Juvenile Reformatory was established in New York in 1825. First schools for deaf and blind were respectively established in 1817 and 1830.
- Emergence of the private agencies, e.g., YMCA.

1900–1935 AD

Social welfare programmes were developed during the first half of 20th century such as:

- Rise of philanthropic foundations: Carnegie Foundation, Rockefeller Foundation, Russell Sage Foundation, Commonwealth Foundation were founded;
- Growth of public parks, playgrounds, programmes for the conservation of natural resources, boy scouts, girl scouts club programmes, etc.;
- Special Wartime Programmes – American Red Cross Services, National Recreation Association, War Risk Insurance Act came into being;
- Growth and establishment of local departments of public health and vocational rehabilitation;
- Programme planning for the voluntary welfare agencies included the rise of the community chest movement. Cleveland Welfare Federation was organized in 1913;
- Improvement in state institutions for the mentally ill;
- Juvenile courts were established separately;

- Civil liberties and inter-group relations were advanced through National Urban League in 1910;
- Chicago School of Civics and Philanthropy was established in 1901 under University of Chicago;
- Simon College in Boston on Medical Social Work came into being and Dr Robert Clot did pioneer work in relation to medical care; and
- American Association of Schools of Social Work was established in 1919.

The main incident during this period was the economic depression in 1929 and because of that many people lost their jobs. As a result, FERA – Federal Emergency Relief Act in 1933 was passed by the government and it emphasized on the appointment of trained social workers to work in the field of social relief, like family counselling, case work, etc. After that, FERA and Social Security Act, 1935 was passed by the government. So, the professional social work found a prominent place in the history of social work in USA.

Period 1935 Onwards

Anti-poverty programme started both in urban and rural areas from 1960. During this period, anti-oppressive movement was going on in USA and for this concern, lot of individual personalities like Martin Luther King, the leader of the congress, along with other leaders pressurized the government to provide equal rights to every citizen irrespective of being black or white. Now many voluntary organizations are working for the needy in the welfare areas and for practicing it they need to have license and without it no person can practice social work in voluntary or in government agencies.

Evolution of Social Work in India

Social work profession is not Indian by birth; it should, however, not be considered completely without a glorious past in India. India had a tradition of philanthropy and social services in the past and it was a natural result of the prosperity and intellectual ferment which prevailed in ancient India. So, we can say social work in India is as old as the Indian society itself. Every aspect of Indian culture is predominated by humanitarian philosophy. But, social work in the form of institutional services is of recent origin. Poverty, economic backwardness and political dependency have been the main obstacles in the smooth development of social work in India. But especially after political independence, it has assumed a new dimension in India. To understand the evolution of social work in India we have to go back in our traditional ancient period. So, here we can discuss the evolution of social work with reference to some phases of Indian history such as:

1. Ancient and Medieval Period
2. Muslim Period
3. British Period
4. Social work after Independence

Ancient and Medieval Period

Social work in ancient India grew under organized or unorganized charity movements started by individuals, groups, and rulers. Charity was the common factor as the country was prosperous. There was a widespread tradition of giving alms and donations to the needy people and the responsibility towards community welfare was shared by the government and certain individuals of the community. Welfare work was considered as the integral part of religion. Basically, the charity and welfare work included teaching, medical relief, looking after orphans, widows, old, infirm, dependent and physically disabled, donating during natural calamities to the poor, etc. By and large, India had a laissez-faire economy which made charity a personal choice.

India had a rich and glorious tradition in ancient time. The description of Yajna, Howana and Dana clearly indicate that the affluent Indian society was full of a sense of community living and togetherness. Varnashram system was making it obligatory for the Grihasthas (house-holder) to look after Sanyasis (saints) and Brahamacharies (student, scholars and ascetics). Some scholars believed that welfare system in ancient India had three-tier system, namely:

1. The joint family at the primary level;
2. The local bodies in village and towns at primary and secondary levels; and
3. State at the secondary and tertiary levels.[2]

The ancient philosophy reveals that good thoughts, good feelings and good deeds led the saints in the upward journey towards salvation. In *Geeta* it is said, "Reach the salvation by assisting each other in life. Ultimately, the help rendered and received should culminate in self-help … . So a person even when he is helped by others should personalize and internalize that help, get strengthened and help himself". *Geeta* also says that holding together of human beings in a society was not possible without perpetual give and take and small or big acts of sacrifice. It emphasized on innate dignity of man.

Upanishads also talked about the same things. During this period, the concept of 'Ishtas' and 'Apartas' were introduced. Ishtas were individual goods and Apartas were social goods like constructing a well, rest house, etc. Apartas were considered greater virtues than 'Ishtas' as they helped the community. Various types of 'Rina' (debts/obligations) were also accepted. These preached the ideal of interdependence. Some accepted ideals of that time were:

- Doing good deeds without expecting any rewards;
- Non-attachment to worldly affairs and adopting dispassionate attitude;
- Modesty and emotional stability;
- Supremacy of the society and lesser importance of individual interest but more on social interest; and
- The total interdependence on each other in society. That is why, Bhiksha (charity or alms) was not considered a favour but a matter of right.

Even in the post-Vedic period *Manu Smriti* along with some other 'smritis' was written, where it described 'Sadharana Dharma' (routine duties) as non-violence, truth, non-stealing, personal hygiene and control of passions. This was the code of conduct of a common man.

The joint family system and caste organizations also used to provide help and assistance to the needy and disabled people. Social welfare became the most important activity during the time of Ashoka. He made hospitals for men as well as for animals. He prepared shelters for orphans, destitute and disabled persons. He had a group of welfare workers who looked after the daily affairs of these places. He also built national highways, rest houses and wells for the common people. Similarly, during Gupta period, there were village republics in the form of village panchayats. In addition to village administration, village panchayats were also responsible for the protection of weaker sections and minors. The Gupta kings also did many works for the good and welfare of the people, made arrangements for irrigation and opened hospitals providing free medical facilities to the common people. There were many charitable institutions maintained by the state. During the period of Parmaras, many works of public utility were undertaken. In the same way, during the Rajput period, village administration was looked after by village institutions. The village assemblies contributed to the safety and security of the people. Gram panchayats also did arrangements of education, hospitals and sanitation.

Muslim Period

Muslims came to India in the 8th century. From the 13th century to the middle of the 19th century, India was ruled by Muslim rulers who introduced a different kind of religion and moral set-up. Through this period, India witnessed the spread of Islam, but welfare activities remained as an integral part of religion. Many welfare activities were undertaken during the reign of Sher Shah. He introduced effective reforms in the system of communication and built roads and 'sarais' at frequent places; besides this, many charitable institutions were established. Charity was given to needy people. He personally took interest in the problems of cultivators and helped weak, disabled and destitute persons. Then welfare measures were again organized by Akbar, who stopped the evil practice of 'sati' and child marriage and also encouraged widow remarriages. The practice of enslaving the war prisoners was also stopped.

Muslim rulers introduced *zakat* and *khairat,* and basic simplicity and equality of Islam. Islam was a new school of thought which attracted many people. It is needless to say that most of the Muslim rulers were not religious and puritan Muslims. It was a unique phenomenon that Islam and Hinduism remained in contact with each other and both could retain their identity and distinction. During this time, composite Indian culture also grew. They helped in developing a new system based on social justice and broader social interest. During this period only, many reformists like Kabir, Ramdas, Tukaram, Dadu, etc., gave a new meaning to compassion, tolerance and concern for humanity.

British Period

Social work evolved in the form of social reform movements in India during the British period. According to historians, British rule was, the main inspiration for social reform movement. In the beginning of 19th century, the condition of India became deplorable. Own native rulers and Nawabs established their small kingdoms and they always used to fight with each other. After the battle of Plassey, East India Company established its hold on the major portions of India. Their main intention was basically for commercial gain and as a result they could not pay attention towards the well-being of common and vanquished people. On the other side, Indian society became orthodox and custom-bound. People had immense honour towards Shastras and Karma Kandas and every kind of customs received sanction under the cover of religion. The custom of *sati*, dedication of women to temples, untouchability and castism and other obnoxious customs were widely prevalent during this time. Christian missionaries spread education, brought the theory of equality. There was no property right for Indian women. Early marriage, inequality and lack of education were the main problems which were leading India into a barbarian culture. So many social reformers came up to wipe out such social evils from the society.

Reform Movements

During this time many social reform movements came into limelight to uproot the social evil and the main ones are as follows:

Brahmo Samaj: The movement was started against the social evil customs and practice of Indian society like *sati* system. It is often called the protestant movement of Hindu religion. It raised public opinion against the practice of *sati* and prohibition of widow remarriage. So, the new era marked its beginning by the social legislation "Regulation XVII of 1829", i.e., for prohibition of *sati*. The Printing Press and Charter Act of 1813 were significant efforts for popularizing education and especially introducing English education in India.

Arya Samaj: In the middle of the 19th century, Swami Dayanand Saraswati advocated self-reliance and propagated Vedic religion to the people.

Ram Krishna Mission: Ram Krishna Mission was also involved in the welfare activities in the society. Ram Krishna Paramhansa preached his teachings through examples. According to Ram Krishna, the mystery of religion and its essence is experience of God. When there is experience of God, all discussions of Shastras, 'karma kanda' and precepts are extinguished.

Social Legislations

Besides these movements, many actions were undertaken towards the social legislation by the British during their reign. They are as follows:

Child Marriage Act: An Act related to child marriage, was passed in 1919. According to this, at the time of marriage, the boy and girl must have attained the age of 18 and 15 years respectively. Another Act, relating to marriage was passed in the year 1933 which conferred validity on such marriages performed by the persons of different castes, religions and communities after adopting Arya Samaj.

Hindu Woman Right of Property Act: It was passed in 1933 and it brought many valuable and desirable reforms relating to the rights of Hindu women.

Hindu Succession Disability Removal Act: This Act was passed in 1928 wherein it was provided that no Hindu could be deprived of succession rights of the property of joint family on the ground of disease or disability.

The19th century should also be remembered for the introduction of many social legislations under the British reign like Widow Remarriage Act of 1856, Leprosy Act of 1889, Reformatory School Act of 1897, etc.

In spite of all these reforms, the sufferings of the masses, their problems and miseries remained unsolved. Providers were making some efforts but they were mostly to satisfy their own conscience. No social reformer thought of creating a just system in the society. Suffering and poverty were considered inevitable and also a test of the sufferer by the Almighty.

Social Work after Independence

After independence social work had got a new orientation in the field of social welfare and development.

The first school of social work was started in 1936 in the name of Sir Dorabji Tata Institute of Social Sciences by Clifford Manshardt with the help of Sir Dorabji Tata at Bombay (now Mumbai). It offered professional training in social work but those workers were Gandhian social workers. Later on, officially many trained social workers emerged and practised in various government and non-government welfare offices. Gradually, many schools of social work came into being in Delhi (later on named as Delhi School of Social Work), Calcutta (at Sriniketan as department of Social Work under Visva Bharati University), Lucknow, Varanasi, Baroda, Agra, Indore, Udaipur, etc., which imparted professional training in social work. Thus, social work in India emerged as a socially oriented professional.

The Constitution of India was enacted and lots of provisions were introduced related to social welfare programmes. Many schemes are being implemented for the development of welfare programmes and social services. Here some of the main measures have been discussed:

Social Legislation

In order to encourage social reforms, many Acts have been enacted by the Parliament. The Special Marriage Act, 1954 has been passed for the interest of those persons who solemnize marriage not as a religious sacrament, but in a civil court. That is why, this Act is also known as the Civil Marriage Act. It has prescribed a minimum age of marriage. In 1955, Hindu Marriage Act was passed which was applied to all religious communities except Muslim community. This Act prescribes a definite age for valid marriage, monogamy, guardianship of mother and provision for divorce. Thereafter, the Dowry Prohibition Act, 1961 was also passed which states that if a person gives and takes dowry, he is liable to be punished. Later on, the central government passed the Untouchability Offences Act, 1955 for the purpose of enforcing Article 15 of the Constitution. This Act was amended in 1976 and it proscribes the practice of untouchability in any form or manner.

Central Social Welfare Board (CSWB)

The Central Social Welfare Board was established in 1953 to promote and accelerate voluntary action throughout the country. Its main focus were survey of the needs of social welfare organizations, evaluation of their programmes and co-ordination of assistance and render assistance to voluntary welfare agencies.

Social Welfare

Immediate after the independence, there has been immense development and intensification of social welfare activities. These activities promote the welfare of the people by securing and protecting a social order in which justice and equality shall be secured to every citizen. Welfare services and rehabilitation were also extended to the weaker sections of the society, especially socially and physically handicapped, women and children in both rural and urban areas.

Social Education

Special emphasis was given to social education and women education in India which was also laid down in the Constitution. Various courses at undergraduate and postgraduate as well as the research level are being run by various universities and their affiliated degree colleges all over the country. The changing socio-economic and cultural scene in the country demands development of human resources. The programme of social education has been promoted to meet these new demands of society as well as of individuals. Presently, social work constitutes the essential approach of a welfare state. Even social work programmes are being implemented by the various government departments with the networking of welfare agencies and NGOs.

Social Work Interventions at Present in India

In the present scenario, many social changes are occurring with new emerging social problems also originating. Along with these changes also emerge many social problems of various dimensions which lead to social action whose main objective is to make adjustment with fruitful changes in the society. Some of the areas of focus have been described here:

Solution of Individual and Family Problems

The main focus has been given on the solving of individual and family problems which may occur because of the effect of globalization. Government has also given this top priority. Even the private sector has given their focus towards this with the help of social action method.

Removal of Social Problems

The government has now taken many initiatives to solve the social problems which are the obstacles for development. From this point, there are large scopes for social action in Indian society. Indian society is confronted by many social problems like castism, untouchability, child labour, child marriage, prostitution, drug addiction, women-related violence, etc. These problems should be solved in accordance with democratic ideals, though the government has been enacting and introducing new laws to control it from time to time.

Social Reform

With the help of social action, social reform can be possible through the improvement of social conditions. State governments have been focusing more on panchayat, education, health, housing, welfare of disadvantaged group, welfare for rural and urban people, etc., for general development and standard of living.

Spread of Democratic Values

The main base of social work believes in democratic values and ideals. Social justice, equality, liberty are the philosophy of social work. Practically, these ideals and values should be available to our entire citizens. In order to accomplish these democratic values, rapid changes in our social structure is inevitable and social action can be used as the means.

Encouragement of Organizational Functions

In the present scenario, social action is a process having various forms as well as modes of execution. Social process could be integrative or disintegrative. So with the help of integrative social process, the speed of social action can be increased more.

Social Organization

Social organizations are one of the most important mechanisms to understand our society and its different ideology. So we have to analyse those social organizations. All religions have there social organizations and they need to perform their duty towards the development of the society.

Philosophy of Social Work

Webster's *New International Dictionary* states that philosophy is, "the science which investigates the most general facts and principles of reality and human nature and conduct especially, and now usually, the science which compromises logic, ethics, aesthetics, metaphysics, and the theory of knowledge". The introduction of the concept and philosophy of democracy further strengthened the need to recognize every human being as an individual, worthy of respect and recognition; the individual being given the rights as well as responsibilities of an equal citizen in a democratic society. The consent of the government, rule of the majority, respect for the creative minority, freedom of assembly, speech and religion supported the development of the individual in his own right. Underlying these factors lay the social philosophy of justice, liberty, equality and fraternity. It is in the background of this philosophy of life that the methods of social work have been developed by the practitioners. Social work is thus a democratic, value-based humanitarian profession. The philosophy of social work practice imbibes in itself the significant features of inherent dignity and self-respect of an individual; pursuit of democratic values; and respect for human rights.

According to Burtrym, "Social work needs to be philosophical in order to be real". The very philosophy or a perspective of social work relies on democratic principles through which it approaches to fulfil its purpose of creating a self-sufficient society. Being democratic in nature, it firmly believes in the dignity of an individual, liberty, equality of all, right of self-determination; and social and distributive justice. So, these constitute a thought that not only include natural rights of an individual, but also emphasizes his or her role in achieving similar environment for others also. Thus, rights as well as duties form the complete theme of being democratic in theory and practice. Another aspect of social work practice focuses on its 'value' aspect which is socially approved principles. The third aspect of social work practice that really reflects its core is its humanitarian approach towards its objectives. Being humanitarian in nature, it discards the 'Social Darwinism' that believes in the survival of the fittest. It also disapproves 'Malthusian principle' that poverty is inherent and cannot be eradicated.

Social work is required as a response to common human needs which include the provision of physiological, psychological and developmental needs. Social work practice creates an atmosphere where these needs are easily met. Social work provides better understanding and atmosphere for human diversity.

Social work includes the concepts of a larger system. As a helping process, social work concentrates its efforts to develop better adjustment between individuals, their subsystems and larger systems. This is done through the interaction of client and worker. Social work plans to provide social justice and bring about change. It also seeks to enhance social functioning of individual, group, etc., which means meaningful and rewarding role of individual in a particular social set-up. This role should improve his self-image. It should help society and its development.

Right from the beginning, we assume that social work focused on adjustment of people in their environment. In 1973, Pincus and Minahan formulated four categories of tasks which are essential objectives of social work profession such as:

1. To enable the people to develop their capacities for solving their own problems and meeting their needs;
2. To enhance people's access to the resource system;
3. To act as dispenser of material goods and services; and
4. To contribute to the formulation and modification of social policies.[3]

The above functions are usual functions of social work which are almost global. To make it very simple, the functions of social work may be divided into:

1. *Caring:* It implies caring of vulnerable groups like children, handicapped, aged and women.

2. *Curing:* It basically involves the problem-solving activities in nature.
3. *Changing:* Here role of a social worker is as a 'change agent'. They motivate people relating to different issues through awareness generation programmes, advocacy, fighting against social evils, etc.

Keeping all these functions in our mind, we may define social work as "professional assistance to risk prone individual, groups and communities for adjusting themselves in the environment, and changing the client or environment whenever it is necessary for better adjustment".[4]

Every human being consciously or unconsciously has certain philosophy that determines his/her perspective on life. Social work has a deep concern with the 'way of living' and his humanitarian touch is naturally the base of the philosophy of social work. The philosophy of social work is constituted of concepts, attitudes and values of social work profession.

A philosophy of social work in every country bears in it the unique realities of that particular culture and socio-economic life and it makes difference in the interpretations of our concepts regarding the relations of men with other men; to what life really and deeply means; to the perspective on world and to the shape and form of socio-economic and political system in which we live. That is why, Bruno rightly remarks that "social work is a practice with common techniques but not a common philosophy".

Pumphery has classified two basic values, 'abstract' values, i.e., those that should or ought to be and are normative in nature and 'instrumental' values, i.e., those values which are the means to achieve those ends.

Herbert Bisno has described the philosophy of social work in his book *The Philosophy of Social Work* in detail where he narrated the philosophic tenets of social work in four areas:

1. the nature of an individual;
2. the relations between groups, groups and individuals, and between individuals;
3. the functions and methods of social work; and
4. social maladjustment and social change.

Values of Social Work

Generally values in social work profession are commonly linked with the notion of system. Frequently we use 'values' to refer to ordering and orienting ideas of the life to be led by an individual which provides a worthwhile way of life for any particular society.

Values are the implicit and explicit ideas about what we cherish. Values determine which goals and actions we evaluate as 'good' and, our values shape our belief and attitudes.

Values may be defined as a conception of a standard cultural or merely personal by which things are compared and approved or disapproved in relation to one another.

Values are socially approved desires, goals that are internalized through the process of conditioning, learning, socialization and that become subjective, a preference, an aim and aspiration.

Values in general may be looked upon as the core component of a clustering of attitudes which direct behaviour towards some goals in preference to others. They express what is expected and what is desired. These also act as 'referral norms' against which the right course of action is to be judged and performed. Values need to be internalized through the process of conditioning, learning or socialization which gradually takes the form of preferences, aims and aspirations of life. That is the reason why values of tolerance, modesty and cooperation are giving place to social competence, self-assertion and conflictual attitudes thereby resulting in the progress of materialistic culture on the one side, while causing the subversion of humanitarian and democratic values of life on the other in the age of globalization. So, in any contemporary society, values have their significance as they provide rules for social adjustment, uniformity in conduct to an extent, ethical and psychological foundation to life, identification of roles and functions in the society, as well as proper assessment of constantly emerging problems. Various scholars have delineated the values of social work as under:

Konopka

(i) Respect for every person and the right of each person to the fullest development of his/her potential; and

(ii) Mutual dependence of individual and responsibility towards each other according to their abilities.

Friedlander

(i) Conviction of the inherent worth, the integrity and dignity of the individual;

(ii) The right to determine oneself what one's needs are and how they should be met;

(iii) Firm belief in equal opportunity for all, limited only by the individual's capacities;
(iv) The right of self-determination; and
(v) Social responsibility towards oneself, one's family and society.

In 1960, the National Association of Social Work in United States gave a code of ethics where it discussed value base in social work in the preamble as, "Social work is based on humanitarian democratic ideals. Professional social workers are dedicated to serve for the welfare of mankind, to the disciplined use of a recognized body of knowledge about human beings and their interaction and the marshalling of community resources to promote the well-being of all without discrimination".

Social work values are not very different from general values in the society. The discussion on values is very subjective because values cannot be totally logical or scientific. There is no method or technique with which one could be forced to uphold a particular set of values. These values are preconceived notions or assumptions. If people do not believe in them, they should not choose the profession of social work as their career. Values are must to student of social work whenever they practice.

Sometimes, it appears that social work propagates values of controversial nature. On the one hand it speaks of the basic worth and dignity of human being, his right of self-determination, and on the other hand it propagates social responsibility of every individual. But rights and duties go together. Very broad values which have been accepted by Americans are given by Johnson (1995):

1. People should be free to make choices;
2. Individual needs and concerns should not be totally subjected to community needs;
3. Worker should use non-judgmental approach to persons and their concerned needs and problems;
4. Social worker's role is helping or enabling not controlling;
5. Friendly and warm relationship is important; and
6. Persons have responsibility for others for their need and concern.

Kohs

(i) The worth and dignity of individual;
(ii) The capacity of human nature to achieve full human potential;
(iii) Tolerance of individual differences;
(iv) Satisfaction of basic human needs;

(v) Liberty;
(vi) Self-direction;
(vii) Non-judgmental attitude;
(viii) Constructive social cooperation;
(ix) Importance of work and constructive use of leisure; and
(x) Protection of one's existence from the dangers caused by man and nature.

The Worth and Dignity of Individual

These values have many interpretations and these can be examined in the Indian context.

The first value in Indian context means some thinking and behaving pattern on the part of social worker who gives the client a feeling as a dignified and useful person in the society. It also tries to make them understand that social workers are not doing any favour to the client by helping them, rather it is their right as a unit of society. This value also includes the process of eradicating all discriminations and favouritism because it is not good in the longer interest of the society.

The Capacity of Human Nature to Achieve Full Human Potential

This indicates the ideal for self-realization and self-fulfilment which is a right and a requirement for satisfied and contended life. Many social problems prevailing in India especially overpopulation, poverty and unemployment, which creates a situation that compelled us to choose any career for surviving. Besides economic reason, other problems like social stigma, castism, sex which make us liable for certain services. In this situation, this value creates positive atmosphere for identifying and developing talents to make them self-fulfilling and self-realizing.

Tolerance of Individual Differences and Non-judgmental Attitude

It is very difficult to practice in a society like ours where multi-cultural and multiple social problems are prevailing, but it is also essential for us. In Indian context, this value means that there is no comparison between individuals and groups and no one's culture and background is better than that of others. The concept of superior and inferior culture will have to be given up when social workers are practising. They should not have any biases towards any culture. In the fieldwork, all sorts of variety entertainment programmes, folk dances and folk songs will be used to exhibit tolerance for differences, and direct and indirect messages of communal harmony may be conveyed through entertainment programmes. The value of 'non-judgmental attitude' above also emphasized the same ideas. They should not judge any client according to their own sense of morality.

Satisfaction of Basic Human Needs

This value has a great importance in Indian context because it aims towards social justice. A decent life is the right of every individual, which in India a big percentage of people are not getting. It is not the role of a social worker or an organization to provide facilities for decent living; rather in order to achieve a just social system, they (social worker or agency) will pressurize the government to put social welfare and services in the priority list for the people.

Liberty and Self-direction

It talks about personal independence of every individual. It is a birthright and a part of democracy and it required self-actualization and self-development. Our society is full of social pressure and control, and as a result, individual and free will have been curbed to the maximum extent. So, a little exposure to democratic decision-making process is much needed in India. It is not only upholding the democratic values, but is a part of social work training. Both these values regarding personal freedom are very important but like other values they are also not absolute. Discipline is equally important but unfortunately it has not reached to the downtrodden. They do not live a required decent life because they cannot think of anything more than food and related basic needs. It is difficult to create a fearless society and it also becomes difficult to guide them how to take advantage of democratic liberty and expression. So, there should be a situation where they could have full liberty with self-judgment.

Constructive Social Cooperation

This is highly important and necessary in a segregated society like ours. The social work methods like group work, community organization and social action do play the role of cooperation and collaboration in the society. Social workers through social movement can provide both economic independence and constructive cooperation and integration in the society.

Importance of Work and Constructive Use of Leisure

It is related to hard work, efficiency and honesty of labour, though it has not so much influencing factor for social workers in India.

Protection of One's Existence from the Dangers Caused by Man and Nature

Natural calamities are a common phenomena in India like earthquake, tsunami, flood, riots, etc. So disaster relief is needed and more emphasis should be given to prevention and treatment activities. Health and proper sanitation also comes under this value. Social workers can play the role as planners and policy makers through direct and indirect activities under group work, community organization and social action.

Social work always taught against favouritism, prejudices and stereotypes whether it is in India or Western countries. It is true that more emphasis should be given to establish welfare state and securing social justice with democratic values. Actually in Indian context, we do not need a different value because our Constitution and social policy should create a positive atmosphere for social work practice automatically. It is practical that it becomes very difficult to uphold social values but in the West, people think it is outdated. We as Indians are dissatisfied because we have limited resources and the required suitable atmosphere, but in the West they have a feeling that all the values in social work are very vague.

From these perspectives, Shardlow has said, "Much to do is obscure or confusing; not least the very concept values ... Many social workers would prefer to ignore the difficulties and to take refuge in old certainties. It is far easier to subscribe to the ideas that there is indeed a finite number of values specific to social work such as found in Biestek's List of seven principles". Later, Shardlow adds, "However, recognizing the lack of agreement about the constituent of values in social work or reaffirming their importance, does little enough to advance our real understanding".

So values are fast changing with the growing scenario of liberalization, privatization and globalization (LPG) in the field of social welfare in the West but in India it is very significant because social change is not so fast. In India, changes would not be in values, principles and assumptions; they would be in models, strategies and nature of social welfare.

Principles of Social Work

According to IASSW and IFSW, following are the major principles of social work:

Human Rights and Human Dignity

Social work is based on respect for the inherent worth and dignity of all people, and the rights that follow this. Social workers should uphold and define each person's physical, psychological, emotional and spiritual integrity and well-being. This means:

(a) *Respecting the Right to Self-determination:* Social workers should respect and promote people's right to make their own choices and decisions, irrespective of their values and life choices, provided this does not threaten the rights and legitimate interests of others.

(b) *Promoting the Right to Participation:* Social workers should promote the full involvement and participation of people using their services in ways that enable them to be empowered in all aspects of decisions and actions affecting their lives.

(c) *Treating Each Person as a Whole:* Social workers should be concerned with the whole person, within the family, community, societal and natural environments, and should seek to recognize all aspects of a person's life.

(d) *Identifying and Developing Strengths:* Social workers should focus on the strengths of all individuals, groups, and communities and thus promote their empowerment.

Social Justice

Social workers have a responsibility to promote social justice, in relation to society generally, and in relation to the people with whom they work. This means:

(a) *Challenging Negative Discrimination*: Social workers have a responsibility to challenge negative discrimination on the basis of characteristics such as ability, age, culture, gender or sex, marital status, socio-economic status, political opinions, skin colour, racial or other physical characteristics, sexual orientation, or spiritual beliefs.

(b) *Recognizing Diversity:* Social workers should recognize and respect the ethnic and cultural diversity of the societies in which they practise, taking account of individual, family, group and community differences.

(c) *Distributing Resources Equitably:* Social workers should ensure that resources at their disposal are distributed fairly, according to needs.

(d) *Challenging Unjust Policies and Practices:* Social workers have a duty to bring to the attention of their employers, policy makers, politicians and general public situations where resources are inadequate or where distribution of resources, policies, and practices are oppressive, unfair or harmful.

(e) *Working in Solidarity:* Social workers have an obligation to challenge social conditions that contribute to social exclusion, stigmatization or subjugation, and to work towards an inclusive society.

Friedlander has described generic principles that apply to the three primary methods of social work (i.e., Case Work, Group Work and Community Organization).

1. Conviction of the inherent worth, the integrity and the dignity of the individual;
2. Right to determine himself, what his needs are and how they should be met;
3. The firm belief in equal opportunity for all, limited only by the individual's innate capacity; and
4. Social responsibility towards himself, his family and his society.

According to Cohen:

1. Self-direction and self-determination. The individual, group or the community must be helped to help himself or itself, with the professional worker playing an indirect or enabling role rather than a manipulative one;
2. Beginning at the level where the individual, group or community stands and proceeding at a pace, that is meaningful to him or it;
3. Deal with the total individual – professional worker must focus not merely on the immediate problem as seen by the individual, group, or community but on its relation to the total situation;
4. Understand and take into account the fact of difference among individuals, group, or communities; and
5. Recognize that the welfare of any individual, group or community is inextricably interwoven with the welfare of the whole. All individuals, groups, communities, must be concerned with the development of material, human and social resources to meet all the needs of all the people rather than the vested interest of any individual, any particular group or community.

Bradford W. Sheafor, Charles R. Horejsi and Gloria A. Horejsi in their book, *Techniques and Guidelines for Social Work Practice* has mentioned 21 social work principles which have been divided into two sections, one as 'social worker as a professional person' (which contains the first five principles) and principles that 'guide practice activities' (rest of the 16 principles). The principles are:

Social Worker as a Professional Person

1. *The social worker should practice social work:* Social worker should practise social work within the boundaries of social work profession. Yet, it is not uncommon to find these and other professionals extending their activities into the domain of another profession. Basically, this principle warns the social worker to do what he or she is sanctioned and trained to do.
2. *The social worker should engage in conscious use of self:* The social worker's primary practice tool is self (i.e., his or her motivation and capacity to communicate and interact with others in ways that facilitates change). The skilled social worker is purposeful in making use of his/her unique manner and style of relating to others. In professional relationships, workers reveals – verbally or non-verbally, directly or indirectly – their values, lifestyles, morals, attitudes, biases, and prejudices. They should be consciously aware of how their own beliefs, perceptions, and behaviours may impact on their professional relationship and these attributes will develop the ability of the client.
3. *The social worker should maintain professional objectivity:* Sometimes the worker becomes emotionally attached with the client and as a result fails to energize clients or discourage clients from investing the energy necessary to achieve change. Then the social worker can be best maintaining this balance through a controlled emotional involvement. It is also important for social worker's mental health. A degree of emotional detachment is needed, allowing the worker to set aside the troubles of clients and society and separate the professional and personal aspects of one's life. Professional objectivity is, perhaps, the best antidote to worker burnout.
4. *The social worker should respect human diversity:* Every society is diversified on the grounds of culture, class, ethnicity, religion, range of physical and intellectual ability, sexual orientation and age, etc. So the social worker should understand and respect such differences and human uniqueness and recognize that what may appear to be deviance or unusual behaviours from one perspective, may be quite appropriate on the other perspective.
5. *The social worker should seek personal and professional growth:* Social work is a contemporary discipline and its focus is on the, here and now, concerns of ever-changing people living in a dynamic

environment. Social worker should be updated in the growth and ever-changing scenario. New theories, concepts, and interventions appear regularly in the literature, workshops or in conferences. The social worker must be updated with the professional information.

Principles Guiding Practice Activities

1. *The social worker should do no harm:* Social work practice is about the facilitation of desired change. However, there is always an element of risk in any effort to bring about change. The social worker must anticipate such possibilities and have a plan for dealing with the things that can go wrong in an intervention. In the effort to do good and enhance the social functioning of people, the social worker must be careful to do no harm.
2. *The social worker should engage in conscious knowledge-guide practice:* The society expects the professional social worker to bring in and employ the latest and most appropriate knowledge in the practice. A social worker cannot possibly stay abreast with all the knowledge that relates to the many dimensions of social work practice. The worker is obliged to be familiar with the most current knowledge that directly relates to his or her practice activities and should also know how to retrieve needed knowledge in related areas. It is also important that social workers are careful consumers of the knowledge presented in the social work literature and at social work conferences. After all, it is the client who is most at risk if practice assessment and intervention is based on faulty information.
3. *The social worker should engage in conscious value-guided and ethical practice:* The social worker should address key ethical issues as a part of social work practice. Values are the centre for this profession. They should recognize that one's values are powerful forces in human behaviour. Helping client clarity and understanding the value issue in their lives can be a critical step in bringing about change. However, in many cases, if clients are to change themselves or their situations, they must take some action to adjust or adapt their values to be more congruent with those of others in their lives.
4. *The social worker should be concerned with the whole person:* Most professions focus on a single dimension. Social work should be concerned with whole person such as biological, psychological, social, spiritual, etc. It requires attention to the client's past, present

and future. Social worker should focus on both the problems and strengths.

5. *The social worker should treat the client with dignity:* The clients should be treated with dignity, respect and understanding. The phrase 'accept the client as he or she is' reminds and encourages the social worker to approach clients as people with dignity who deserve respect.
6. *The social worker should individualize the client:* Every individual is unique and the social worker has to accept it when practising. This means that the worker must be in tune with and pay attention to what the client is thinking and feeling and how he or she is behaving from moment to moment and from session to session. They should be sensitive to each client's unique history, characteristics, and situations. They must also appreciate the differing ability and readiness of clients to participate in a particular intervention strategy.
7. *The social worker should lend vision to the client:* A central feature of professional helping is to bring new ideas, new perspectives, and more effective change strategies to a problem situation. If an individual or group is to invest in the change process, they must be convinced that the outcome will be worth the efforts. Social worker must introduce and nurture a sense of hopefulness and offer a vision that change is possible and that there are new and better ways to deal with the situation. While offering new perspectives, encouragement, and support and techniques for change, the social worker must also be realistic and honest about limits and possibilities.
8. *The social worker should build on client strength:* To change the situation by the client, the social worker should accept and encourage the ability and potentiality which they have. The emphasis on maximizing and building on client's strengths helps change the tone of the helping relationship from one of gloom over problems and pathology to one of optimism. Thus, social worker should carefully assess the strengths.
9. *The social worker should maximize client participation:* 'Helping your client to help themselves' is a principle based on the belief that if meaningful and lasting change is to occur for an individual, group, community, or any other client system, the people who will need to change must be active participants in the change process. It is the responsibility of the social worker in guiding the process to be sure that, as far as possible, all relevant persons participate in

identifying the problem, formulating a plan of action, and implementing that plan. In order to maximize the participation of the client, the social worker should 'do with the client and not to or for the client'.

10. *The social worker should maximize client self-determination:* This principle assumes that the client is capable and legally competent to make decisions in relation to self and others. Some clients may not understand the consequences of an action or may lack the mental capacity to make sound judgments and might, therefore, make choices that are clearly harmful to themselves or others. At that time, the social worker must take on a decision-making role for these clients. The social worker should reluctantly assume the responsibility for taking decisions on behalf of clients and then only after careful review of the situations, after consultation with others.
11. *The social worker should help the client learn self-directed problem-solving skills:* The change in social functioning made by a client with the assistance of a professional worker can become unravelled unless the client is prepared to sustain that change over time. Ideally, a social work intervention helps prepare clients to cope successfully with future difficulties and to engage in self-directed problem-solving when faced with another problem so they will not need to return to the social worker for additional assistance and help. Social worker also teaches the clients how to utilize resources.
12. *The social worker should maximize client empowerment:* The goal of helping people, both individually and collectively, to gain power over their lives has been a part of social work's philosophy since its founding. However, use of the term 'empowerment' to capture this commitment to working collaboratively with people to attain their goals by increasing their personal and political power to influence their life situations has gained prominence in recent years. It is a continuous challenge for the worker to empower their clients.
13. *The social worker should protect client confidentiality:* There are two forms of confidentiality: absolute and relative. Absolute confidentiality refers to a situation when information imparted by the client can never go beyond the social worker. This degree of confidentiality is rare in social work practice. It is only under the protection of some professional licensing statutes that a client can claim a legal right to privileged communication. Most social work practice

involves relative confidentiality, meaning that the most a social worker can promise is to act responsibly within the profession's code of ethics, adhere to existing laws, and follow agency policy concerning the handling of client information. The social worker must be prudent regarding what information is placed in agency files, and care must be taken in preparing clerical staff to respect the confidential nature of any materials they may type. The social worker must carefully select the plan, the location of interviews and cautiously select the information to be discussed during consultations and case conferences.

14. *The social worker should adhere to the philosophy of normalization:* Many clients may be suffering from mental and physical disability. Because of these limitations, they often experience discrimination and social isolation. The philosophy of normalization is a powerful force in efforts to integrate persons with disabilities into the life of the community and ensure that their lives resemble that of the so-called normal person as much as possible. This philosophy originated in the field of mental retardation but has spread to programmes serving other groups such as the elderly, the physically disabled, and mentally ill.
15. *The social worker should continuously evaluate the progress of the change process:* Social work is far from an exact science and it involves working with ever-changing people and ever-changing situations. The objectives of helping activities, therefore, must be clearly delineated and regularly reviewed to be certain that they remain relevant to the client's needs. It is not enough to set the course of an intervention strategy and assume that the desired outcome will be achieved. Rather, a continuous monitoring and evaluation of the change process by both the social worker and the client is necessary.
16. *The social worker should be accountable to clients, agency, community, and the social work profession:* Social workers are obliged to give their best service at all times and therefore, must be accountable to those individuals, families, and groups they directly serve. In addition, since the social worker is employed in social agency or is part of a private practice group, they are also responsible for carrying out the programmes and procedures of that organization. In addition, the existence of a professional monopoly demands that the members of the profession also be accountable to the community. For many social workers, this accountability is

formalized through licensing, for others, it is less structured but nevertheless expected. Even the code of ethics clearly states that social work profession expects accountability to clients, colleagues, employers, the profession and society.

Social Work as a Profession

Social work profession is more than seventy years old in India, but it is still not strongly recognized as a profession. In USA too, social work had to struggle for its existence and recognition. Is social work eligible to be a profession? This question was posed by Flexner in 1915. He thought it is not a profession. In 1906, the American Sociological Society felt the silent growth of another discipline. Sociology was advancing towards pure and abstract nature whereas social work was moving towards social reform and individual development. Elean Young Husband had felt that it was basically moral boosting. Social work, according to her was shockingly paternalistic, moralistic and authoritarian.

But, in this age of liberalization, privatization and globalization (LPG), be it a developed or developing country, the emphasis is on specialization, competency and effective attainment of desired objectives and it has influenced the discipline all over the world to justify their applicability to the human problems. Consequently, social work as a discipline has gradually emerged into a practice with professional characteristics.

It becomes imperative to know about the 'profession' and its characteristics. It is unfortunate that some laymen or even educated people use the term 'profession' as a negative connotation and in a superficial sense conceptualizing that it is a business-oriented and has a profit motive attached to it. But in reality it is not.

A profession is characterized by:

1. specialized body of knowledge,
2. scientific methods,
3. techniques and skills,
4. an identified area of operation,
5. code of certain ethics,
6. degree of organization, and
7. social approval.

A profession is an occupation which requires a higher educational degree, diploma or certificate, to be specifically used for the welfare of the people.

Elliot has differentiated between professional and non-professional occupation as:

Criteria	*Professional Occupation*	*Non-professional Occupation*
Knowledge	Broad, theoretical knowledge used in application to human problems.	Craft or Skill.
Task	Non-routine situations.	Routine.
Decision-making	Unprogrammed decisions.	Programmed decision.
Authority	Ends (derived from knowledge) decided for society (or institution within it).	Ends decided by society (or other institutions).
Identity	Occupational group or specialized services.	Other or non-specialized.
Work	Central life interest and problem-oriented.	Means to non-work ends.
Career	Individual achievement which involves meeting initial entry qualifications.	Occupational/class advancement.
Education	Extensive education, showing skill and meeting other latent status requirements.	Limited.
Role	Total role (expectations extend beyond expertise and work situation).	Specific role.

So, in a profession, both theoretical and practical knowledge and situations are used intensively in a wider perspective. But Elliot in his description did not mention the significance of the 'Social Approval' though social approval provides the all-important social recognition to the social work practices.

Professions are no longer viewed as mere vocations having professed knowledge or intellectual techniques. Talcott Parsons viewed a profession as 'a cluster of occupational roles' in which the incumbents perform certain functions valued in society in general, and by these activities typically earn a living as a full-time job.[5]

Theodore Caplow and Harold L. Wilensky do not consider 'knowledge' or 'skills' to be of any consequence in the emergence of any profession or in the making of a professional. Caplow identified sequential development of certain characteristics that mark the steps in the professionalization process as:

1. Establishment of a professional association;
2. Assertion of a monopoly over some of the services;
3. Development of a code of ethics;

4. Political agitation for certification and licensing;
5. Control of training facilities; and
6. Development of working relationships with other groups.

Similarly, Wilensky asserted that occupations begin to professionalize as soon as they:

1. Emerge as identifiable specializations;
2. Are sufficiently in demand to sustain the full-time remunerative employment of some number of persons;
3. Acquire a set of technical skills and encourage the development of general principles that can accumulate into a body of presumed fundamental knowledge;
4. Generate around these livelihoods, skills and knowledge a sense of identity with others similarly engaged in the specialization; and
5. Share the conviction that a necessary social function can best be executed through the occupational group.

Wilensky thus considers the 'knowledge' accumulated by a profession as a kind of 'presumed fundamental knowledge', more important is the sense of identity of the group engaged in certain modes of livelihood and a conviction that some necessary social functions can be performed by them alone. Caplow too considered 'assertion of a monopoly over some of the services' by a group important for professionalization.[6,7]

From the above discussion, the basic components that emerge for an occupation to be called as a profession are:

1. Systematic and scientific knowledge;
2. Basic skills, techniques and tools;
3. Social work education;
4. Professional organization;
5. Professional training;
6. Code of ethics; and
7. Social approval or recognition.

From the above discussion, the question that comes to our mind is whether social work is to be called a profession or not? Here we will try to justify the answer that social work is really a profession by analysing all the characteristics of a profession mentioned above.

Systematic and Scientific Knowledge

It is based on specific procedure for understanding the human problems thereby establishing the cause and effect relationship between psycho-social variables in order to diagnose and treat those problems effectively. Since social work practice endeavours to improve the social functioning of human beings, the experimental tools are not applicable due to ethical considerations, even though the scientific methods of enquiry like observation, interview, case study, field experiments are used to draw inferences about the effects and their causes. The data and findings collected from the field are compiled and quantified and then it is tested by using statistical tests like t-test, z-test, chi-test, f-test, etc. Thus, statistical tools form the characteristics features of social work research with scientific principles implicit in their application. So, social work covers a wide range of knowledge relating to human behaviour.

For any profession there should be a particular knowledge base which may be derived from various other sciences but basically every profession must have its own core knowledge base. In India, this knowledge is not indigenous. Most of the theories of social work philosophy and methods are imported, and for this reason the position of social work profession is slightly weaker in India.

Basic Skills, Techniques and Tools

Every profession must develop some skills and techniques in the professional field. Skill is the professional's capacity to apply effectively the knowledge and understanding to the given situation. It is the attainment of a harmonious balance between needs, capacities and resources of the individuals, groups or communities through a constructive relationship between a social work professional and the target people. Skill imparts smoothness to achieve the desired goals. Skill renders the required services and effective use of insight in relation to the problems of his/her client through programmed sequences of action. Social work has in its command the techniques of individual conscientization, group conscientization, organization and planning, and maintaining counter system and administrative techniques.

Professionals should perform such an activity which non-professionals cannot do, for example a doctor can operate or an advocate can plead a case. Unfortunately, social worker could not develop such special skills which grant them the special position. Most of the social workers who are working or practising in India are untrained.

Social Work Education

Social work as a professional course is gradually gaining its momentum in the realm of education. Social work in the form of BSW, MSW,

M.Phil and PhD is taught in various universities in India. With the present emerging scenario, where the emphasis has shifted from the government responsibility to the non-governmental organizations and voluntary sector, the education in social work can be a fruitful avenue for students of various disciplines. Even social work courses have been designed purposefully based on emerging social problems to impart theoretical as well as fieldwork knowledge so that the principles of theories are tested and the students become aware about the social conditions. Students are placed in different areas for fieldwork like schools, hospitals, welfare agencies, communities, etc., and they convert their theoretical knowledge into practice for intervention.

Professional Organization

Every profession must have a common platform for its professionals which would reflect the feelings of co-professionals. Such associations are very much strong in developed countries. In social work both in national and international levels, there are number of professional associations. The most important associations in international scenario are International Federation of Social Workers (IFSW), International Association of Schools of Social Workers (IASSW), American Association of Social Workers, British Association of Social Workers, whereas in India there are Association of Schools of Social Work in India, Indian Association of Trained Social Workers (IATSW), National Association of Professional Social Work in India (NAPSWI) etc., who are functioning well to promote social work and in the interest of social work professionals.

Professional Training

There should be proper training for the professionals. A lot of technical input is required because anybody cannot be a social worker. He/she needs to be properly trained to become a realistic social worker. Proper training and acceptance of trained people by the community is an important attribute for the profession. Students are trained by the social work educators in the class and also students get trained in the field with supervision.

Code of Ethics

Code of ethics for any profession acts as an important instrument in guiding the conduct of persons involved in the functioning of the organization. In the same way, social work has some code of ethics which social worker students maintain during their fieldwork or during any intervention with clients. Such code of ethics are like code of conduct towards seniors, colleagues and subordinates in the organization, towards clients and other needy people, towards inter-agency relationship, towards its profession, towards themselves, etc.

Social Approval or Recognition

Ultimately any profession really exists only when people accept it. It is the people's acceptance of social work practice as a profession that will ensure its professional validity and social recognition to its identity in the realm of professions. The impetus on the growing role of NGOs and other welfare organizations shows that social work has been accepted in the society. In every corner, social work and its significance are accepted and respected.

From the above discussion it is quite evident that though social work practice inculcates all the essential virtues and features to be accepted as a profession, still a lot more needs to be done because of some factors which are responsible for the slow progress of this profession in India. Rather we can say that social work is struggling to get this status in India. Those factors are as follows:

1. In India, a long tradition of charity-oriented culture has created a unique Indian psyche where material gifts are accepted easily and services are rendered free of cost. People give charity in the name of social work and that is why professional-oriented service is not easy because people still think providing charity is social work.
2. We are still not able to produce grass-root level workers as professionals. Those who are working in the rural or remote areas are non-professionals and they do not have social work degree or training. Hence, the great portion of masses feel that for doing social work, no special training is required and anybody with such intention can do it.
3. In our country, social workers have adopted a line of least resistance. They do not want to do it from their heart and they have certainly lost their broader perspectives; rather they just want to earn money which gives an unworthy image to social work profession.
4. Social workers are sitting in an ivory tower which means they have urban bias. They are taking the profession only as a career and not as a humanitarian service. Social workers are working for

micro-level activities and do not want to be involved in mass issues. So, in return masses do not recognize them.

5. People/students join social work profession not because of devotion to social work, but because of the opportunities to have easy jobs. Social work and welfare activities need a lot of resources and money. So people think that only policies are there, programmes and activities are very few. When social workers try to intervene in this situation, people feel that social work is perhaps a farce and they cannot solve their problems. As a result, social workers do not get much importance in the heart of the masses.
6. In India, social work profession suffers from a political shadow. Sometimes it has provided a stepping stone for a political career; as a result, people are very skeptical about welfare efforts because they have experienced the selfishness of these workers. Political parties, while helping during natural calamities also utilize the work as a propaganda base. As a result, it becomes difficult for the masses to envisage that the social worker would come to help them out with a selfless attitude.
7. The mushrooming of NGOs has also become another problem for this profession. Most of the NGOs are not engaging professional social workers regularly; rather they appoint other persons who do not have social work background. Sometimes NGOs do not prefer social worker because they think that such professionals are more expensive, they might be less devoted, they might be more methodical and less flexible, they might be process-oriented and not result-oriented and they have nothing specific to offer which non-professionals can not perform.
8. Sometimes welfare agencies and NGOs are involved in unfair deals and corrupt practices to which social workers might not adjust in this situation.
9. Due to its interdisciplinary nature, social work has been unable to create a genuine space for itself. The skills, techniques and tools have been drawn from other disciplines which also hampers its unique identity and entity. The training has failed to inspire and instil the right attitude in the social workers which is also a cause of serious concern now. Because of increasing materialism, individual ambitions often predominate that of non-profit and hamper the real purpose of this value-based profession.
10. We have seen that social worker does not enjoy a level of remuneration commensurate with related professions, nor does he/she

enjoy a desired prestige and status, comparable to even low-paid related professions. They also do not reveal the type of self-image which reflects personal satisfaction.

11. The lack of indigenized teaching material based on Indian case studies is one of the major factors in the slow process of professionalization of social work in India.
12. All the social work theories, models, techniques are borrowed from western countries and those are not relevant to the Indian scenario because the problems, factors, ideology and intervention mode are different from western countries. So, Indianization of theory, models, techniques have to be developed to solve their own local problems.
13. Empirical research work in India has still not developed so far.

Skills in Social Work for Practising in Different Phases

Skill in social work terminology is nothing more than a social worker's capacity of utilizing his/her professional knowledge and values for practising as social worker in an efficient and expert manner. It is obvious that skills are largely based on the approach, such as radical approach, existentialist approach, problem-solving approach, etc. Nevertheless, some common skills may be traced. The skills applied by the social workers during their practice in different situations has been discussed below.[8]

Basic Helping Skills

The helping process when it starts, makes use of the skill of understanding the focus of the problem, because very often we get confused about the issue – Who the client is? What is the core problem? Understanding the depth of the problem is based on experience. The second skill used from the beginning till the end of the helping process is the skill of developing a warm and purposeful relationship. This professional relationship includes acceptance and right of self-determination.

Involvement Skills

It is very difficult to involve the client in the helping process. To make involvement of the client in case work is easy compared to group work and community organization. The worker should have deeper understanding of culture, sub-culture, dialect, public opinion, prejudices, superstitions, felt needs and unfelt needs, etc. Besides these, social worker should have warm and pleasing personality with an extrovert behaviour in the helping process. In Indian context, all these are very important because Indian masses are very sensitive about their culture and ethnic group. To involve the client, the worker should develop a professional self also.

Observation Skills

In the helping process, observation skills are always used. A layman's observation may be narrow and subjective whereas, a social worker should have a more objective and keener observation. A social worker observes body gesture, unsaid words, psychology of the client, and physical conditions of the individual, group or community. Especially a group worker or a community organizer must have much more developed observational skills, because he/she is observing a lot of things and out of that they have to discard useless points and keep useful ones.

Communication Skills

This skill is the most important skill for social workers. Knowingly or unknowingly they are using it at all times. Both verbal and non-verbal communication is important for the worker and it becomes a continuous process. This skill includes interview, discussion, meaningful silence and correspondence, notes, minutes, telephonic message, etc. Interpretation of communicated message is another aspect of communication. In India, it is very difficult to both communicate and understand, because of some reasons like hypocrisy in society, prejudices and biases in the mind of the people. Language which changes after every five yards is another problem of communication. The worker has to interact in every language to work with such diversified people.

Empathy Skills

Controlled and conscious empathy enhance the helping process. It is used basically for case work but at the same time for understanding a group or community psyche; empathizing skills may be required because a social group is also 'individual' and unique because every group and community has its individuality. Empathy also helps in developing non-judgmental attitude towards the client.

Monitoring and Evaluating Skills

Sometimes the social worker may go wrong, so monitoring and evaluation at every stage is required to understand the real status of the worker. Social work process which is not so much time-bound, target oriented and quantitative should be scrutinized and screened at every step against subjectivity. This is only possible with proper monitoring and evaluation. Evaluation mechanism may develop with the idea that either person should improve or environment should change accordingly. We should work more on environmental change as our society is changing continuously.

Skill in the Action Phase

- Elaborating skills
- Empathic skills
- Sharing worker's feeling skills
- Sharing information skills
- Analysing and convincing skills
- Persuading skills

Skills at the Final Phase

At this phase various management and organizational skills are required. As Schwartz describes, "In the final phase of work – that which I have called transition and ending – the worker's skills are needed to help the members use him and each other to deal with problem of moving from one experience to another". To make this phase more productive, evaluation and analysis of the achievement are required. For this the worker should have analysing and evaluating skills. If there is a need then the new person may be introduced by the old worker. At this point the skills of purposeful relationship would be utilized, because this relationship is not forever. It has both the beginning and an end. In Indian situation other skills are also required to deal with clients, which are:

- Crisis management skills
- Collaborative skills
- Supervisory skills
- Analysing skills
- Resource mobilizing skills
- Relationship skills like listening, feeling/sensing, referring, responding, information gaining, etc.
- Problem-solving skills like problem identification, problem assessment and goal setting, selecting and implementing, intervention, termination, planning, data collecting, evaluating, etc.
- Political skills like advocacy, providing evidence, demonstrating, taking legal action, bargaining, etc.

- Skill in linking with individual, group and other social agencies
- Rapport building skill
- Budgeting and fund raising skills

Conclusion

It is understood that social work profession is beset with many problems and those are inherent in nature. The emerging trends of social conditions and reality in the society are also not going to be very challenging. The future trends of society could be like more of consumerism, more urbanization and industrialization, more dirt in politics and subdued role of honest leaders, more privatization in the field of economy and less permanent jobs, movement of welfare state towards more of welfare society, development of new professions and advancement of existing profession, increase rate of poverty, more of economic recession and unemployment problems. As a result, the problems also will be very grave. So, social work profession still has opportunities and challenges to be faced in future. The future society will become even less compassionate and more individualistic than at present. Instability will increase in social, economic and political system and the process of change will be difficult. Social work must follow the Indian culture and reject those models which are not related to our culture. Professional organizations or associations should be so motivated as to make them work for the upliftment of social work profession. Such efforts may involve more workshops to identify and generate indigenous teaching materials, updating the present data base, more practice-base creative writings, consideration of such literature in selection and promotion of teaching and field staff, and enhancing interaction between social work educational institutions with field practitioners. We have to create subject-specific library, intranet and internet and should create 'Social Work Information Exchange Network' (SWIENET). Through this network, the existing literature could be transmitted in electronic form, so it would be accessible to all. Today's urgent need is to take up the task of promoting researches.

Notes

1. Werner W. Boehm, "Objectives of the Social Work Education Curriculum of the Future", *Curriculum Study* (New York: Council of Social Work Education, 1959), p. 54.

2. M.V. Moorthy, "Philosophy of Social Work in Changing India", in *Social Work Education and Social Work Practice in India,* ed. by T. Krishnan Nair (Madras: Association of Schools of Social Work in India, 1981), p. 28.
3. Allen Pincus and Anne Minahan, *Social Work Practice Model and Method,* (Itasca, ILL: Peacock Publishers, 1973), p. 9.
4. Aronando Morales, Malcolm E. Scott and Bradford W. Sheafor, *Social Work: A Profession of Many Faces* (5th ed.) (Boston: Allyn & Bacon, 1989), pp. 13–15.
5. Talcott Parsons, *Essays in Sociological Theory* (Glencoe, Illinois: The Free Press, 1959), p. 372.
6. Theodore Caplow, *The Sociology of Work* (Minneapolis: University of Minnesota Press), 1954.
7. Harold L. Wilensky, "The Professionalization of Everyone", *American Journal of Sociology,* 70 (2), 1964.
8. Hajira Kumar, *Social Work: An Experience and Experiment in India,* (New Delhi: Gitanjali Publishing House), 1994.

4 Domain of Fieldwork in Social Work in India

Proper field education gives a social worker critical understanding of how socio-structural inadequacies, discrimination, oppression, and social, political and economic injustices impact human functioning and development at all levels. It also imparts global knowledge of human behaviour and the social environment, with particular emphasis on the person-in-environment transaction, lifespan development and the interaction among biological, psychological, socio-structural and cultural factors in shaping human development and behaviour; knowledge of the social welfare policies and services of the locality, country and/or region. Besides, a clear comprehension of social work's origins, purposes, practices and development, sufficient knowledge of related occupations and professions to facilitate inter-professional collaboration and teamwork is also visualized.

Fieldwork

With regard to standards regarding programme curricula, schools should consistently aspire towards the following:

1. The curricula and methods of instruction are being consistent with the school's programme objectives and its expected outcomes.
2. Clear plans for the organization, implementation and evaluation of the theory and field education components of the programme and specific attention to the constant review and development of the curricula have to be taken.
3. Ensuring that the curricula will help student social workers to develop skills of critical thinking and scholarly attitudes of

reasoning, openness to new experiences, paradigms, and commitment to lifelong learning.

4. Field educational contexts that provide for clearly designed and purposeful learning experiences will contribute to the holistic development of student social workers.
5. Planned coordination and cooperation between the schools and agencies that are selected for fieldwork education has to be taken care of. The planning and implementation of orientation sessions for fieldwork supervisors or instructors will focus on educating non-social work fieldwork instructors or supervisors of the programme objectives and expected outcomes, and the ethical principles of the profession.
6. There should be provision for the inclusion and participation of field instructors in curriculum development, especially with regard to field education. A partnership between the educational institution and the agency in decision-making regarding field education and the evaluation of student's fieldwork performance could be developed.
7. Making available to fieldwork instructors or supervisors, a field instruction manual that details its fieldwork standards, procedures and expectations has to be developed.
8. Ensuring that adequate and appropriate resources to meet the needs of the fieldwork component of the programme are made available.

Domain of Social Worker

- The development of the critically self-reflective practitioner, who is able to practice within the value perspective of the social work profession.
- The recognition of the relationship between personal life experiences and personal value systems and social work practice.
- The appraisal of national, regional and/or international social work codes of ethics and their applicability to context-specific realities.
- Preparation of social workers within a holistic bio-psycho-social-spiritual framework, with generalist skills to enable practice in a range of contexts with diverse ethnic, cultural and racial groups, and with both men and women.

Methods of Practice

- Practice skills in, and knowledge of, assessment and intervention at micro, mezzo and macro levels for the purposes of developmental, protective, preventive and/or therapeutic intervention.

- The application of social work values, ethical principles, knowledge and skills to confront inequality, and social, political and economic injustices.
- Knowledge of, and skills in, social work research, including ethical use of relevant research paradigms, and critical appreciation of the use of research in social work practice.
- Supervised fieldwork education, with due consideration to the provisions of the above-mentioned item.

Paradigms of the Profession

Of particular salience to social work education, training and practice are the following theoretical/epistemological frameworks that should form the core curricula. These frameworks are not necessarily mutually exclusive:

- An acknowledgement and recognition of the dignity, worth and the uniqueness of all human beings (*person-centred approach).*
- Knowledge and understanding of the inter-connectedness that exists within and across all systems at micro, mezzo and macro levels (*ecological systems perspective*).
- Development of knowledge and skills in working in a wide range of contexts, with different sized 'client' populations across all system levels (*holistic, generalist or integrated approach*).
- An emphasis on the importance of advocacy and changes in socio-structural conditions that disempower, marginalize and exclude people (*social justice/human rights approach*).
- The capacity-building and empowerment of individuals, families, groups, organizations and communities through a human-centred developmental approach (*social development perspective*).
- Problem-solving and anticipatory socialization through an understanding of the normative developmental life cycle, and expected life tasks and crises in relation to age-related influences (*developmental lifespan perspective*).
- The assumption, identification and recognition of strengths and potential of all human beings (*strengths perspective*).
- An appreciation and respect for diversity in relation to race, culture, religion, ethnicity, linguistic origin, gender, sexual orientation and differential abilities (*respect for diversity).*

Standards with Regard to Student Social Workers

In respect of student social workers, schools should endeavour to reach the following standards:

- Clear articulation of its admission criteria and procedures, which should be compatible with those of the training institution.
- Student recruitment, admission and retention policies that reflect the demographic profile of the locality that the institution is based in.
- Due recognition should be given to minority groups that are underrepresented and/or underserved.
- Facilitation of articulation across institutions by specifying the recognition of credits obtained at other training institutions.
- Provision for student advising that is directed toward student orientation, assessment of the student's aptitude and motivation for a career in social work, regular evaluation of the student's performance and guidance in the selection of courses/modules.
- Making provision for and encouraging the participation of all students, including mortality rates, migration, gender and age profiles, and how these impact social policies and social service delivery.
- 'Minority groups' may be defined in terms of numerical representation and/or 'minority' in terms of socio-economic and/or political status. It remains an ambiguous and contested concept and needs to be defined and clarified within specific social contexts those in distance, mixed-mode, decentralized and/or internet based programmes in relation to the development of its core purpose or mission and the programme objectives, and in the formulation and modification of policies that affect academic and student affairs. Such participation should be consistent with the policies of the training institution.
- Ensuring that, in offering distance, mixed-mode, decentralized and/or Internet-based teaching, the quality of the educational programme is not compromised.
- Mechanisms for locally-based instruction and supervision should be put in place, especially with regard to the fieldwork component of the programme.
- Explicit criteria for the evaluation of student's academic and fieldwork performance.
- An indication of how students evaluate their own values, attitudes and behaviours in relation to its accepted and relevant code of ethics.
- Making available, to all students, the school's grievance and appeal procedures. Such procedures should be compatible with those of the training institution.

- A specification of the school's policy and procedure with regard to the termination of a student's enrolment in the programme. Poor performance and/or the failure to uphold the values and ethical principles of social work may render the student unsuitable for the profession.
- Non-discrimination against any student on the basis of race, colour, culture, ethnicity, linguistic origin, religion, political orientation, gender, sexual orientation, age, marital status, physical status and socio-economic status.

Fieldwork in social work educational programmes involves multiple learning pedagogies and activities. Most popular components in the domain of fieldwork programme are: (i) Orientation Programme, (ii) Concurrent Fieldwork, and (iii) Block Fieldwork. In addition to these three, some schools organize additional components such as: (i) Rural Camps, (ii) Study Tours, (iii) Supportive Fieldwork Instructions, (iv) Skill Development Workshops, and (v) Summer/Winter Placements.

Fieldwork Practices

In India, different schools of social work have developed their own programmes of fieldwork depending upon the kind of communities/agencies and opportunities available in the area and the differences in curricula and fields of specialization. But, the broad outlines of fieldwork programmes in most schools of social work in India are on the following lines. The requirement of putting in about 15 hours of fieldwork per week is compulsory in most schools of social work, during the two-year period of training. In some schools the fieldwork is carried on in the afternoon of week days while in some others, two days in the week are exclusively set apart for fieldwork. Orientation classes are generally held prior to the commencement of fieldwork in order to initiate the students into the methods and contents of fieldwork. Group meetings, panel discussion and seminars are later conducted to discuss problems and effect improvements in fieldwork programmes.

Orientation Programme

Most of the schools of social work organize orientation programmes varying from 5 days to 14 days for the newcomer students in the profession and before starting the course curricula. Orientation provides information regarding the importance and place of practicum in the educational programme. Orientation programmes also clarify purpose, functions, and ethics in social work professional practices. Some schools name these as 'induction programmes'.

Agency Visit

It is the practice of many schools of social work to begin the fieldwork programme by organizing a series of visits to social welfare agencies in the area. This is particularly useful to those students who never had an opportunity to visit similar agencies. Such visits will give the students concrete instances of social welfare programmes. During these visits they study the objectives of the agency, administration of programmes, sources of finance, areas of strength and weakness, etc., and get a total picture of the institutions. This will particularly be helpful because some of these students are likely to be placed for fieldwork in these agencies and this prior study and contact is very useful.

When in the course of such visits or during educational tours, the students should remember that they are neither, sightseers nor overseers. They are going into the agencies by the kind courtesy of the agency personnel, to study the working of these agencies as they are, and not as they should be. They should be able to learn by listening to people and observing closely, but must remember their job is not that of inspectors, critics or advisors. If suggestions are asked for, realistic and practical ones may be given. It must be remembered that many of these agencies are functioning under various kinds of limitations and the visitors may be disappointed if one expects to find ideal conditions in all of them. The questions put to the agency personnel should be simple and straightforward and only to elicit needed information. They should not be cynical in approach or critical in tone. Well-written and comprehensive reports on these visits will indicate how much one has been able to learn as a result of these visits. The agency visits will enlarge the breadth of their vision while report writing will develop the facility of expression.

Fieldwork Placement

Fieldwork placement in the first year is generally intended to provide learning opportunities for students in the practice of basic social work methods such as case work, group work and community organization. Fieldwork manuals or outlines prepared by each school for use in the various field help to guide the students, who are also individually supervised by faculty supervisors. The students get opportunities depending upon their preference and the existence of sufficient number of agencies, to gain experience in one or more of these methods. Fieldwork at this stage involves the students in a detailed study of the structural and functional set-up of the agency and learning experience wherever practicable in the administration of the agency programmes. The extent of learning opportunity naturally depends upon the opportunities available in the agency and the goodwill of the agency personnel. In some cases, they have no opportunity other than to copy down information from official records, whereas in some others the students actively participate as part of the agency. The fields of specialization are usually labour welfare, rural welfare, correctional administration, tribal welfare, family and child welfare, psychiatric social work, etc.

In retrospect, those who are in charge of placing students for fieldwork will find it difficult to be able to satisfy all students with regard to the field in which they are to be placed and the particular agency in which to work. The anxiety of the students is placement and the particular agency in which to work. The anxiety of the students to be placed in such fields which they believe to be better than others and in such agencies which have been described to them by their seniors or friends as 'good' agencies is understandable. But, at the same time, they must be helped to understand that the success of their fieldwork does not depend entirely on their opportunity to work in any one field or agency, but in their ability to learn to use the social work principles and techniques in any setting and in any agency. The purpose of fieldwork is to generally acquaint them with the practice of social work principles and skills. Oftentimes what is more significant, specially while moving into any of the many fields of social work after the training, is not so much the special and limited experience in any one agency but rather the general and cumulative effect of a varied programme of fieldwork in a variety of agencies. This is so because in India, unlike in USA, UK and other countries the special conditions and needs of our country seem to require a general practitioner in social work rather than a specialist in case work, group work, etc.

The specific objectives of agency placement are as follows:

1. Expose the student to the nation's various developmental problems.
2. Create a growing social consciousness in the student in order to develop an attitude of commitment and sensitivity to problems.
3. In keeping with the needs of the community, participate in the planning and organization of simple and specific tasks, and learn to involve individual and groups in the same.

4. To learn by being a part of the implementing, monitoring and evaluation team.
5. To experience the service delivery system in reality and integrate it with knowledge gained in theory, thereby enabling the student to sharpen skills essential for the social workers.
6. Finally, agency-based field practicum is on the job training for the social work students.

One of the most covered agencies for fieldwork among the majority of students is the factory. In schools of social work where specialization is offered, maximum numbers opt for labour welfare. Thus, both in the course and fieldwork, there is a great rush of students for labour specialization. This is understandable in India because labour field is an expanding one with increasing job opportunities. This will be confusing to those in other countries who believe that labour is not really a field of social work and that the practice of social work, as such, in a factory is more ideal than practicable. But we in India have come to accept labour as a field of social work and the government has given a statutory stamp on this approach by making the appointment of labour welfare officers compulsory and also by requiring them to have a degree or diploma in social work with no specialization in labour, those who have no social work training but rather a general training in labour field, and also those who had in addition to social work courses, a specialized course in labour.

Besides the agency placement, the department also gives importance to the community placement in all the schools of social work in India. There is no single school that provides only agency placement or community placement. All the schools provide community placement especially in rural community, urban community or urban-slum community. The main objectives of community placement are to understand about the holistic purview of the community, its structure and function from all perspectives.

Agency Response to Social Work Practicum

The academic institutes expect the agency supervisor to check and sign the dairy and discuss the progress in learning of the students for achieving the objective of field practicum in social work. The agency's response towards facilitating the training of the social workers is an important variable in the endeavour of professional education in the country. The response from the organizations in this regard has not been encouraging so far owing to the following reasons:

- That many agencies even today do not have trained social workers employed in the organizations to guide and facilitate the process of learning on mutual interests. The mutual interest means engagement of the trainees in organization's projects and programme in progress, with or without any cost but making it mutually beneficial to each other.
- Many organizations feel that it is a burden for the professional engaged, as they have to spend time and energy for the learning of the students from the educational institutes.
- The agencies have adopted the people-centred movements leaving aside the method-centred practice in social work, thereby resulting in mismatch in the process of fieldwork needs of the institute of learning.
- The process of liberalization, privatization and globalization (LPG) has placed the clients, groups and communities in vulnerable situation; increased unemployment, underemployment in this poverty-stricken country where management of social services has to depend a lot on the government and funding agencies, curtailing the grants for people-centred development projects.
- Some organizations take fieldwork placement of students as an invited encroachment to the field of their work and avoid or refuse such placement.
- Considering the proximity and availability of professional organizations the institutes have very few choices of fieldwork agencies for placement of students.

Cooperation with Agency

The active cooperation of agencies is crucial to the success of fieldwork. It is true that the vast majority of the agencies is very cooperative and does its best to enable and assist social work students to organize fieldwork activities useful to the clients of the agency and to themselves in terms of learning experience. Where fieldwork requirements include the task of initiating students into the theory and practice of agency programme and administration, it is considered by a few of the agency personnel as interruption of their routine schedule of work. But, even though it entails some loss of time it must be borne in mind that the service they render is not something, which is helpful to the students only, but something, which will cumulatively benefit the whole field of social work. The agencies are participating in the development of competent, practical-minded and professionally qualified social workers and the time spent on them is not wasted but well-spent in the interest of the development social work. It is a good investment because in course of time it will yield fruits in terms of effectiveness of social welfare programmes, and the development of a good cadre of social workers, who will be able to help people in distress and groups in difficulties more effectively and efficiently. The students and the authorities of the schools of social work should appreciate the goodwill shown by the agencies and must be very considerate and cooperative so as not to cause inconvenience in any way. The details of the fieldwork programmes must be worked out in consultation with the agency personnel and must be gone through under their guidance and supervision. The faculty supervisor must keep in touch with the agency supervisor so as to help the students to have as much practical experience as possible, keeping in mind the limitations of the agency, if there are any.

Supervision

Effective and helpful supervision in future is a very important factor contributing towards the success of fieldwork programmes. But to many students of social work in India, the personalized supervision is a source of headache and to a few nearly a nightmare. This is partly because of the background of many students on whom attention was never focused earlier. Often their nearest contacts with the teachers were usually from the last benches in the classroom. They were awarded marks or promoted to higher classes in the most secretive and anonymous manner. But, in the school of social work, the student can no more hide himself in a crowd of students, nor can protect himself from the searching eyes of the teacher by sitting behind a classmate. Here, he is not known intimately, is watched carefully, and helped directly. Thus, coming out into the limelight is very embarrassing to many. To be involved in an individual supervisory session, in which he and somebody else are looking closely and intimately at his work is not so easy for a beginner.

These difficulties are there in good many cases, and the helpful and supporting role of the supervisor is to assist such students to note these problems and gradually help them out of these difficulties. Some supervisors may have too high expectations of the student and may forget that he should also begin where the student is. Sometimes, when they throw light on how the client has to be made comfortable, accepted without reservations and helped continuously, they may forget that the students also deserve to get these from the supervisors. Since many are the fields in which students are placed for fieldwork, some supervisors will not be able to help effectively or guide properly if they themselves do not have sufficient experience in the field and may not be able to fully appreciate the difficulties which the students face. Supervision is essentially a helping and enabling process. It should not be merely a mechanical and monotonous probing into the work as is done by an inspector, but a process of sharing the facts and situations between the two, as a result of which the student is gradually able to develop and function effectively on his own.

Some students tend to lean too much on the supervisors for suggestions, etc., and at every stage would like to be told what to do next. But if there is too much of spoon-feeding by the supervisor, the student will not get a chance to develop initiative or have independent thinking and take action. On the other hand, to think that the student knows everything and needs no guidance is also an extremely wrong position to take. The role of the supervisor is to educate the student according to his pace, building on his areas of strength and using the greater experience and competence he himself has in the field. He should be able to create a sense of trust and confidence in the student towards the supervisor so that the student feels free to communicate and by the recognition of positive factors should be able to eliminate the weak points in his functioning.

If high standards of performance and conduct are to be expected from the students, still higher standards in supervision is also called for. In the course of supervision the supervisor should be able to imbibe the qualities of regularity, sincerity, honesty, uprightness, etc., and should be able inculcate these sovereign qualities in the students not by preaching but by his own example. Some students may think that the quantity of fieldwork is more important. But what is really important is quality, how a thing is done being more important than what is done. The most significant thing is the regularity and responsibility, sincerity and seriousness, brought to bear on the fieldwork. For example, someone might ask: "Why this great fuss about submitting the fieldwork report exactly on time, what if I submit it any day I finish writing?" On the one hand without regular reports, conferences and discussions will be meaningless. Even more important than this is the fact that such insistence is to enable the students to form regular habits and systematic ways of working. By submitting the fieldwork reports exactly on time, week after week and month after month, it becomes a habit with him, and in any job situation he will be able to carry out the work as regularly and systematically.

In the words of R.R. Singh (1985), supervision is "a two-way process between supervisor and supervisee in which the supervisor instructed, enabled, guided, supported and communicated with the student in his quest for developing social work skills, knowledge and attitudes".

So, the fieldwork supervision generally involves: (i) the supervisee (a student of social work) undergoing formal training in social work which may lead to the award of some degree, diploma or certificate; (ii) supervisor of school/department under whose auspices formal social work education and training are imparted; (iii) some specifically designated personnel of some social service/social welfare/social development/human development agency which exists in the community for the purpose of providing services/promoting social and human development; (iv) clients/and/or people in the community whom services are to be provided and/or with whose cooperation the student must learn to practise social work.

Some schools have introduced group supervision system to guide students. Group supervision can take two forms; one is that it may be treated as a substitute or supplement to individual supervision to effect economy in time, and extends benefits to students for a longer duration; the other is that it uses the group as a means for individual and collective awareness, growth and action, and also as a source of mutual support for the members of the group. This also helps, in a way to dilute the authority of the school or the agency supervisor, and the students get a feeling of being an equal partner in a formal programme.

It was found from all the schools of social work that most of the educators pay weekly supervision in the field.

Table 4.1

Opinion of the Educators about Supervision in the Fieldwork

Supervision	*Frequency*	*Percentage*
Yes	80	88.9
No	10	11.1
Total	90	100

It was found that around 90 per cent educators pay their weekly supervision in the fieldwork but only few of the respondents were of the opinion that they do not pay supervision in the field.

Transport/Communication Facility for Supervision

All the schools of social work do not have transportation facilities for fieldwork but some schools provide transport especially for observational or rural camp. Some schools give it for students' fieldwork or for faculties' supervision and some schools do provide it occasionally to the students. It was seen that the students from most of schools manage the transportation on their own. This is one of the dilemmas of social work in India, where although fieldwork is considered as the heart and soul of social work, transportation facilities are not provided to the students (sometime students need to go very far from the main destination for fieldwork and most of the time they spend just in coming and going to the community or agency and very little work is capitalized in practice) as well as to the faculty members (who loose interest in such supervision because of the lack of transport facilities in the department).

From the educator respondents it was found that most of the schools of social work in India do not have communication facility for supervision.

Table 4.2

Opinion of the Educators about Communication Facility in the Department

Communication Facility	*Frequency*	*Percentage*
Yes	35	38.9
No	55	61.9
Total	90	100

It is clear from the table that only 38.9 per cent teacher respondents are of the view that they have communication facility in the department to supervise their students in the fieldwork but ironically it shows that around 62 per cent respondents are of the view that they do not have any communication facility for supervision of the students in the field.

Individual Conference

The aim of Individual Conference (IC) is to guide and help the students to integrate social work theory and practice, help to express the experiences in theoretical terms, to review the work in accordance with the plan and to monitor the performance of the students. The supervisor focuses on the learning needs of individual student and directs the course of supervision accordingly. The students should make note of the instructions, observations and comments given by the supervisor and should clarify their doubts related to the work with the supervisor. Hence, the students should come prepared for the ICs and further their learning. The agency supervisor must hold at least one IC with the students every week to understand the progress of learning and advise the learners accordingly.

Group Conference

Group Conference (GC) intended to increase the horizon of knowledge and input of the student by learning from the experiences of other students. GCs help to increase the horizon of knowledge of the students by learning from the experiences of other students. It helps to demonstrate professionalism in discussing presentations made by fellow students, develop the skills of articulation and presentation.

It also provides opportunity to chair and conduct sessions and in the process learn to deal with group dynamics. Each student is required to make a presentation in the GC. The GCs will help the students to learn skills in presentation, chairing and recording. GCs will be generally held once in a week or fortnight depending on the departmental conditions. Attendance in GCs is compulsory for all the students.

From the educators of all 15 schools of social work in India, researcher got the information about the ICs and GCs.

Table 4.3

Opinion of the Educators about Holding ICs/GCs in the Department

Holding ICs/GCs	*Frequency*	*Percentage*
Yes	75	83.3
No	15	16.7
Total	90	100

The above table shows that overwhelming percentage (83.3) of respondents is of the opinion that they take regular ICs/GCs in the department and rest of the respondents (16.7%) mentioned that they do not take regular ICs/GCs because they are often involved in the activities of the department as well as of the university.

Mid-term Sharing/Evaluation

The supervisor conducts a sharing session by the middle of the academic session. The aim of a mid-term sharing is to monitor the progress of the student and give further direction to the work by identifying areas of improvement and tasks for the next term of fieldwork.

The mid-term sharing session is held in the middle of the session of each term of concurrent fieldwork. The students prepare a self-assessment report as per the guidelines and submits it to the supervisor before the sharing session. Similarly, the supervisor will also prepare an assessment report about the student. These reports are shared between the supervisor and the student during the mid-term sharing. Most of the schools have their own timings and criteria for evaluation and sharing.

Recording

Recording provides an opportunity to the student to organize and present information, observations, reflections and actions in a systematic manner. It is useful for reflecting on one's own role and reactions in an interaction, in administration and research. In fact these are the bases for any evaluation. Process recording is stressed by all the schools. This form of recording is the product of the practice of social case work in the early years of professional social work, and with minor adaptations has been followed in group work and community organization also.

Every student should maintain a small diary during fieldwork, Individual Conferences (ICs) and Group Conferences (GCs) and note down significant aspects of work done including supervisory inputs. The dairy should clearly indicate the date of fieldwork, the hours devoted and activities taken up. The student should get the diary checked periodically by the respective supervisor and show it to other supervisors during field visit supervisions for making their comments/remarks. The students should properly maintain the field diary, as it is a document submitted for evaluating the performance of a student.

Students placed in agencies/communities should write separate or comprehensive daily records depending on the assignments undertaken in the agency/community duly signed and authenticated by the agency supervisor or sometimes by the community supervisor. The approach of recording deserves careful consideration by the schools of social work so that flexible guidelines are developed to record and document practice experience.

Fieldwork Reports

Well-maintained fieldwork records enable the student and the supervisor to objectively review the work done and to improve the same in future. Acceptance of objective criticism and constructive suggestions and the ability to bring about the necessary chances in work and outlook is the required prior condition which will help the student to learn more in the process of supervision. To think that one is above correction is not only incorrect in point of fact, but also inadmissible, in terms of approach. The reports should be honest, clean and clear and bring out the process of work in any setting and faithfully record the factual details, correctly reflecting the areas of success and the difficulties faced. But it has to be admitted that an extent of exaggeration or an element of story telling may creep into the reports of some, even though they are naturally in a very small minority. Sometimes, this tendency is due to very high expectations on the part of the supervisors about the professional performance of the students. Having got from a few conferences, the lines of the supervisors' criticism and suggestions, a few of them tend to write reports not as the work actually turned out but more in a manner which is likely to meet with the approval of the supervisor. Cases of totally cooked up and fake reports, which sooner or later will be discovered, are exceptions and even this is no justification for distrusting the students generally, and having a sort of police inspection. Supervisory visits should not be so much to check whether the students do the work, but rather to see them working and render help or assistance if needed. If, in the course of social work training it is not possible to inculcate honesty and uprightness in the students, that training is not worth anything. But honesty cannot be expected if honesty is penalized as when an honest effort and report in fieldwork is criticized while a dishonest one is praised. But here also dishonesty will never pay in the long run. The outlines provided, the orientation classes and supervisory guidance should help the students to write honest and systematic reports.

Evaluation

Fieldwork is subjected to continuous process of evaluation in the course of conferences between the supervisors and students. But towards the end of each term or academic year the student and the respective supervisors jointly evaluate the total performance of the students in fieldwork and record the same for reference. Both the student and the supervisor must be as objective as possible.

These summary evaluations at the end of the term or year is not likely to lead to any new finding but rather would help to sort out the positive and weak points which must have been observed and discussed in the course of previous conferences. What is needed at this stage is to have a view of the totality of the performance over a period and to assess the same in such a way as to help in the course of next placement or job situation. Even the person, who has been functioning well, can do still better if properly helped by objective evaluation and if strengthened by achievements.

Many schools ask the students to write out a self-evaluation report following an outline prepared for the purpose or are encouraged to raise points which will help in evaluating their work. The evaluation is a joint work and the points in the report prepared by the supervisor and the self-evaluation reports or points indicated by the student are jointly discussed and the final form of the report will largely reflect the thinking of both. These are later discussed with the head of the institution and other staff members, who help in finalizing the grades or marks. In some schools in addition to individual or group evaluation conferences, a viva voce examination on the fieldwork performance is conducted and the performance in these oral tests and the report of the supervisor forms the basis for the final marks or grades.

The outline developed by the various schools for evaluation is naturally very helpful. But it is very difficult to develop criteria which will be cent per cent successful. One difficulty is that it is not so easy to divide the persons working into watertight compartments and assess them separately. Even though individual items of performance and relationship are to be looked into, the attention must necessarily be rather on the total performance and overall functioning over a period of time. The criteria developed in various schools lay down that evaluation of fieldwork must naturally assess the student's personal qualities such as honesty, sincerity, regularity, ability to establish and maintain positive relationship with clients, agency personnel, etc., ability to integrate theoretical knowledge with practical work in the field, responsibility in the use of social work skills, success of professional performance and development of professional discipline, ability to work within agency limitations, positive use of supervision, willingness to admit mistakes and learn therefrom and student's overall performance. The evaluation must naturally lay emphasis on the positive and strong points and at the same time should not overlook the weak spots in work and the personality of the student. Most of the schools of social work have both internal and external evaluation system.

Criteria for Evaluation

Attendance: Punctuality and regularity in attending concurrent fieldwork, ICs, GCs, seminar, submitting worksheets, reports and fieldwork diary.

Field Performance: It would be based on the number of criteria such as ability to adjust with the agency/community, acquiring knowledge about the vision, mission, programmes, activities and service delivery system of the agency, perception, comprehension and conception, developed professional approach to work assigned and assessment of the functioning of the organization.

Ethics and Values: Student should have sense of responsibility and professional commitment, capacity to take initiative, respect for social work values and ethics; team spirit and team work should be inculcated along with setting an identity of being a social work professional in a broader aspect.

Quality of Records: Quality of records involves project work report, presentation of data, mode of presentation of data, analysis and interpretation of data, suggestions drawn and its rationality, language and style of recording.

Seminar: This includes content, style of presentation; language, clarity, defense, participation, etc., which are the assessment parameters for a student in a seminar.

Contents of Evaluation: The contents of evaluation covers recording and other documents related to fieldwork, punctuality in fieldwork, receptibility and initiative in launching field programmes, resourcefulness and responsibility towards their field programmes, extent of involvement in carrying on the experimental or other field-related programmes, use of social work skills and techniques, ability to organize fund raising and promoting public relation and development of capacity to use and utilize supervision.

Supportive Fieldwork Instruction

In order to expand horizons of practice learning, students are provided inputs from experienced practitioners so that they may learn appreciations for practice and understand deeper insight and self-awareness as well as positive and negative aspects of practice performance. This basically intends to supplement students' knowledge and quest to become like their role models. Though these interactions do not require much resources but demands proper planning to organize in an orderly manner.

Skill Development Workshop

In any professional education and training, skill development is one of the prime objectives. It helps learners to acquire specific skills for situations encountered during practice as well as acquire skills for their concurrent fieldwork learning. These may be for problems/concerns, issues or situations like, working with alcoholics or people living with HIV/AIDS, adolescents for life skills development, youth for leadership development and couples for marital relationship and enrichment, support for the aged and disabled elderly people. From all the schools of social work it has been found that only three schools of social work, i.e., TISS, Delhi School of Social Work and Jamia Milia Islamia are providing skill development programmes and workshops from time to time.

Study Tour/Camps

Some schools hold a three-to-five or ten days' camp, the main purpose of which is to provide an experience in group living and group participation. It gives learning opportunities in democratic management under the guidance of one or two members of the faculty, and enables students to assume full responsibility for the organization of the various activities, in the planning and execution of which students are given full opportunities. This can be a very useful experience for those who had never participated in such group activities and provide an opportunity to practise group work principles among themselves. But some schools consider that these objectives can be realized in the course of the general and extra-curricular activities of the school.

Study tours mostly in the second year are an integral part of the training programme in most schools of social work in India. This also provides an opportunity for group participation and planning and specially helps to widen the mental horizon of the students and acquaints them with the problems of social welfare and programmes of social welfare agencies in other parts of the country. Seeing things is the best way of learning and the study tours help the social workers to grow out of narrow regional considerations and develop a national approach and get an overall picture of the field of social welfare in India. The amount of time, energy and resources that must necessarily go into planning and execution of study tours are tremendous. But, the educational components and learning opportunities in such tours are well worth the trouble and expenses that necessarily go into it. From the study it was found that out of 15 schools of social work, 11 schools have education tour and rural camp.

Summer and Winter Placements

In some of the schools in India, summer and winter placements are optional (like in Delhi School of Social Work winter placements are optional for both MA Previous and Final Year students and summer placements is compulsory for MA Previous students) for both the MSW Previous and Final Year students. But most of the schools of social work in India do not have the system of winter and summer placements. These placements aim at building the confidence in working with different groups or people by enhancing their competence and broadening their basic knowledge, skills and also developing critical perspectives of social work practice. Throughout these placements, students are expected to undertake field action-cum-study projects within an organization of their choice or with selected NGOs which provide many experiences in the field of social work practicum. Students are also expected to identify some specific components and mechanism of the projects with the consultation of agency staff and faculty members of the respected department of the schools to develop their professional competence.

Block Fieldwork

The pattern of block placement, like the concurrent fieldwork varies form school to school and in other context it is either compulsory or voluntary but it is generally organized at the end of two years of social work. This learning activity enables learners to integrate learning and generate newer learning by participating in the intervention processed over a period of four to six weeks continuously, in a specific agency. Students generally give their options for placement agencies. Sometimes these options are guided by considerations of variety of experience, depending on concurrent fieldwork experiences, likely opportunities for employment in the agency and own convenience or relation with an employee or resource persons. Majority of the schools ask their students to undergo block fieldwork training at the end of the two-year programme and it is more treated as pre-employment training. Therefore, most reputed schools have made it as non-credit activity but ensure that everyone completes this learning exercise. Some educational institutions offer such an opportunity at the end of the third or prior to the examinations of the fourth semester as they do consider it worth evaluation, as part of their professional development. In a narrower point of view, block fieldwork is the weakest link in the entire fieldwork programme, because supervision is not possible from the school, and has to depend on agency. During the block placement, students are required to submit reports of the work done (some schools want fortnightly report or some want report after completing the fieldwork). These reports have to be sent to the respected departments duly signed by the students and countersigned by the agency supervisor. Most of the schools will provide University degree to the students only after completing and submitting the comprehensive block fieldwork report to the department. From the study it was found that all the schools of social work (15 schools under this study) have a system of block placement.

5 Issues Addressed, Programmes and Assignments Undertaken and Outcomes

During fieldwork, students are placed in different settings according to the presence of those settings near the schools or on availability of intervention by the department. As the problems are varied and different connotations of the interventions are needed, the students need to work both at micro as well as macro levels. Thus, the system at large that includes the individual, group, community people and administrative work, has to be considered holistically in dealing with cases, issues, programmes and assignments during fieldwork by the students. On the other hand, the training and practice system need not restrict itself only with the three basic methods of social work (Case Work, Group Work and Community Organization) but the holistic view has to be there in the practice of social work like Social Work Administration, Social Action, Social Research or Social Advocacy. For doing that, students under training and during fieldwork practice may be given an opportunity to learn to work at different levels and settings of social work intervention. Basically students are working in different settings like community setting, agency setting, industrial setting and medical and psychiatric setting in most of the schools of social work in India. But the students who were under my area of study, were mostly working in the community and agency setting for fieldwork practice and where they have been working on different issues, programmes and cases and assigning their tasks through social work intervention.

There are two types of system of placement for working in the community, one the students are placed directly in the open community by the schools and another is that students are placed by the community attachment or through an agency. In the open community setting the students will get an exposure to the various problems which would certainly help him/her practice in an integrated manner. Here, the students would see and cover different innovative practices and training models such as integrated approach, crisis intervention, holistic approach or developmental fieldwork in the community setting. The community setting certainly helps the students to visualize and internalize the problems at the micro level. The community setting will develop their social outlook and social perspective and also it will teach the students to practice the professional social work with an integrated approach. The student in the community setting through community organization prepares them to participate in the community welfare activities and thereby helps to improve their quality of life by way of actively involving and participating in different developmental programmes, or income generation programmes for total community empowerment. The main contents of fieldwork placement and training in the community setting are: (1) establishment of rapport and contacts with community people, (2) understand the community (in terms of physical, socio-economical, cultural, educational, political connotation), (3) find out and recognize formal and informal leaders in the community, (4) find out the problems and need of the community people, (5) prioritize the actual and felt needs, (6) find out the different causative factors of the problems of the community, (7) enlisting community resources (both internal and external), (8) programme planning according to the resources, (9) ensure community participation, (10) programme implementation, and lastly (11) termination and evaluation of the whole problems and programmes. For doing these, the students need to go through different phases like: (i) orientation phase, (ii) need identification phase, (iii) planning and preparation phase, (iv) implementation phase, and (v) termination and evaluation phase in the community setting.

In this study, the researcher found that out of total respondents, 39.7 per cent students were placed in the community for concurrent fieldwork. During their concurrent fieldwork they worked on different issues and social problems such as dealing with problematic individuals like mentally challenged and behavioural problems; working and dealing with case work, group work and community organization; organizing the programmes for the benefit of the service recipients; working with village structure, cultural pattern, socio-economic conditions of the villages; working with drop-out children and both male and female SHG members in the community; working with old-age pension. They are also working with child related problems in CGC, i.e., child's psycho and emotional problem, child rearing problems, dealing with micro-credit, marital disputes, working with adolescent problems, illiteracy, unemployment, development of child through group therapy; training of youth group and income generation programmes, working with women and child reproductive health, early marriage and family planning, social security of workers, women SHG formation and examining health status of the community and vocational training to youth group, working with mother and child health and problems faced by the pregnant mothers coming for delivery in the hospital, working with local clubs for mitigating social issues, etc.

The value of fieldwork is greatly enhanced and enshrined when the agency itself considers the work and activities of the student primarily as educational rather than as an additional hand to provide services.

Basically there are four types of agencies found for fieldwork training of students. The first type of agency is the agency which has a sound and preferred programme and also has trained personnel on its staff. The agency very often welcomes the placements of the students and at the same time designates one of the staff members to supervise the work of the students. In such situations, the school recognizes the agency staff as an independent supervisor and allots him/her mutually agreed number of students for concurrent fieldwork. He/she will be the responsible person for the day-to-day guidance and supervision of the students, and the schools of social work accept the evaluation of the agency supervisor as final. He/she is regarded equivalent to a member of the field staff of the school and also invited to attend all the fieldwork meetings in the school from time to time. Even the students have to submit their reports to him to evaluate, though there are very few agencies extending such kinds of service because the agency personals are so loaded in their duties that they are not able to find time to read the student's reports and records. There may be some problems in this in a way, that the responsibility for supervision of the students is divided between the agency supervisor and school supervisor and it necessitates a close relationship and liaison between them in the students' interest. In the absence of such relationship, the students are likely to get confused and may get contradictory instructions from the supervisors.

The second type of agencies are those agencies which are neither able to provide a trained worker nor are convinced of the usefulness of trained personnel. Here the school provides its own supervisors and they are responsible for the work of the students placed in those agencies. They introduce the students to the agency, its programmes, policies and selects assignments. They frequently visit the agency to examine the student's work and to ensure the quality of the learning experience. The main problem of this arrangement is the time factor and the students being supervised by a person who is not administratively related to the service he/she is providing. Sometimes students face confusion on how to use the social work values and methods which may not be those followed in the agency. The third type of agency is developed by the school themselves to pioneer and demonstrate the efficacy of a new services in the region. Where the existence of agencies is very less, there the school develops services of its own and share the services among the faculty members to organize the programmes and at the same time supervise the students placed under them. In this situation, the main problems are the availability of the members of the staff for teaching and supervision. The last type of agency makes students to be involved in administrative work. In this regard, students do not learn anything; they rather spend time for the sake of fieldwork and thus loose the interest to work further. These are the agencies of fieldwork pattern based on the agency-school relationship. There may be other types of agencies also.

In my study, out of the total respondents, 181 (60.3%) students were of the opinion that when with the agency they worked on various social issues like working with civil society support programme, participatory and action research, social assessment and participatory monitoring and evaluation. They also undertook working in schools and working methods of agency, working with village development, training for SHGs, training for government projects like SGSY, PMRY, etc., for making the community people self-reliant, working with TB, HIV/AIDS patients and on total human health, working for women empowerment and domestic violence against women, education and problems of slum, hostel for girls, mitigating child labour, working with street children and their health, education, substance abuse, sexual harassment, conducting life-skill education among adolescent girls, etc.

Fieldwork Placement

Table 5.1 shows that more than 60 per cent students are placed in the agency and nearly 40 per cent students are placed in community for their concurrent fieldwork placement.

Table 5.1

Distribution of Student Respondents by Concurrent Fieldwork Placement

Fieldwork Placement	*Frequency*	*Percentage*
Community	119	39.7
Agency	181	60.3
Total	300	100

Dealing with Case Work

From Table 5.2, it is observed that 192 respondents (64%) practised case work during their concurrent fieldwork while other 108 respondents (36%) did not practise any case work. Out of total respondents who have practised case work, 118 respondents (61.45%) practised less than three case works, 49 respondents (25.5%) practiced three to five case works, 19 respondents (9.89%) practised five to eight case works and rest of the six respondents (3.1%) also practised more than eight case works during their concurrent fieldwork.

Table 5.2

Distribution of Student Respondents by Dealing Case Work

Case Work	*Frequency*	*Percentage*
Yes	192	64
No	108	36
Total	300	100

It was found that students usually in all the schools of social work in India practice case work methods on different issues, for example, with handicapped children, TB patients, drop-out children, street children, etc. Their interventions in case work were in the following areas:

1. handicapped patients who need economical support,
2. well-being and welfare of the individuals,
3. proceeding towards development,
4. positive outcome in drop-out students and cataract patients,
5. confronted with various human disablements,
6. develop thinking capability of the client to handle the situation,

7. TB patients received 'cured status' and marital conflict case solved with mutual agreement, and
8. street children were rehabilitated in shelter home.

Till some students are working in the process, some successfully closed their cases.

Dealing with Group Work

Table 5.3 shows that more than two-thirds of students do practice group work method of social work during their concurrent fieldwork. Around 23 per cent students said that they did not practice group work in their fieldwork. Even some students commented that they actually sometimes did not follow the process of group formation and rather did group activities.

Table 5.3

Distribution of Student Respondents Dealing with Group Work

Group Work	*Frequency*	*Percentage*
Yes	230	76.7
No	70	23.3
Total	300	100

In group work, their target groups are children's group and slow learner group, youth group, women SHG group, adolescent group, etc., and the issues they are working on are behavioural problems and sex education with youth group; recreation and personality development through sports and intellectual games with adolescent group and pre-natal and post-natal health awareness, group conflict, team building and motivation with youth and adolescent group; personal hygiene and physical fitness through exercise, recreational activity, crafts and cultural aspects, domestic violence as violation of human dignity, supportive sessions on life-skill education, substantial abuse, health and hygiene, positive and negative acts, anger management, peer pressure, life-skill education among adolescent girls; also on gender issue, RCH, career goals, behavioural modification of adolescent (using slang language), motivation of members to participate, ability to work with coordination, cooperation and facilitate in decision-making at different levels.

The outcomes of the group work were group understanding, group dynamics and interaction pattern, group cohesion through realistic purview; understanding group circumspection which is a platform where the group members nourish their inner potentialities and channelizing those towards positive development; develop personality and leadership quality, enhance creativity and conflict resolution among group members, learn to take responsibility, change behaviour in right way, develop sharing attitude and capacity building, develop own identity; initially members' participation were less but through more interaction and regular intervention, it was easy to deal with social issues, make the children group self-conscious and thoughtful, improve their study, sustainable and psychological development; group started taking responsibility of any task with mutual dependency and willingness to participate in any social cause.

Dealing with Community Organization

Table 5.4 shows that most of the respondents do practice community organization in their field, especially those who are working in the community and even students placed in the agency also practice it. Only few of the respondents comment that they did not practice community organization as they did not have opportunity because they were placed in a structured agency.

Table 5.4

Distribution of Student Respondents Dealing with Community Organization

Community Organization	*Frequency*	*Percentage*
Yes	262	87.3
No	38	12.7
Total	300	100

The issues they dealt with were health and nutrition of the child and mother and RCH, awareness on dengue and malaria in the community, working with youth group on the issues of addiction, sanitation and nutrition problems of the community, parent-teacher-student meeting on education and dropouts, awareness on legal aids and club formulation in the community, mass awareness on TB, STD, physically and mentally handicapped children and their rehabilitation, issues of cattle vaccination, issues of ration card, birth certificate and old-age pension, organizing health check-up camp in the community, superior and inferior complexities between two parties and inter-class conflict, community cleaning, working with pressure group and peace building projects, organized awareness camp on HIV/AIDS, sports competition for children in the community, open training centre for youth, awareness programme and survey on Janani Suraksha Yojna by NRHM (National Rural Health Mission), working on community dynamics and community need assessment.

The outcomes according to the students were utilization of both external and internal resources for dealing with different issues in the community; villagers are now more concerned about their development, quality of mid-day meal, etc. Parent's confidence towards education increased, got motivated towards SHGs and its functions, community consciousness developed in the area of health, distribution of government programmes, etc.

Specific Tasks to be Fulfilled during Fieldwork

Figure 5.1 depicts the distribution of student respondents by specific task to be fulfilled during concurrent fieldwork placement.

Figure 5.1

Distribution of Student Respondents by Specific Task

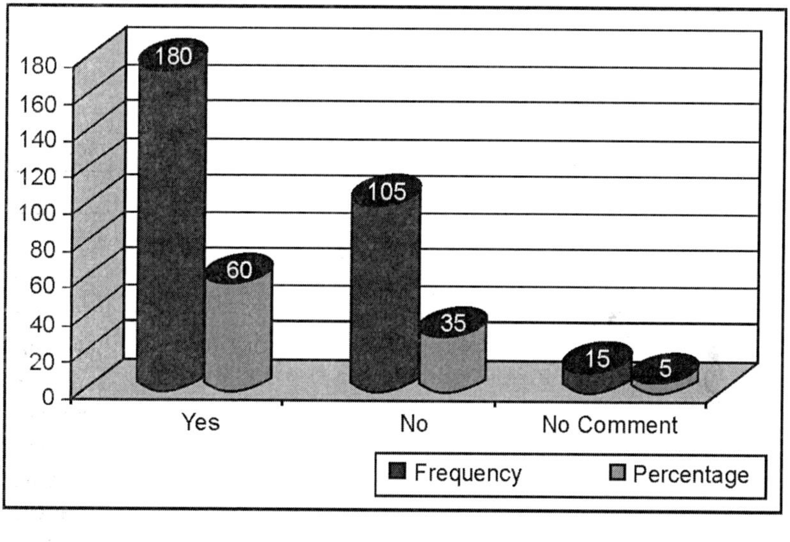

It is seen from the above figure that 60 per cent of the student respondents were of the opinion that they have to fulfil certain tasks in the fieldwork. Around 35 per cent of the respondents opined that they need not fulfil any specific tasks in their fieldwork rather they had enough freedom to work on any issue. Remaining 5 per cent of the respondents did not comment on this issue at all.

It was found that most of the schools of social work in India are imposing certain tasks on the students in the fieldwork and they evaluate also based on the tasks fulfilled.

Students primarily fulfil tasks like case work and case dealing, group work and group activities, community organization and community work, case profile and group profile, to learn socio-economic status of the community, techniques of intervening, rapport building, play certain roles as an educator, guide, facilitator, researcher, motivator in the community, convert their (community) felt needs into real needs, need to understand the political process to provide standardized services, conduct meetings and evaluate its outcomes, research work and survey work in both the community and agency, awareness programmes and campaigning on social issues and provide services implemented by the government at grassroots level, etc.

Supervision

Figure 5.2 indicates the opinion of the students regarding the supervision paid by their department supervisor in the fieldwork either in the agency or in the community.

Figure 5.2

Regular Supervision by the Department Supervisor

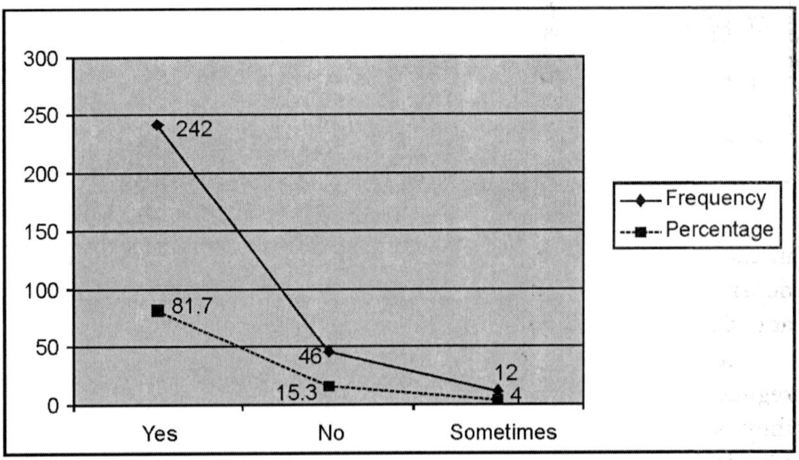

It can be seen from the above figure that 81.7 per cent of the respondents opined that their department supervisor pay supervision visits regularly but 15.3 per cent of the respondents said that their supervisors do not come for supervision at all. On the other hand, it can be seen that a little percentage (4%) of the respondents opined that their supervisors sometimes pay their visits to fieldwork.

It can be concluded that most of the supervisors in the schools of social work in India are very much involved in supervision.

Involvement of Students in Individual Conferences

Figure 5.3 indicates the 'distribution of respondents attending individual conferences in the department.

Figure 5.3

Distribution of Respondents Attending Individual Conferences

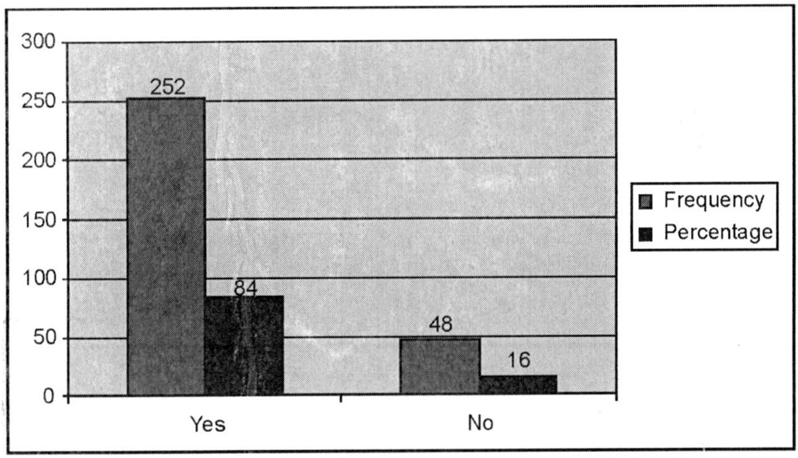

It was found that out of total respondents (300), 252 respondents mention that they regularly attend individual conferences in the department and remaining 48 respondents mention that they do not attend regularly because of the negligence of their supervisors.

It was also found that out of 252 respondents, who were regularly attending individual conferences, 232 (77.3%) said that they attend individual conferences once in a week and the remaining 22.7 per cent said that they attend it twice a week.

From the above analysis it is clear that most of the schools of social work maintain and give importance to organize regular individual conferences in the department.

Involvement of Students in Group Conferences

Figure 5.4 indicates the distribution of respondents attending group conferences in the department.

Figure 5.4

Distribution of Respondents Attending Group Conferences

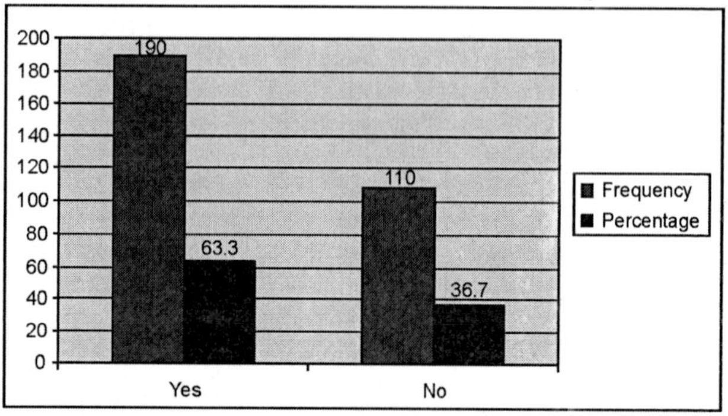

It was found that out of total respondents (300), 190 respondents mention that they regularly attend group conferences in the department and remaining 110 respondents mention that they do not attend group conferences regulalry.

From the above analysis it can be concluded that some of the schools of social work in India do not pay much attention to organizing group work regularly in the department.

Fieldwork in Job Profile

Figure 5.5 shows the opinion of the students regarding how fieldwork would help in job profile in future.

Figure 5.5

Distribution of Respondents Regarding Fieldwork in Job Profile

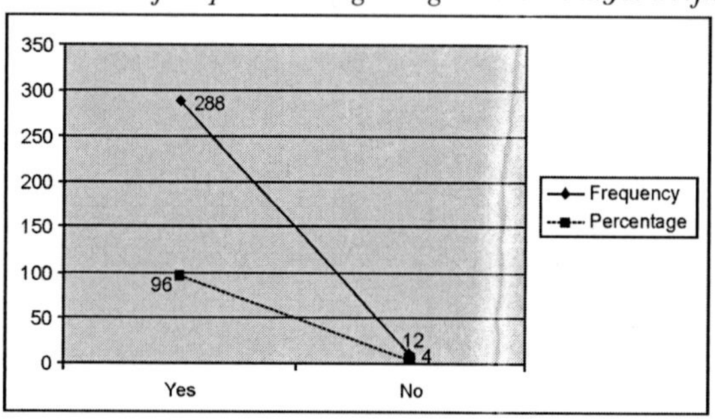

It was found that 96 per cent students have clear opinion that concurrent fieldwork would help job profile in near future and rest of the 4 per cent of the respondents do not consider that concurrent fieldwork would help them in job profile in future.

The students have come out with ways on how concurrent fieldwork would help job profile. It would help through increasing the competency of the students, understanding the reality-based problems solving process, have a scope to relate theories into application, dealing with either problematic or normal individual/group/community in different situations, mastering of adjusting situations, helps and shows the way how to work at grass-root levels, develop skills of rapport establishment with community people, develop confidence and gain expertise in dealing with social issues and develop professional competence. It also develops professional self, gives us strength to accept the people as they are and their problems accordingly, points out our weakness so that we can overcome it before going to professional work or job, gives a very important role of accountability, credibility and time management – it is the world where we are conscious that 'we are being watched' from the usual field of 'we watch how others perform'. With professional social work experiences one can start ones' own career; it helps to observe true picture and reality, builds professionalism with students, and teacher to work in limitations. It also helps to be a professional social worker and to know about the role of social worker in the agency or community, to identify the problems, resources (internal and external) of the organization or community and intervention of the problems, etc.

Satisfaction of Dealing Issues in Fieldwork

Table 5.5 exhibits the opinion of the student respondents whether they are satisfied in dealing with issues and problems in fieldwork or not.

Table 5.5

Distribution of Respondents by Satisfaction in Dealing with Issues in Fieldwork

Satisfaction in Dealing with Issues	*Frequency*	*Percentage*
Yes	238	79.3
No	62	20.7
Total	300	100

It is found that 79.3 per cent respondents are satisfied with their fieldwork especially when they deal with different issues and social problems but rest of the 20.7 per cent respondents were with different views and were not satisfied in dealing with issues and problems. They have also given the reason of dissatisfaction in dealing with issues in their fieldwork such as: inculcating real theory, knowledge yet to come truly, increasing competency still not a ground reality, dealing with only national problems and avoiding local problems, sometimes limitation from client's/beneficiary's part, sometimes problems remain unidentified and are kept hidden, lack of practical knowledge of the students or practitioners, sometimes lack of proper guidance to the students by the department supervisors because of their own work or being busy in their own projects in the department or outside, sometimes placement is done in such a way by the department that the interest of the students is not taken care of. As a result, there is no interest in the fieldwork; the problems sometime become so complex to deal with and there is a limitation of time and resources both from the agency and community. With contradictory departmental perspective, sometimes student cannot do what they want to do, because they do not have the power and authority; sometimes more students are placed in an agency or in a community, as a result there would be more selfish interests among the students when dealing with the issues.

Problems Faced during Fieldwork

Table 5.6 shows the opinion of the student respondents regarding problems faced by them in dealing with issues in the fieldwork.

Table 5.6

Distribution of Respondents by the Problems Faced in Fieldwork

Problems Faced in Fieldwork	*Frequency*	*Percentage*
Yes	184	61.3
No	116	38.7
Total	300	100

It was found that 61.3 per cent students clarified that they faced some problems in the fieldwork but 38.7 per cent students said that they did not face any problems. The main problems faced by the students (61.3%) are problem of initial relation building, problem of mistrust towards students due to earlier experiences, problem of people's participation at optimum level, problem of huge expectation of the recipient/community; timing of fieldwork is another problem for the students, especially for contacting the community where people are working the whole day for their living. Also with a large community sometimes it is not possible to communicate or have a rapport with everyone in a short span of fieldwork especially semester system; sometimes community resources are not utilized properly, wrong ideas and notions are preconceived by the community people that students will work according to them. Some other problems faced are: due to huge pressure on theory, the students cannot do enough in the fieldwork for the diversification of the community like different religious groups, difficult to bring them on one platform, negligence and avoidance of the villagers to some particular problems, non-availability of working men during any fruitful programme, hamper a lot, villagers sometimes careless and indolent in carrying out task that require their attention, lack of networking, communication and language problem, sharing information among co-workers working in the same villages is very less, sometimes senior students set unethical norms in the villages and juniors at times are forced to abide by them, scolding students by the teachers in the community in front of the villagers is another problem faced by the practice students in some institutions; difficult to change destructive mores and tradition of the community, because of some limitation of the agency, decision-making is not possible, no room for innovation and no permission for various things in the field to the students by the agency or the department, and sometimes students cannot take any initiative for any work in the agency of their own, sometimes the limitation of timing hampers intervention of the students; sometimes agency is not working very actively, people are mostly uneducated and with lack of professional knowledge and experience most of the agencies are run by non-professionals only.

Opinion of the NGO/Agency Personnel about the Students and Fieldwork Practice

There are different opinions about the fieldwork practised by the student social workers in their organizations during their concurrent fieldwork. Here are some of the opinions gathered and formulated on the basis of the brief discussions with NGO officials (especially in West Bengal, Andhra Pradesh, Assam, Uttar Pradesh) and my own experiences (during the agency supervision in different places like Delhi, Kanpur and Assam during my tenure of lectureship) as a social work educator.

There is a gap between the theoretical learning and its practicability in the field. The gap is because of the unavailability of trained professionals in most of the NGOs. The NGOs and other agencies in today's developmental activities are basically acquired by the non-professional personnel who do not have any understanding of the social work methods, theories and techniques. In the name of social work, they are grabbing funds from the different government and funding agencies and very little developmental and welfare activities are done with the utilization of the social work students who are doing their fieldwork throughout the year in those agencies.

Fieldwork training is an overall team work which requires the active and effective participation of the schools, students and agency personnel over the year.

According to the opinion of the agency personnel, students need to fulfil certain tasks/assignments. These field assignments not only provide best opportunities to the student social workers to involve themselves at grass-root level in the process of problem-solving, also but they could use the social work techniques and methods. Most of the agency personnel were of the opinion that social work students help in many of the situations using their skills, knowledge and talent during their placement in agencies. The helps are like involvement in community development programmes, fund raising, counselling, helping in project works usually doing investigation, case study, data collection, research, and also administrative works. They are also working in the area of education, health and hygiene, child issues, women issues, family planning, legal aids, vocational training, SHG formation and organizing camps using their core social work methods and techniques.

Even community peoples are of the opinion that social work students have shown a new way of living because now they are aware about their rights, helping in income generation programmes, forming SHGs at their places.

Still some agency personnel are not satisfied about the activities undertaken by the social work students because they sometimes do not abide by the rules and do not follow the parameter and purview of the agency.

But NGO personnel should not have an apathetic approach towards the student social workers placed in their agency and should not comply with the fieldwork responsibilities as an unwanted ritual or practice. They should encourage the students for an active participation in the functional aspect of the agency which will help the development of the inner potentiality of the students but also the agency as well.

Summary

Fieldwork begins with the placement of the student in the field, and education consideration is given more priority than other considerations. It is seen that in the fieldwork in all the schools of social work in India that frequent changes of agencies, communities, supervisors, allotment of number students per agencies/communities, allotment of fieldwork responsibilities to supervisors both in agencies/communities, and allotment of number of agencies/communities to be supervised by a teacher including new agencies/communities assigned. In this chapter the focus is given on the issues addressed, programmes and assignments and outcomes in their fieldwork.

The students are placed particularly in the agency (hospital, school, family planning centre, disaster management cell, District Urban Development Agency (DUDA), municipalities, developmental NGOs, jail, juvenile justice court, Block Development Officer (BDO) office, etc.) and in the community (rural, urban, slum community, etc.) and do developmental works utilizing professional social work techniques and methods. Basically students addressed age-old problems and issues as well as new emerging issues and problems through the utilization of the 'trinity' of social work, i.e., Case Work, Group Work and Community Organization and also the use of Social Research, Social Action and Advocacy.

The issues that had to be taken by the students in the different schools of social work in their respective fieldwork are such as emergence of RTI Act regarding accountability of government and other administrative sections to the common people, emergence of micro-credit as a tool of poverty alleviation, corporate social responsibility, misuse of natural resources, environmental pollution and deforestation, global warming and its impact on social life, terrorism and communalism and its impact on society, human rights violation, female infanticide, relief and rehabilitation on natural disaster and disaster management, eco-tourism, land mafia and land distribution system, problem of working women, degraded status of Hindi, wildlife studies and waste management, extinction of rare species, etc. The students got some achievements and outcomes after assigning those tasks in the fieldwork, as students cannot provide any outcome without learning various relation building elements. The outcomes are intervening and interacting processes, confronted with various human disablement, develop thinking capability of the client to handle the situation, understanding group circumspection which is a platform where the group members nourish their inner potentialities and channelising those towards positive development, develop personality and leadership quality, enhance creativity and conflict resolution among group members, utilization of both external and internal resources for dealing with different issues in the community; villagers are now more concerned about their development, overcoming different situations, etc. During their fieldwork they also faced some problems like the diversification of the community with different religious groups, the difficulty to bring them on one platform, inability to understand the political process of the community, needing more realistic guidance from the department supervisor, negligence and avoidance of the villagers to some particular problems, lack of networking, communication and language problem, non-availability of working men during any fruitful programme. Because of some limitations of the agency, decision-making is not possible in the agency, there is no room for innovation and no permission for various things in the field to the students by the agency or the department, lack of professional knowledge and experiences and most of the agencies are run by non-professionals only.

The students also believe that fieldwork would help their job profile in future because it will increase the competency of the students, understanding the reality-based problems-solving process, have a scope to relate theories into application, mastering of adjusting situations, helps and shows the way how to work at grass roots levels, develop confidence and become experts in dealing with social issues. While developing professional competence, it points out our weakness so that we can overcome it before going into professional work or job; it also gives a very important role of accountability, credibility and time management, and to work in spite of limitations, etc.

Lastly, it is clear that we need to modify our age-old techniques, theory of social work practice based on our own indigenous culture and reality.

6 Fieldwork and Its Emerging Trends Today

Over the past few decades, overshadow of changes has taken place in terms of economic crisis, political instability, cultural changes and ideological differences between states. Irrespective of the dichotomies between micro and macro social work practice model of the region or nation, the field instruction programme seems to have greater consistency cross-nationally in terms of its educational value, pattern of field practice and the accountability of the profession, for the quality of learning of students. In addition to the problems of cultural adjustment, which have been within the purview of social work practice for some time, problems such as the exploitation of women migrants (particularly in domestic service), the harsh treatment of illegal migrants, and the growing attachment of racist sentiment to social policy issues affecting migrants need to be addressed. Paradoxically, globalization has also fostered increased ethnic conflict and violence in many parts of the world. This problem is not only related to the growth of migration, but is also a function of the tensions accompanying economic, political, social and cultural integration. However, incidents of large-scale ethnic conflicts have their roots in the early phases of globalization, when the European powers subjected to the peoples of Africa, Asia, and Central and South America to global imperial rule. This is a far cry from the real truth, and because of this stance, globalization in general is encountering resistance from various interest groups, foremost among them are the environmentalists, union leaders, cultural traditionists, religious leaders of different persuasion, non-governmental organizations (NGOs) and social workers. But globalization (which means, in today's context homogenization of prices, products, wages, rates of interest, and profits to become the same all over) has created new opportunities for social workers in different parts of the world to share experiences and learn from each other. Increased reciprocal contacts would assist social work's development as a profession and, we hope, equip it to exert greater international influence. Globalization offers new opportunities for social work to expand its knowledge base. By engaging more actively in international activities, social work educators can enhance their understanding of pressing contemporary social problems. Problems such as AIDS, homelessness, substance abuse, and child neglect have critical international dimensions that, if properly understood, can provide deeper insights into etiological and related issues. For example, the World Health Organization's effective dissemination of information on international AIDS research has undoubtedly promoted a better understanding of this tragic condition (Midgley, 1990). Social workers can increase their practice effectiveness by critically examining and adapting practice innovation emanating from other countries. Globalization can also facilitate social work's efforts to enhance its own professional development. Greater international contacts will contribute to a greater shared identity among social workers, improved opportunities for collaboration, and a greater commitment to respond collectively to the changes of an interdependent world.

Globalization has also created massive new emerging problems in the world as well as in India like cultural adjustment, large-scale migration, poverty, unemployment, population growth, underemployment, terrorism, human right issues, caste-based problems, problems of urbanization, regional imbalances, youth unrest, etc. Austerity policies have squeezed welfare provisions under the Governments of various parties in India for the last few decades. People are mostly dissatisfied with the old system of welfare. The new denounces, the profligacy and inefficiency of public services while feminists and leftists insist that social welfare provisions must be transferred to establish near democratic forms of socialized provisions. Even in India, large number of developmental and different poverty alleviation programmes have been launched in the context of planned development. With the introduction of New Economic Policy (NEP) in 1990s, lot of socio-economic changes have been brought into India contributing to the erosion of the social safety nets, traditionally a welfare state responsibility. In the light of the still existing economic and social disparities in India, privatization of social and welfare sector programmes would make it difficult to find grassroot solutions to social problems. Certain areas like health, education, rural development, social welfare and so on, have already been facing modifications with reduced allocations from the state funding. Moreover, as responsibility for the well-being of the people is transferred from the state to the private sectors, the burden of survival falls on the initiative of the communities and voluntary groups. Thus, the new economic climate and its realities, inexorable though, will influence the practice of social work and vice versa. It is time for social work to find more viable linkage between the professional function and the changing context of the developmental process of the country. It is suggested that the social work educators be prepared to train students to meet the new challenges.

Today, India is the second most populous country in the world, with about 1.04 billion people, home to one-sixth of humanity. Although, it is difficult to accurately predict population growth rates 20 years to the future, we expect this number to rise by another 300–350 million, in spite of continuous efforts to reduce fertility rates. This would raise the total population to about 1,330 million by 2020. India is in the process of a demographic transition from high fertility, high mortality and stable population to low fertility, low mortality and stable population. This transition is a global phenomenon generated by the improved availability and access to modern health care that sharply reduced mortality rates and increased life expectancy. The crude death rate has declined to one-third of its level in 1941 and the expectation of life at birth has nearly doubled during this period. Falling mortality rates have been followed by a steady decline in birth rates, but this decline has not been as steep as the fall in death rate; even after reaching the replacement fertility rates, the population will continue to grow because of large numbers of young persons entering reproductive age. While, assessing future prospects, it is necessary to take into account the vast regional differences in demographic parameters. Population growth has recently decelerated below 2 per cent for the first time in four decades, but not uniformly across the length and breadth of the country. Several states in South India have already reached, or are about to attain, the replacement level of fertility that would ensure a zero growth rate of population in the long run. On the other hand, in many states in North India, characterized by high fertility rates, it may take several decades to reach the replacement level of fertility. There are also similar differentials in levels of mortality, especially in infant and child mortality. At the national level, two alternate scenarios for achieving population stabilization have been considered. In the optimistic scenario, which is based on achieving the demographic goals of the National Population Policy 2000, life expectancy is assumed to rise to 71 for males and 74 for females by 2020. Under the realistic scenario, life expectancy is assumed to reach 65 for males and 69 for females by 2020. Under either scenario India's population would exceed 1.3 billion in the year 2020. In both cases, the sex ratio of population (females per 1,000 males) would marginally increase from 932 in 2000 to 950 in 2020; reversing the historical trend of falling sex ratio is expected in the 21st century.

Major Challenges for India

1. A targeted approach to bring millions of families above the poverty line.
2. Generation of nearly ten million of new employment opportunities per annum, especially for those in the lower income groups.
3. Eradication of illiteracy.
4. A concerted effort to raise primary and secondary enrolment rates and minimize dropouts.
5. Improved public health to reduce infant mortality and child malnutrition.
6. Massive investment in power generation, telecommunications and other physical and social infrastructure.
7. Accelerated acquisition of technology capabilities to raise productivity in agriculture, industry and services.
8. Becoming a more important player in the world economy in terms of both trade and investments.

In the changed circumstances, the professional social worker requires competence in community work which involves policy analysis, legislative advocacy, community need assessment, project identification, preparation, administration and evaluation. Therefore, the field content should be redesigned to provide these skills and enable the students to function as developmental workers. However, the nature of field training, especially in community work and administration, has been reported to be lacking curricular thrust, field opportunities and adequate educational focus. The need to review and improve the design of students' field assignments was felt long back to promote the involvement of students in fieldwork and to upgrade the quality of field instructions, the key element for the preparation of the professionals of tomorrow (Desai, 1987).

Social work needs to respond to the social problems caused by globalization. The problems of poverty, inner-city decay, unemployment, and increasing despair in the industrial countries are a direct consequence of global economic change and the unwillingness of government to address these problems in ways that integrate displaced people into the productive economy rather than discarding them. Social work also needs to be more active in providing services to immigrant ethnic minorities and promoting a better understanding of the advantages of cultural diversity. Although the profession has previously worked with refugee population, more needs to be done to enhance social work's effectiveness in this growing field of practice.

Since the inception of the social work in India, more importance have been given to development, poverty alleviation, social justice, social development, social policy and planning, unemployment, etc. But these have made very little impact on the field of social work and social welfare. Even the Indian Council of Social Welfare and the Indian Council for Child Welfare have only switched to social development and child development respectively, without even changing their names, aims, and objectives which were framed almost five decades ago. Social work community representing the national voluntary agencies and social work training institutions has now to take stock of the situation. They have to take a conscious decision in order to reorient social work profession to the needs of present-day society. They have to effectively meet the changes of development, and for this, to modify their techniques and methods. They may have to move from Case Work to Social Action, and associate themselves with the work done by social activists, public interest litigants, trade unions, women and youth groups, etc.

In the course of the research study, it has been observed and evaluated that not only educators agreed upon the emerging issues but students also support the changing scenario of issues today. Students also were of the opinion that social work intervention is required to those emerging issues.

In order to study the 'fieldwork and its emerging trends today' the variables taken into consideration are:

- Age profile
- Sex
- Religion
- Mother tongue
- Qualification/specialization
- Relevance of fieldwork in social work
- Complex social problems
- New mechanism to deal with social problems
- Focus on new emerging areas
- Fieldwork process
- Student's assignments and tasks
- Changing concept of fieldwork

This chapter has been sub-divided into two sections to get in-depth knowledge and information on fieldwork and its emerging trends today. Section one includes the view of student respondents on emerging trends and section two includes the view of educator respondents on emerging trends of fieldwork today.

Students' Perspective on Fieldwork and Its Emerging Trends Today

Age Profile

Table 6.1 exhibits the age profile of the student respondents. It was found that 88 per cent of the respondents are from the age group of 20–25 and rest of the 12 per cent of respondents are from the age group of 26 and above.

Table 6.1

Distribution of Student Respondents by Age

Age (in years)	*Frequency*	*Percentage*
20–25	264	88
26+	36	12
Total	300	100

It is concluded that some students (age is more to be a student of MA class) having background of other subjects and holding more degrees opt for social work as their career, because they feel secure in terms of job placement.

Sex

From the table below it is found that compared to male students(45.7%), female students (54.3%) are opting more to social work as their career.

Table 6.2

Distribution of Student Respondents by Sex

Sex	*Frequency*	*Percentage*
Male	137	45.7
Female	163	54.3
Total	300	100

Religion

From Figure 6.1 it is observed that more than two-thirds of respondents, i.e., 216 (72%) are from the Hindu background and 61 (20.3%) are Muslims. On the other hand, rest of the respondents are from Christian (6.3%) and Others (1.3%) background, respectively.

Figure 6.1

Student Respondents based on Religion

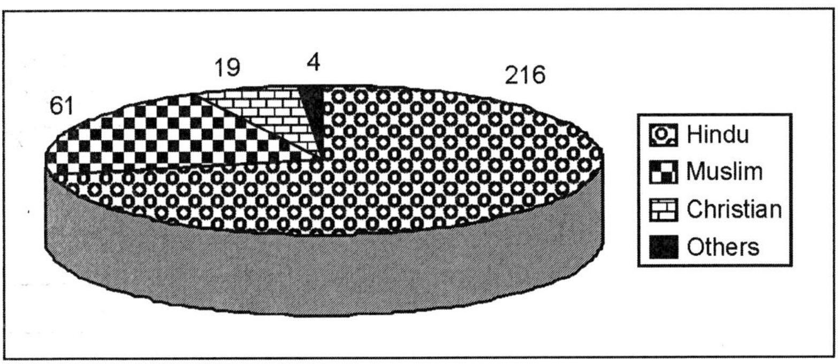

The 'Others' group is comprised of Jain (2) and Buddhist (2).

Mother Tongue

Figure 6.2 depicts the distribution of respondents regarding mother tongue.

Figure 6.2

Distribution of Respondents based on Mother Tongue

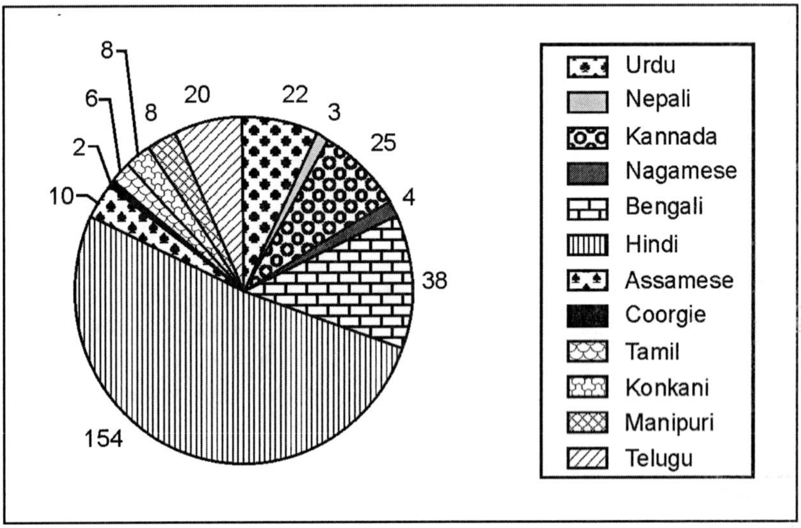

It is found that respondents with Hindi background as mother tongue are covering more than 50 per cent (154) whereas the Bengali-speaking students come around 13 per cent (98). The other language speaking students are as follows: Urdu 22 (7.3%), Nepali 3 (1%), Kannada 25 (8.3%), Nagamese 4 (1.3%), Assamese 10 (3.3%), Coorgie 2 (0.6%), Tamil 6 (2%), Konkani 8 (2.6%), Manipuri 8 (2.6%) and Telugu 20 (6.6%).

It was also found that the number of Hindi-speaking respondents is more with five schools and two schools of social work being selected from Hindi belt states like Uttar Pradesh and Delhi respectively under the study. On the other hand, Kannada-, Tamil- and Telugu-speaking students were also covered with more than 15 per cent respondents as five schools of social work were selected from Karnataka and Andhra Pradesh.

Qualification/Specialization

Figure 6.3 shows the specialization taken by the students in MSW in different schools of social work in India.

Figure 6.3

Distribution of Student Respondents Regarding Specialization

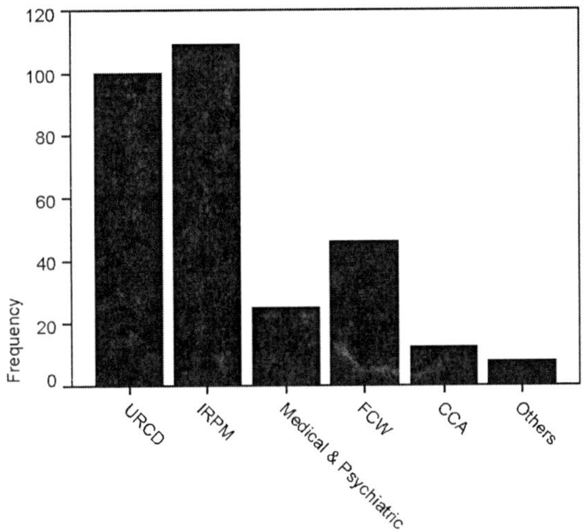

It is seen from the graph that students are more interested to opt for Urban and Rural Community Development (URCD) and Industrial Relation and Personal Management (IRPM). They feel that as India is a rural-based country and different NGOs and voluntary organizations in India mostly are working in the area of rural development, the scope of job placement would be more in terms of URCD as specialization. Students also feel that as India is going into industrialization in a broader aspect and foreign companies are also coming in rapidly, the specialization of IRPM has a great scope for job placement. On the other hand, Family and Child Welfare (FCW) is also gaining importance in the student community, especially among female students.

Out of total student respondents, 100 (33.3%) students opted for URCD as their specialization, 109 (36.3%) for IRPM, 46 (15.3%) for FCW, 25 (8.3%) for Medical and Psychiatric Social Work and 12 (4%) for Criminology and Correctional Administration (CCA). The rest of 8 respondents (2.7%) opted for social work with the elderly and cancelling work. It was found that CCA as specialization for MSW is provided by Tata Institute of Social Sciences, Mumbai.

Relevance of Fieldwork in Social Work

Table 6.3 depicts the opinion of the student respondents about the relevance of fieldwork in social work and it is the most relevant part also.

Table 6.3

Opinion of the Student Respondents about the Relevance of Fieldwork

Relevance of Fieldwork	*Frequency*	*Percentage*
Yes	286	95.3
No	14	4.7
Total	300	100

It is clear from the above table that overwhelming percentage (95.3) of the student community are of the opinion that the fieldwork is the most relevant part of social work and only 4.7 per cent students feel that fieldwork is not the most relevant part of social work.

The students elaborated the reasons of fieldwork being the relevant part of social work: as most lively and core portion of social work, it deals with human being, most real scenario for intervention, actual place to comprehend problems and issues, gives knowledge about various fields, judge about own capacities and capabilities, deals with various social problems and learning how to solve it from professional point of view, exposes to the worker practical problems of the society, strengthens analytical power and relationship skills and enriches observational and listening skills, challenges to face any situation, 'learning by doing' helps to make one perfect, helps to learn the uniqueness of individuals, provides more competent service and helps to conduct research, enriches our experience in future from practice viewpoint, raises empathetic sensitivity of the students, useful to sharpen one's perceptual ability, helps to inculcate the philosophy which is centric to social work, helps to identify our gaps in learning and then to rectify it, it gives the real picture of the society and to judge ourselves, helps to know the actual needs of the individual and people and helps to grasp the root cause of the problem, helps to collect primary statistical data regarding issues and problems, helps to observe the social problems that a single community faces in various dimensions, adventure-oriented, give more confidence to understand individual, group and community, gives a practical application and approach and increase professional competence, helps for future understanding and also fieldwork gives a better understanding of the emerging social issues and problems today.

Complex Social Problems

Table 6.4 indicates the opinion of the student respondents about the complexity of social problems in India today.

Table 6.4

Opinion of the Student Respondents about the Complexity of Social Problems Today

Social Problems are Complex	*Frequency*	*Percentage*
Yes	283	94.3
No	17	5.7
Total	300	100

It was found that around 95 per cent students are of the opinion that social problems in our society today are most complex and sometimes it becomes very difficult to apply social work tools and techniques in an accurate manner and also the utilization of the principles and techniques of basic methods of social work becomes irrelevant thereof. On the other hand, only 17 students (5.7%) are of the opinion that problems are not complex to deal with, rather new problems have developed today because of the influence of liberalization, privatization and globalization (LPG).

Hence, it is concluded that the students are more interested for the introduction of new theory and mechanism in the Indian perspective.

New Mechanism to Deal with Social Problems

Figure 6.4 indicates the opinion of the student respondents regarding the adoption of new mechanisms to deal with new social issues and problems today.

The figure shows that 195 students (65%) are of the opinion that to deal with new emerging social problems today there is a need to introduce some new mechanisms in the fieldwork. But 81 students (27%) were of the opinion that there is no requirement of introducing any new mechanisms to deal with those issues and problems. They feel that if proper help and coordination from both, the department as well as from the NGOs, or community people is there and if social work methods with their varied techniques and principles are channelized properly, then there would be no need for introducing any new mechanism. It was also found that 24(8%) respondents did not comment on this issue.

Figure 6.4

Opinion of the Student Respondents about New Mechanisms to Deal with Social Problems

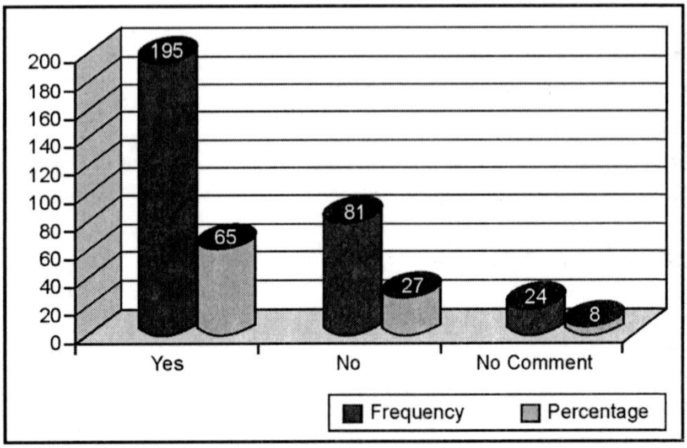

The student respondents tried to interpret and thought about some new mechanisms and theories which could be useful to deal with those issues and problems today. These needful mechanisms are: (1) reality-based approach, (2) balancing two phenomena for positive interest, (3) more ethical and morals dominant theory, (4) rationality inculcation theory, (5) provision of effective implementation of PRA method, (6) dealing with social problems according to the nature of the problems, (7) theory related to human behaviour, (8) theory for maximum utilization of human capital, (9) theory related to mind set up towards the sustainable development, (10) more democratic theory, (11) regular workshops and seminars on fieldwork, (12) identifying and solving single problems at a time, (13) use of electronic media to collect data and awareness, (14) democratic decision-making should be stressed upon, (15) emphasis should be given on research and research methodology, (16) bottom-up approach in decision-making process, (17) local service delivery institutions should be strengthened, (18) task-centred approach should be focused, (19) services should be given to right and needy persons, (20) proper use of legal aids, (21) more PHC and education centre should be opened in the community, (22) more scope for adult education and basic problems should be focused in the community/society, (23) advocacy component must be included and practised, (24) new legal mechanism and its application process with regards to social problems must be introduced, (25) instead of 'sense of competition', there must be 'sense of cooperation' in the civil society sector to solve the target problems, (26) theories should set separately for different problems, (27) theories should be adaptable to changing circumstances, (28) problems should not be generalized and one mechanism cannot deal with all social problems together, and (29) there should not be abundant resources and commitment should be there from all sides.

Hence, it could be concluded that because of the new emerging problems in our society, we need some kind of new mechanism to deal with such problems because sometimes social work methods and principles do not apply and are not relevant in the Indian conditions.

Focus on New Emerging Issues/Problems

Table 6.5 shows the opinion of the student respondents on emerging issues/problems today.

Table 6.5

Opinion of the Student Respondents on Emerging Issues/Problems

Need to Focus on Emerging Issues and Problems	*Frequency*	*Percentage*
Yes	132	44
No	168	56
Total	300	100

It is seen from the above table that 44 per cent students feel that there is a need to focus only on new emerging issues/problems today but 56 per cent students do not have the same opinion about it.

The students also focused on new emerging areas and issues where more intervention is needed. These are:

- Child labour and child rights
- Protection of women and women harassment
- Emergence of Special Economic Zones (SEZs) and its effect
- Issue regarding reservation policy in educational institutions
- Evaluation and implementation of 'Bharat Nirman' programme for rural development
- Emergence of RTI Act regarding accountability of government and other administrative sections to common people
- Emergence of micro-finance and micro-credit as a tool of poverty alleviation; evaluation of NREGA scheme/programme
- Corporate social responsibility; school social work, medical and psychiatric social work and mental health

- Child marriage and girl child trafficking
- Unorganized labour migration
- Unemployment problem and mechanical life and its problems
- Corruption and corrupted mind of the people
- Crime related to eve-teasing
- Sex and homosexuality, rape and kidnapping
- Misuse of natural resources
- Environmental pollution and deforestation
- Global warming and its impact on social life
- Terrorism and communalism and its impact on society
- Human rights violation, disability, social planning
- Weakening family ties and social and cultural impact
- Relief and rehabilitation on natural disaster and disaster management
- Displacement of people especially tribal
- Eco-tourism; livelihood management
- Gay and lesbianism
- Building an effective and accountable civil society organizations
- Participatory research
- Prostitution and child abuse
- Slum improvement
- Land mafia and land distribution system
- Industrialization and its problems and impacts
- Poverty, homelessness and starvation death
- Increasing communalist feelings in people
- Need-based intervention programme for hospitalized children
- Level of aspiration and self-concept in juvenile delinquents
- NGO management
- Problem of working women
- Degraded status of Hindi
- Wildlife studies and waste management
- Increasing drug addiction in call centre
- Increasing prostitution among college students
- Extinction of rare species

The students, who have the opinion about the need to give focus only on new emerging issues/problems, mention the reasons for that opinion as well. The reasons are:

- Modern social problems are providing new dimensions to existing old problems.

- Need to explore whether the people are getting proper access to all government programmes/schemes/facilities.
- It needs immediate action to resolve it; unless and until it is misrouted, the problem will crop up even more.
- Management subjects like IT sector, need informed services.
- So many NGOs/VOs/developmental organizations are working on old issues only.
- Early intervention will give fruitful results, so that issues do not spread much.
- Easy to get attention and emerging issues gets importance than other issues etc.

Fieldwork Process

Figure 6.5 indicates the opinion of the students in favour of change in fieldwork process for the betterment of student's career today.

Figure 6.5

Opinion of the Student Respondents in Favour of Change in Fieldwork Process

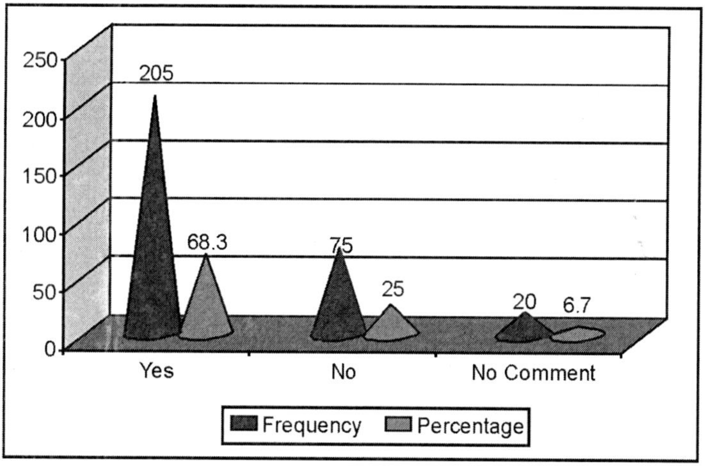

It gives a clear picture from the above figure that out of total respondents, around two-thirds, i.e., 205 (68.3%), of student respondents are of the opinion that fieldwork process should be a change for the betterment of student's career and 75 respondents (25%) are not in favour of change of fieldwork process. It also indicates that 20 respondents (6.7%) did not comment on this issue.

The students who supported (i.e., 68.3%) the view that fieldwork process should be changed for the student's betterment have highlighted on the new process. According to students, new processes might be:

- Provision for rural camp in new villages in all the institutions in India and there should be anonymity.
- Provision for summer and winter placement for both MSW first and second year in all schools of social work.
- To make fieldwork more attractive, schools could introduce small incentives for the students who do well in the fieldwork because this could be a motivational factor.
- Frequent workshop and seminar should be organized regarding fieldwork in schools of social work.
- Days of fieldwork can be increased but hours of work can be minimized so that regular touch with community exists.
- New community, slum or village should be adopted for social work intervention.
- Strict supervision is required.
- Block placement could be introduced at BSW level also.
- Regular 'focused group discussion' should be organized to build confidence in the students.
- Various organizational visits should be mandatory, so that they can get the latest data regarding the field of intervention.
- Fieldwork should be more community-based, agency and advocacy-based.
- Students' interest should be taken care of.
- First six months should be theory classes and next six months should be regular fieldwork.
- Fieldwork placement should be based on the interest of the students.
- Exposure should be given to the students in different settings instead of placing them in the same setting more than once.
- Special classes and examination should be for fieldwork.
- Specialist teacher should be there to deal with fieldwork.
- Laborious students should be entertained with awards like 'best field worker', etc.
- Documents of fieldwork should be kept for future references.
- Special funds for organizing programmes should be kept in the department so that students could utilize it for their programmes in the field.

- Small research/study should be given to the students.
- It should have more impact of management, like financial management should be taught to the students as they need to do it in the job in later period.

Educators' Perspective on Fieldwork and Its Emerging Trends Today

Age Profile

Figure 6.6 shows the teacher respondents covering all the fifteen schools of social work in India in terms of age group under this study.

Figure 6.6

Distribution of Educator Respondents by Age Group

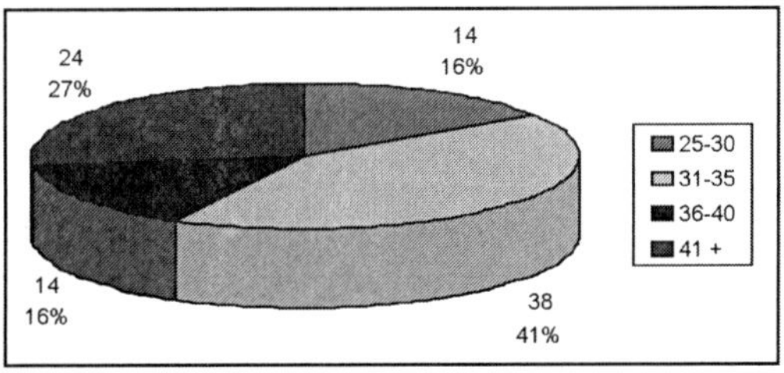

It was found that most of the teacher respondents are in the age group of 31–35 constituting 41 per cent, 27 per cent comes under the age group of 25–30 and on the other hand both 16 per cent comes under the age group of 36–40 and 41 and above respectively.

It is concluded that some teachers make social work as their profession just after completing their MSW degree with National Eligibility Test (NET).

Sex Profile

Table 6.6 depicts the distribution of sex of the teacher respondents.

Table 6.6

Distribution of Educator Respondents by Sex

Sex	*Frequency*	*Percentage*
Male	62	68.8
Female	28	31.2
Total	90	100

It is found that compared to female respondents (28), male respondents (62) are more.

It is concluded that still the female counter part is gradually increasing.

Religion

Figure 6.7 indicates the background of the teacher based on their religion.

Figure 6.7

Distribution of Educator Respondents based on Religion

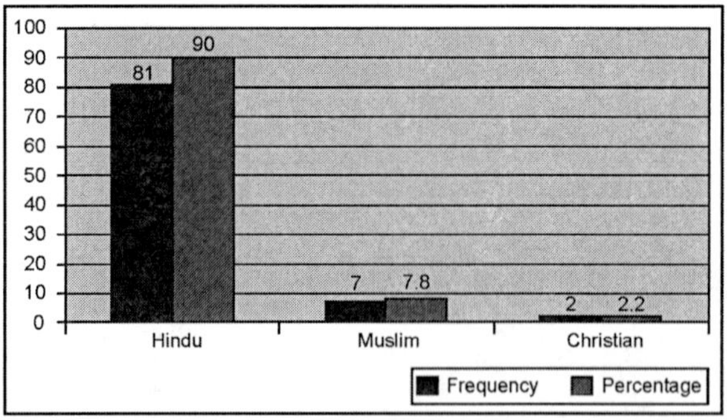

It is seen that 90 per cent of the total respondents comes from Hindu background and 7.8 per cent teachers are of Muslim background. On the other hand, only 2.2 per cent teachers indicated their religion as Christian.

Mother Tongue

Figure 6.8 indicates the percentage of teacher respondents about their mother tongue.

Figure 6.8

Distribution of Educator Respondents based on their Mother Tongue

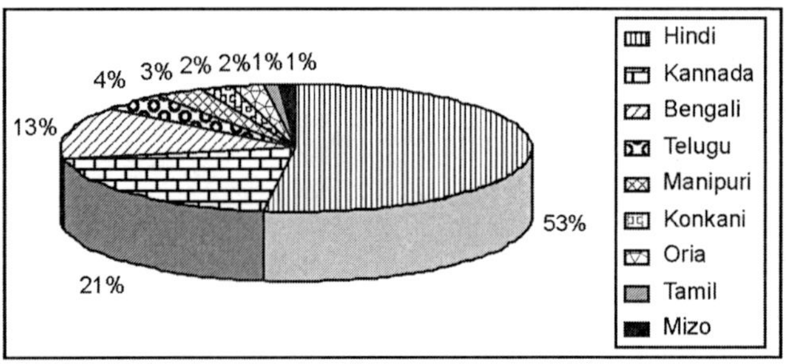

It is very much clear from the above that more than 50 per cent (53) teacher respondents' mother tongue is Hindi whereas 21 per cent is Kannada, 13 per cent is Bengali and rest of the teachers are Telugu (4%), Manipuri (3%), Konkani (2%), Oria (2%), Tamil (1%) and Mizo (1%) respectively.

It was analysed and concluded that Hindi as the mother tongue of respondents is more because most of the teacher respondents of the schools of social work are from Delhi and Uttar Pradesh. On the other hand, rest of the percentage of Telugu, Konkani, Tamil and Kannada languages are from Karnataka and Andhra Pradesh.

Specialization

Figure 6.9 shows the specialization of educators before joining the profession.

Figure 6.9

Distribution of Educator Respondents Regarding Specialization

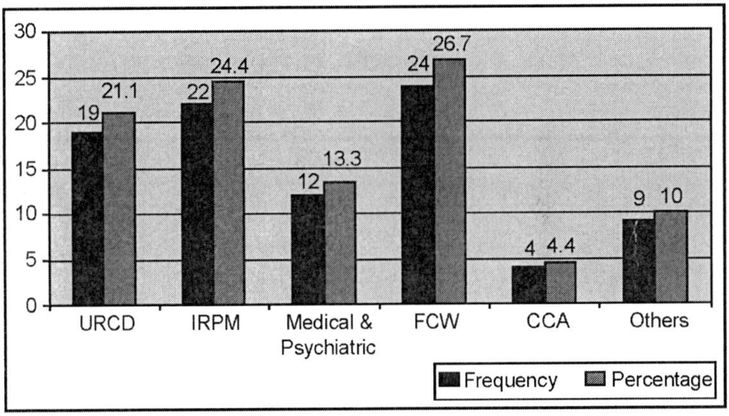

It is seen from the above figure that except for Criminology and Correctional Administration (4.4%) other specializations are more or less equally distributed among the educators like 21.1 per cent educators have Urban and Rural Community Development background, 24.4 per cent have Industrial Relation and Personal Management, 13.3 per cent have Medical and Psychiatric social work and 26.7 per cent have Family and Child Welfare. It is also seen that rest of the 10 per cent educators do not have any specialization because they are from sociology background (especially in the schools of Banaras Hindu University (BHU) and Mahatma Gandhi Kashi Vidyapeeth where social work is affiliated with department of sociology from the beginning).

Students' Assignments and Tasks

Figure 6.10 explains the opinion of the educators regarding the student's assignments and tasks in the fieldwork, whether students are assigning their tasks in accordance with the new emerging areas of intervention or not.

It is seen that 80 per cent of the total educator respondents totally agreed with the statements about the assignments and tasks assigned by the students in their fieldwork but 15.6 per cent respondents do not agree with the above statements. Whereas 4.4 per cent educator said that their students assign their tasks sometimes, i.e., not always.

Figure 6.10

Opinion of Educator Respondents Regarding Student's Assignments and Tasks

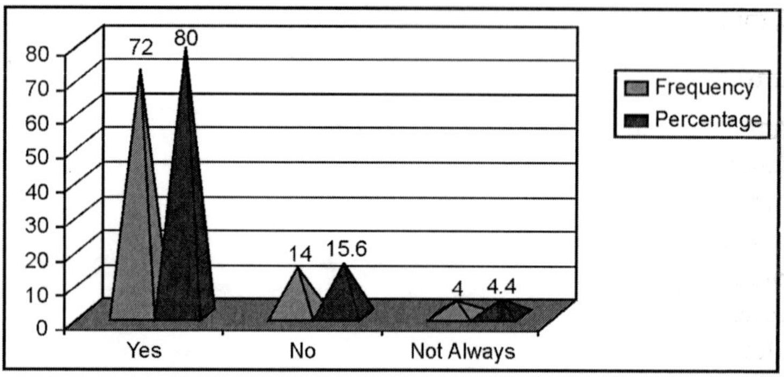

The educators also mentioned the new emerging areas where their students are assigning the tasks for social work intervention utilizing the basic social work methods, principles and techniques such as combatting HIV/AIDS, total literacy campaign, Self-Help Group, women and adolescent health, advocacy, domestic violence, homelessness, drug abuse, informal and unorganized labour, new government programmes and schemes, human rights, etc.

It could be concluded that nowadays students in many of the schools of social work in India do assign their tasks in the new emerging areas for social work intervention.

Changing Concept of Fieldwork

Table 6.7 exhibits the opinion of the educators regarding the changing concept of fieldwork today from traditional ideas to new modernity.

Table 6.7

Opinion of Educators Regarding the Changing Concept of Fieldwork

Changing Concept of Fieldwork	*Frequency*	*Percentage*
Yes	82	91.1
No	8	8.9
Total	90	100

It is found that overwhelming percentage of the educators (91.1%) feel that the concept of fieldwork should be changed from traditional ideas to new modernity, taking care of new emerging areas in the present society. They say that as the gradual escalation of new areas is taking place, the social work also should shift its idea towards new modernity. On the other hand, only 8.9 per cent educators were of different opinion, i.e., they do not want a change in the concept of fieldwork.

Summary

From its inception, social work education in India is comprised of teaching, fieldwork practice, project work, etc. Initially, fieldwork practice was generally agency-based, where students were involved in different types of work relating to remedial, rehabilitative services and promoting development with equity and justice. But with the advent of emerging socio-economic, political and cultural situations undoubtedly opened up greater opportunities of functioning for professional social workers, both in terms of target groups and issues for operation.

New emerging target groups such as disabilities, unorganized sections, migrant workers, street and working children, drug and HIV/AIDS, violence and their families, communal disharmony, terrorism, disaster, poverty, environmental degradation, increasing social complexities, effect of globalization, political corruption, caste violence, etc., have added for pracice and for that need the interest of professional social workers to make them visible and to develop their focus for effective functioning.

This chapter clarifies the opinion of the respondents on the relevance of fieldwork practice in emerging areas. They are fully agreed that social problems are more complex today and for that we need to have well adjusted new mechanisms and theory to deal with those issues and problems. Overwhelming percentage of both the teacher and student respondents feel that there are many more new emerging areas which need to have professional intervention in our fieldwork such as: emergence of Special Economic Zones (SEZ), issue regarding reservation policy in educational institutions, evaluation and implementation of 'Bharat Nirman' programme for rural development, emergence of RTI Act regarding accountability of government and other administrative sections to the common people, emergence of micro-credit as a tool of poverty alleviation, corporate social responsibility, crime related to eve-teasing, sex and homosexuality, rape and kidnapping, misuse of natural resources, environmental pollution and deforestation, global warming and its impact on social life, terrorism and communalism and its impact on society, human rights violation, female infanticide, weakening family ties and social and cultural impact, eco-tourism, building an effective and accountable civil society organization, land mafia and land distribution system, industrialization and its problems and impacts, etc. They have also given the reasons for practicing in the new emerging areas of fieldwork, as modern social problems are providing new dimensions to existing old problems. There is a need to explore whether the people are getting proper access to all government programmes/schemes/facilities. NGOs and developmental organizations are working on old issues only, therefore, early intervention will give fruitful results, so that present issues do not spread much. Respondents have given their suggestions about the introduction of new mechanisms and theories based on the emerging social problems for effective practice such as need for reality-based approach, more ethical and morals dominant theory, provision of effective implementation of PRA method, theory related to human behaviour, regular workshops and seminars on fieldwork, identifying and solving single problems at a time, use of electronic media to collect data and awareness, emphasis should be given to research, and research methodology should be adopted, bottom-up approach in decision-making process should be strengthened, task-centred approach should be focused, advocacy component must be included and practised, instead of 'sense of competition', there must be 'sense of cooperation' in the civil society sector to solve the target problems, etc.

We are still focusing on the techniques and methods of European countries and especially USA. These approaches and models are not suitable for Indian emerging situation and for that we need to change our practice technique models and approaches in the changing paradigm.

We need to change our focus from conventional aspect to developmental fieldwork, rights-based and issue-based fieldwork intervention and for that social action and advocacy will be the essential method for fieldwork practice.

7 Discussion and Conclusion

The Role of Social Worker in the 21st Century

Now the question is what should be the role and status of a social worker in the 21st century India. The social worker in the 21st century should be a confident and competent professional committed to working with and alongside people who use social work services, with their advocates and other professionals helping them to achieve the best possible outcomes in their lives. The primary responsibility of the social worker will remain as: the protection and promotion of the welfare and well-being of children, vulnerable adults and communities.

Social workers operate within the codes of practice for social service workers and employers and subscribe to the value base most recently set out in the International Federation of Social Work Code of Ethics, which is based on respect for the inherent worth and dignity of all people, and the rights that follow from this. Social workers should uphold and defend each person's physical, psychological, emotional and spiritual integrity and well-being. They should work holistically taking into account the individuals, their family and their community. They would build supportive relationships with people in order to help them effect change in their lives and work collaboratively with other professionals. They are committed to continuously developing their own professional skills, knowledge and expertise.

Social workers are skilled in coordinating complex networks of integrated service delivery, particularly in those situations of uncertainty where relationships are complex and where there is a high degree of risk to the person using social work services and to the wider community.

Social work will continue to be a demanding profession. Social workers must possess the maturity and strength of character to confront challenging and complex situations; the emotional intelligence to establish relationships with people in these situations and the intellectual curiosity to acquire and use research evidence to achieve better outcomes for people who use these services. Their employing organizations must recognize the importance of the social worker's role and ensure that they are properly equipped and supported to operate effectively.

Social workers constantly manage the twin roles of care and control in discharging their duties in a varied and complex environment. It is important that service users and the general public understand the complexity of balancing the two roles. This means, there must be a robust evidence base for the decision-making process, for example, through using consistent approaches to risk assessment. The ability to identify acceptable levels of risk and put in place appropriate risk management mechanisms is a highly skilled task. This involves respecting individuals rights while balancing these with public safety. There must also be collaboration, transparency and openness with clients, particularly in relation to using statutory powers.

Social workers must uphold public trust and confidence in social services. They must be aware of society's values and operate in accordance with legal obligations. In seeking to achieve the best possible outcomes for people who use social work services, social workers will use the knowledge and skills and understanding which are set out in the standards in social work education in order to:

- prepare for and work with, individuals, families, careers, groups and communities to assess their needs and circumstances;
- plan, carry out, review and evaluate social work practice with individuals, families, careers, groups and communities and other professionals;
- assess and manage risk to individuals, families, careers, groups, communities, self and colleagues;
- demonstrate professional competence in social work practice; and
- manage and be accountable with supervision and support, for their own social work practice within their organization; and support individuals to represent and manage their needs, views and circumstances.

They must also contribute to the development of effective policy, practice and research within social work services and in the context of working partnership.

Social workers should work more in statutory, voluntary and private settings and as independent practitioners. While this will continue to be the case, the evolving nature of service delivery will inevitably have an impact on where social workers are located. Given the nature of the complexities in different dimensions, interactions and risks involved in the lives of people using social services, social workers do not and must not work in isolation from their colleagues in health, education, housing, employment and justice services as well as with voluntary and private sector providers. Increasingly, services are being integrated around the individual needs of people who use services in order to produce better outcomes for children and adults. Integrated service delivery requires a high level of sharing of skills, knowledge and roles, involving a wide variety of professionals in working with, assessing, recommending and reviewing action plans for vulnerable children and adults. This, in turn, requires professionals to have a clear and well-developed understanding of their own distinctive contribution and those of others.

The rural social work curriculum should be injected with problems of tribal and rural socio-economic and political aspects along with social forestry, water management, problems related to women, children, handicapped, elderly, migrant labour, weaker sections, domestic child labour, rural unemployment, etc., and a good amount of fieldwork training. It is also assumed that if the present trend continues, it will pose serious challenges for the social worker in the future, because future society will be less compassionate and more individualistic than at present.

Viewing people's conditions on the ground includes recognizing the effects on them of having to engage with a variety of agencies, and assessing where action or change by other agencies may open up opportunities, remove barriers to achieving the outcomes they seek. Social work skills are often deployed to good effect in collaborative work with other professionals, either in on-going multi-disciplinary teams or in ad hoc joint work around the needs of an individual or family. The distinctive social work contribution combines a developing body of knowledge and skills, a set of core values and priorities, and a range of personal qualities and includes working through the medium of a qualitative personal relationship.

While majority of social welfare personnel in most of the countries especially in India, function at field levels in multiple roles and do not try to possess graduate level education, social work is heavily biased towards university-based education.

Overlooking those problems, it will be very difficult to deal the problems in future. However, the social workers can use their skills, principles and knowledge to encourage the clients not to be dependent upon the welfare services, rather they should be more productive and fruitful to themselves and as well as for the society at large.

The professional practice of social workers should always be underpinned by the following principles:

- The primary responsibility of the social worker is the protection and promotion of the welfare and well-being of children, vulnerable adults and communities.
- Social workers should use their professional knowledge and expertise to make judgments and decisions for which they are professionally accountable.
- Social workers must have access to professional consultation through line management arrangements which provides support and advice from appropriate, experienced social workers. This consultation should focus on assisting practitioners to reflect on their practice, use their powers effectively and make complex decisions for which they are personally and professionally accountable.
- The level of complexity and responsibility carried by social workers should be reflected in the career structures and remuneration available to them, and the continuing professional development they undertake.
- Leadership within local government for social workers undertaking protected functions should be exercised.

What Social Worker's Role and Functions Should be Today?

Developing Effective Relationships

Adopting a holistic approach and forging therapeutic relationships are not unique to social work. What makes the role of the social worker distinct is that it combines both. The social worker seeks to understand the person's entire situation (holistic approach) and to work with this. Developing an effective helping relationship with people who use services is central to the role of the social worker in order to ensure better outcomes. Social workers need sufficient time to combine knowledge of skills and values and demonstrate the effective listening, respect and sensitive engagement which this involves. The ability to form and maintain such relationships can be eroded by a workload which exceeds resources, by over management of risks and by increasing expectations from people who use services of the social worker's capacity to meet their needs. The development of a staged and tiered approach to social work intervention should ensure that the time and skills of social workers are invested appropriately in supporting those with the most complex needs, i.e., where there are multiple risk factors and vulnerability.

Social workers have a key role in working alongside people to help them take more control of their lives where this is possible and appropriate. Social workers should always aim to promote independence for users, even if this is a long-term goal. However, it will always be the case that for some people, creating a long-term supportive relationship with social work services may be an appropriate response to managing risk and promoting the well-being of vulnerable children or adults. Some people will need high levels of support throughout their lives in order to achieve their full potential.

Social workers may work with people who have no wish to engage with social services but who are required to do so in the interests of the protection of their own or other's safety. In these circumstances, the development of a therapeutic relationship or working alliance with the involuntary service user is an essential element in bringing about the achievement of positive change in their lives.

Generalist or Specialist

Social work services work alongside a range of universally provided services. There are many points of entry to these universal services. Part of the social worker's task is to assist people maximize the opportunities available to them from universal services, for example, education and health and to advocate for them with these services. Not every person looking for assistance from social services will need the level of intensity or duration of contact central to developing a therapeutic relationship with a social worker. For some, engagement with social services is purely a means of accessing a necessary service or resource. For this group of people, any necessary support may be more appropriately delegated to another social services worker.

Social work is and should remain a generalist profession, with a strong common values, skills and knowledge base. Individuals' social problems are often multifaceted and vulnerable people should expect to find continuity of service from their allocated social worker and be confident that worker will in turn be able to draw on the specialist knowledge and expertise of colleagues.

Generalist professionals need the back-up of specialist expertise and knowledge. A good generalist service depends on good supporting specialist services. However, we also recognize that social workers need to build up their knowledge, skills and expertise in specific areas (for instance, substance misuse, autism, bereavement counselling) as they operate in increasingly specialist environments. Their knowledge and expertise must be available to people who use services as well as to colleagues elsewhere in social work services and within other professions. In order to do this:

- Teams and organizations need a comprehensive knowledge base about the skills and expertise of the workforce, both to provide ready access for advice and consultancy and to identify and fill any gaps.
- Individual professionals need to know the limit of their own competence. Professional consultation should provide a vehicle to support this and encourage practitioners to seek expertise when and where they need it.
- We must clearly define accountabilities in this process and the parameters within which this happens.
- We should recognize that there may increasingly be sharing of expertise across sectors, both in terms of sharing good practice and in providing access to particularly scarce specialist expertise.
- Organizations should ensure access to specialist expertise when and where that is required. This may be in giving advice to a practitioner or in taking over responsibility for users with particular needs.
- We should promote the development of generalists with specialist interests – similar to the model increasingly developing in general medical practice.
- If we are to maintain social work as a generalist profession, whilst ensuring that each social worker has the necessary competence to fulfil their current role effectively, then we will need to undertake the following actions:
    (a) Provide the necessary training opportunities to allow social workers to develop excellent knowledge and skills.
    (b) Develop a contemporary and relevant educational framework that allows people to develop the competence to undertake their current role and to add additional competencies required for new roles.

Access to Services

Social workers are legitimately involved in making decisions about how services are deployed. However, it is recognized that social workers and users can see this 'gate-keeping' function as a barrier to building effective therapeutic relationships. In order to make this function more effective, a number of actions are proposed:

- Develop more effective collaborative approaches to decision-making with service users and carers which are built on openness and transparency and develop individual and community capacity.
- Ensuring the provision of services is fair and equitable through effective communication between front line staff and finance, and strategy leads, including influencing where resources are inadequate and recommending where resources could more effectively meet need.

All of these require effective communication, financial controls and sound governance which the review group will need to address in considering systems and processes.

Now, let's discuss the major findings, suggestions and recommendations.

Major Findings of the Study

The findings of the study has been elaborated both from the educators' and students' perspectives.

Educators' Perspectives

Background

Age

Age profile of the respondents revealed that nearly 43 per cent educators came under the age group of 31–35 and nearly 27 per cent educators were in the age group of 41 and above. However, equal percentage, i.e., 15.5 per cent of educators were in the age group of 25–30 and 36–40 respectively.

Sex

Out of total respondents (90), 62 respondents, i.e., 68.2 per cent are male and 28, i.e., 31.2 per cent respondents are female educators. It was found that still female educators are less in social work education except in Tata Institute of Social Sciences and Delhi School of Social Work where female respondents were more compared to male respondents.

Religion

Religion-wise distribution revealed that 90 per cent respondents, i.e., 81 educators were Hindu while 7.8 per cent respondents were Muslim and 2.2 per cent respondents were Christian respectively. Christian respondents were found in schools of social work in South India only.

Caste

Caste distribution has shown that more than 50 per cent respondents were from general category. On the other hand, scheduled castes and scheduled tribes were very less compared to general category which were only 13.3 per cent and 5.6 per cent respectively. The percentage of other backward classes is more, i.e., 17.8 in comparison. It was found that 11.1 per cent respondents did not mention their caste at all.

Mother Tongue

It was found that 47 educator respondents (52.22%) were from Hindi background, 18 respondents (20%) were from Kannada background and 12 respondents (13.33%) from Bengali background. Rests of the respondents were from Telugu (4.44%), Manipuri (3.33%), Konkani (2.22%), Oria (2.22%), Tamil (1.11%) and Mizo (1.11%) background.

Qualification

The qualifications of the respondents were varied. It was found that out of total respondents, 36 respondents were holding PhD which represents 40 per cent. Around 21.1 respondents were having PG degree in social work and 17.8 per cent respondents were also holding M.Phil degree. Only 11.1 per cent respondents noted that they did BSW at the initial stage. Surprisingly, it was found that 10 per cent respondents were holding a degree other than social work degree. This percentage of respondents were having the degree of sociology; some of them even a PhD degree in sociology. It was analysed that some of the schools of social work such as Aligarh Muslim University, MGKV Varanasi, and BHU, etc., are having affiliation with sociology department; rather it can be said that department of sociology initiated the start of social work in their university, and still continue running and coordinating the social work department.

Additional Qualification

Additional qualification aspect showed that 23 respondents were having other extra qualifications rather than social work qualification. Out of 23 respondents, 12 respondents, i.e., more that 50 per cent have PG Diploma in Rural Development and Human Resource Management and 4 respondents have Certificate Course in Computer Application. Rest of the respondents were having Degree in Economics (8.69%) and 21.73 per cent respondents have other certificate courses in Research Methodology, LLB and MBA.

Family Background

It was found that more than 60 per cent respondents, i.e., 55 are from urban background whereas 38.9 per cent respondents were from rural background. It was also analysed that educators from urban background in schools of social work in India cover most of the rural areas.

Type of House

Type of house reveals that only 37.8 per cent respondents have their own house whereas 62.2 per cent respondents are staying in rental houses. It was evaluated after discussion that those ever coming from rural background and teaching in urban areas are mostly staying in rental houses.

Teaching Experience in Social Work

It appears that 30 respondents, i.e., 33.3 per cent had less than five years teaching experiences and 28.9 per cent of respondents had more than five to ten years teaching experiences. A few respondents, i.e., 10 per cent, 13.3 per cent and 6.7 per cent respondents had teaching experiences of ten to fifteen, fifteen to twenty, and twenty to twenty-five years respectively. Only 7.8 per cent respondents were having teaching experience of more than twenty-five years. It is concluded that young social work educators are coming into this profession.

Research Experience

Here research experience covers only doing research in terms of job or any projects other than PhD work. It was found that around 50 per cent were having less than five years of research experience and 22.2 per cent were having less than five to ten years experience. On the other hand, equal number of respondents, i.e., 13.3 per cent respondents have ten to fifteen and fifteen to twenty years of research experience respectively. It was also found that only 2.2 per cent respondents do not have any research experience and they directly joined teaching.

Involvement in Organization/Project before Joining Teaching Staff

It was found that out of total respondents, 51 respondents were of the opinion they did not join any organization or projects before joining the teaching staff but 39 respondents said that they joined an organization or project work before joining teaching staff. It was found that out of 39 respondents, only 2 respondents had less than one year experience and 19 respondents had one to three years experience. On the other hand, 12 respondents and 6 respondents had three to five and more than five years experiences respectively in any organization or any project in different parts of India.

Association with Professional Organization

A majority of educators, i.e., 62.2 per cent responded that they are associated with professional organizations in different capacities such as: a member of governing body which consisted of 25 per cent; 12 respondents as a consultant (21.42%); 4 respondents as an advisor (7.14%); 24 respondents as a member (42.85%); and 2 respondents (3.57%) as evaluator and secretary of organizations. It was concluded that educators not only involve themselves in teaching but they are involved in different associations or organizations in different capacities and some of them are also having their own NGOs working in developmental issues involving their students in project work.

Specialization

It appears that 19 respondents (21.1%) are having specialization in Urban Rural Community Development (some schools call it Community Development) and 22 respondents (24.4%) are having specialization in Industrial Relation and Personnel Management (some schools call it Human Resource Management). It also appears that 12 respondents (13.3%), 24 respondents (26.7%) and 4 respondents (4.4%) are having specialization in Medical and Psychiatric Social Work, Family and Child Welfare and Criminology and Correctional Administration respectively. On the other hand, 9 respondents had Sociology background, and did not have any specialization in social work. It was concluded that specialization in Criminology and Correctional

Administration familiar to the educators and also this specialization is not provided by any schools of social work, except Tata Institute of Social Sciences.

Concurrent Fieldwork and Supervision

Placement of Students in Fieldwork

It was found that 74 respondents (82.2%) said that their students were placed both in the community as well as in the agency. On the other hand, 10 respondents (11.1%) and 6 respondents (6.7%) said that their students were placed in the agency and in the community respectively.

Placement Ratio of Students

An overwhelming majority of the educator respondents, i.e., 90 per cent have said that their schools do not maintain an equal proportion of placement ratio in the agency and in the community while only 9 respondents, i.e., 10 per cent said they maintain an equal proportional ratio of student placement. It was concluded that majority of the schools of social work do not have any criteria being followed for the placement of the students either in the agency or in the community.

Specialized Agency Near the Department

A majority of the educator respondents, i.e., 66 (73.3%) were of the opinion that they have proper and specialized agencies for the placement of the students near their department, while 16 respondents (17.8%) said that they do not get proper and specialized agencies close to their department. There was a small percentage of respondents (8.9%) who were of the opinion that they have some agencies near their department which are proper and specialized. It is concluded that specialized agencies are working on social issues with social work personnel using social work techniques and methods for intervention.

Regular Contact with Agency and Community Supervisor

It was found that a majority of the respondents, i.e., 68 (75.6%) have regular contact with agency or community supervisors and 20 respondents (22.2%) do not have regular contact with agency or community supervisors because of their busy schedule in the department, overburden of the classes and being busy with own project works. On the other hand, 2 respondents which constitute only 2.2 per cent said that occasionally they had regular contact with agency supervisors or community supervisors. It was analysed that some schools only have community supervisor, like Tata Schools of Social Sciences and Delhi Schools of Social Work, whereas most of the schools of social work do not have community supervisors.

Fieldwork Agency with Trained and Experienced Personnel

Majority of the respondents (75.6%) fully agreed with the statement that they have fieldwork agencies with trained and experienced personnel to guide students in the agencies. But 20 per cent respondents said that they do not have trained and experienced personnel in the agency to guide the students. On the other hand, only 4.4 per cent respondents said that they know some agencies that have trained and experienced personnel to guide the students in the agency. It is concluded from the above that many agencies do not have trained and experienced social work background personnel who could use social work techniques and methods to deal with social issues and could guide the student trainees.

Supervision in Fieldwork

It was found and concluded that a majority of the educator respondents (88.9%) supervise their students and only 11.1 per cent respondents said they do not supervise students because of their involvement in other activities of the department. The ratio of the supervising students varied also, like around 44 per cent respondents said that their ratio of supervision is ten to fifteen, 30 per cent said the ratio of student under their supervision is about five to ten. On the other hand, only 12.6 per cent and 13.8 per cent respondents said that their ratio of supervision is one to five and fifteen and above respectively. So, it is concluded that most of the educators in different schools in India have more ratio of students to be supervised in the fieldwork. It becomes very difficult for the supervisors to supervise all the students in the same manner as the ratio is very high and they are also overburdened with their classes.

Fieldwork Visit

It was found that more than two-thirds of the respondents, i.e., 70 (77.8%) visit the fieldwork regularly to supervise and guide the students. Only 22.2 per cent respondents said that they do not visit the field regularly but sometimes they pay a visit when it is most needed. It was also found that out of total respondents (70), 53 respondents pay a visit mostly to the field once in a week and 14 respondents visited two days in a week. But 3 respondents said that they pay a visit only once in a month. It is clear that those who do not visit the field regularly may be because of negligence by the schools or due to the attitude of the educators towards fieldwork.

Regular Individual and Group Conferences

It was found that a great majority of the educators (83.3%) do organize regular individual and group conferences in the department to evaluate and guide the students, but there are 16.7 per cent educators who do not organize these regularly. Around 60 per cent educators, who organize regular conferences in the department, do so once in a week and 23.3 per cent do organize them for two to three days in a week.

Teacher-Agency Meetings and its Frequency

The majority of respondents (72.2%) said that they organize teacher-agency meetings to know the requirements from both sides on related issues and problems while dealing with the students, and only 27.8 per cent said that they do not organize meetings because of the negligence of the department and the negative attitude of the agency. Out of total respondents who do organize meetings, 1 respondent said it was once in a fortnight; 2 respondents said they organize meetings once in a month; 34 respondents organized meetings once in a quarter whereas 6 respondents once in a year. On the other hand, 22 respondents said that they organized teacher-agency meetings but did not have any fixed schedule. From the above scenario, it is clear that no schools have an actual fixed date to organize teacher-agency meetings.

Changing Concept of Fieldwork and Approaches

Change of Fieldwork

Almost all the respondents (91.1%) were in favour of changing the fieldwork from traditional concept to modernity. They say fieldwork should not be only based on helping and preventive measures but it should focus on the new concept according to modern issues and problems which is emerging today. According to their view now the idea and intervention of fieldwork should be based on factors like, examining the needs of the society, as per global situation, issue-based activities, to face new challenges which are emerging, job-oriented fieldwork, new areas has to be addressed incorporated in the syllabus, impose more responsibility on student related to project management, more research-based fieldwork, right-based approach in fieldwork and therapeutic approaches should be adopted. On the other hand, only 8.9 per cent respondents say that they do not feel the need to change the concept of fieldwork. It could be concluded that most of the educators want their own concept of fieldwork in accordance with the changing scenario, and focus on social work intervention on emerging issues and problems.

Different Fieldwork Approaches besides Concurrent Fieldwork

Cent per cent of the respondents (100%) opined that they practiced different fieldwork approaches other than concurrent fieldwork such as agency visit, rural camp, research project, educational tour and block fieldwork. Around 28 respondents said that they practiced all the fieldwork approaches.

Emerging Areas

About 80 per cent of the respondents said that their students assigned their tasks in fieldwork in accordance with the emerging areas of intervention, but 15.6 per cent respondents felt that students are not assigning their tasks in accordance with new issues but they are still working in the areas of education, health, etc. It was found that 4.4 per cent respondents said that their students sometimes assign their tasks in accordance with new areas and it depended upon which issues needed to be tackled first. Some analysis came from the educators that if the main problems of a community consist of issues like health, education, etc., then students cannot neglect these issues either and they should intervene first. The educators highlighted the emerging areas like working with HIV/AIDS patients, total literacy campaign, evaluation of government programme for rural development, childrens rights, advocacy, juvenile justice, domestic violence, mental health, informal and unorganized labour, drug abuse, etc.

Students' Perspectives

Background

Age

Age profile of the student respondents revealed that out of total respondents (300), 264 (88%) respondents were in the age group of twenty to twenty-five and only 36 (12%) respondents were in the age group of twenty-six and above.

Sex

It was found that female students were more interested in opting for social work profession as their career. Around 55 per cent (163) respondents were female and rest of the 45 per cent (137) respondents were male students.

Religion

Religion-wise distribution reveals that the percentage of Hindu students was more than any other religion. It was found that 72 per cent (216) respondents were Hindu and 20.3 per cent (61) respondents were Muslim whereas 6.3 per cent respondents belong to Christian religion. Only 1.3 per cent (4) belong to other religions that include Jain and Buddhist.

Caste

Caste distribution reveals that more than 50 per cent (154) student respondents belong to general category, 19 per cent (57) students belong to Scheduled Castes, 5.3 per cent (16) belong to Scheduled Tribes and 17 per cent (51) belong to Other Backward Classes. It was also revealed that 22 respondents (7.3%) did not mention their caste.

Mother Tongue

As the sample was collected from different states (15 universities of seven states), automatically the mother tongue became varied and different. It was found that Hindi as mother tongue was more constituting 51.3 per cent (154), Urdu 7.3 per cent (22), Nepali 1 per cent (3), Kannada 8.3 per cent (25) and Bengali 12.6 per cent (38). Rest of the respondents belonged to Nagamese (1.3%), Asamese (3.3%), Coorgie (0.6%), Tamil (2%), Konkani (2.6%), Telugu (6.6%) and Manipuri (2.6%).

Previous Qualifications

It appears that students coming for admission in social work have varied qualifications in their graduation and some of the students even come after obtaining a master's degree. It was found that 27.3 per cent (82) respondents have the background of BSW, 33 per cent (99) of BA, 11.3 per cent (34) of BCom, 12 per cent (36) of BSc, and 2 per cent (6) have the background of other qualifications like BBM and LLB and 14.3 per cent students (43) join social work after having another MA degree. They noticed that they took admission in social work (MSW) to secure their job.

Additional Qualifications

It was revealed that a great majority of student respondents (82.6%) do not have any additional qualifications, only 6.6 per cent students have additional qualification of diploma that includes Computer Science, Instrumental Music, Fashion Designing and Office Management, PGD HRM and Computer Application. On the other hand, 2 per cent students have additional qualifications, i.e., LLB and 6.6 per cent students have Certificate Course in Human Rights and Industrial Labour. Rest of the 2 per cent had additional qualification in Bachelors of Education.

Specialization

It was found that 33.3 per cent (100) students opted for Urban and Rural Community Development as their specialization, 36.3 per cent (109) opted for Industrial Relation and Personal Management, 8.3 per cent (25) opted for Medical and Psychiatric Social Work, 15.3 per cent (46) opted for Family and Child Welfare and 4 per cent (12) opted for Criminology and Correctional Administration. Rest of 2.7 per cent (8) opted for other specializations such as Social Work with Elderly, HIV/AIDS and Counselling

Concurrent Fieldwork and Issues Undertaken

Placement in Fieldwork

It was found that more than 60 per cent students were placed in the agency for the fieldwork and rest of the students placed in the community. It was also found that 54 per cent students were placed in the agency in the first year with 46 per cent in the community. Again 41.3 per cent students were placed in the agency in the second year along with 58.7 per cent in the community also in the second year as well. Most of the students were of the opinion that their placement was against their interest, but some students opined that they were placed in their interest. They also added that the department does not follow any particular criteria for placement of the student for fieldwork except, Tata Institute of Social Sciences and Delhi School of Social Work. But most of the schools followed the principle that whoever is placed in the agency, he would be placed in the community next year or vice versa. Some schools also had fixed placement like in the first year student will be placed in the agency and in the final year placement will be in the community or vice versa.

Dealing with Case Work

A majority of the student respondents (64%) said that they practiced case work and 36 per cent respondents were of the opinion that they did not practice it. It was also found that students who practiced case work, out of them 61.45 per cent dealt with less than three cases, 25.5 per cent dealt with three to five, around 10 per cent dealt with cases between six to eight and only around 3 per cent dealt with more than eight or above cases during their fieldwork.

Dealing with Group Work

More than two-thirds of respondents (76.7%) revealed that they practiced group work and rest said that they did not practice group work. Some students also added that they practiced group work but they did not follow the stages of group formation rather they simply did group activities in the fieldwork.

Dealing with Community Organization

It was found that an overwhelming majority of the students (87.3%) responded that they practiced community organization in their fieldwork and rest of the students did not practice it. Some students said that they maintained the principle of community organization when dealing with social issues like health and nutrition of the child and mother and RCH, awareness on dengue and malaria in the community, working with youth group on the issues of addiction, sanitation and nutrition problems of the community, parent-teacher-student meeting on education and drop-outs, awareness on legal aids and club formulation in the community, mass awareness on TB, STD, physically and mentally handicapped children and their rehabilitation, issues of cattle vaccination, issues of ration card, birth certificate and old-age pension, organizing health check-up camp in the community, prenatal and postnatal care with women, etc.

Relevance of the Theory in Fieldwork

A majority of the students were of the opinion that theory taught in the class has a great relevance in the fieldwork dealing with social problems and issues and 7.7 per cent students said it had no relevance in the fieldwork. But 10.3 per cent students did not offer any comment on this issue.

Supervision by the Supervisor

More than two-thirds (81.7%) of total respondents were of the opinion that department supervisors supervised regularly and guide them, but 15.3 per cent respondents were of the opinion that their supervisors did not come for supervision. Around 4 per cent student respondents said that some times their supervisor visited the field.

Fieldwork Conferences

A great majority of the students (84%) responded that they attended individual and group conferences in the department regularly, but 16 per cent students did not involve themselves in regular conferences.

New Mechanism Dealing with Emerging Issues and Job Profile

Regarding Complexity of Social Problems

An overwhelming percentage (94.3) of students have said that social problems are more complex today than it was before, whereas the remaining students respondents (5.7%) did not agree.

Need for New Mechanism or Theory

It was found that majority of the students (65%) were of the opinion that we need a new mechanism and theory to deal with emerging issues today and 27 per cent were against it, whereas 8 per cent respondents did not comment on it. They pointed out about the mechanism and theory such as: need were reality-based approach, balancing two phenomena for both positive interest, more living and attracting theory to deal with issues, more ethical and morals dominant theory, rationality inculcation theory, provision of effective implementation of PRA method, dealing with social problems according to the nature of the problems, theory related to human behaviour, theory for maximum utilization of human capital, theory related to mindset up towards the sustainable development, more democratic theory, etc.

Relevance of Fieldwork

As many as 95.3 per cent of the total respondents said fieldwork is the most relevant part in social work whereas the rest of 4.7 per cent went against this view.

Guidance in Fieldwork

There were 69 per cent student respondents with the opinion that they get proper guidance in fieldwork from the department supervisor, but 21.7 per cent students said that they did not get proper guidance from their department supervisor. Rest of the 9.3 per cent said that they got occasional guidance from the department supervisor.

Specific Tasks to be Fulfilled during Fieldwork

It was found that 60 per cent (180) out of total respondents were of the opinion that they need to fulfil specific tasks during their fieldwork such as community organization and community work, group work and group activities, and case work, etc. But 35 per cent (105) mentioned that they do not need to fulfil any specific tasks in their fieldwork. Rest of the 5 per cent student respondents did not comment on it.

Fieldwork Helps in Job Profile

Almost all the student respondents (96%) think that concurrent fieldwork would help in their job profile as it increases their competence, helps in understanding the reality-based problem-solving process; gives a scope to relate theories into application while dealing with either problematic or normal individuals, group and community in different situations; helps and shows the way on how to work at grass-root levels; develop skills of rapport establishment with community people, etc. Only 4 per cent student respondents commented that fieldwork did not help much in a job.

Days of Fieldwork

Around 39.3 per cent student respondents were of the opinion that the number of days of fieldwork should be increased and they are in favour of three days in a week rather than two days, but more than 60 per cent student respondents did not favour increasing of fieldwork, as it would effect their theory classes.

Satisfaction with Fieldwork

It was found that around 80 per cent students were satisfied with their fieldwork in dealing with social issues and problems, because they got help from the department as well as from the agency, but 20 per cent students were not satisfied with their fieldwork dealing with issues because they were very often helped by the department as well as by the agency.

Change in Fieldwork Process

About 68.3 per cent (205) student respondents were in favour of change in fieldwork process for the betterment of their career today. They also mentioned that some processes like fieldwork placement should be based on the interest of the students, exposure should be given to the students in different settings instead of placing them in same settings more than once. There should be special classes and examination for fieldwork, specialist teacher should be there to deal with fieldwork, hard working students should be given awards like 'best field worker', small research/study should be given to the students, etc., but 25 per cent students (75) were not in favour of change of fieldwork process. On the other hand, a small percentage of total student respondents (6.7%) did not give any comment on this issue.

Problem Faced in Fieldwork

It was found that 184 respondents (61.3%) faced problems during fieldwork and it was concluded that problems were like mistrust towards students due to earlier experiences, female students getting more and unnecessary importance, problem of huge expectation of the recipient/community; timing of fieldwork is another problem for the students especially for that community where people are working the whole day for their living and earning, and the difficulty in contacting them. Because of the diversification of the community like different religious groups, it was difficult to bring them on one platform, needing more realistic guidance from the department supervisor with regard to negligence and avoidance of the villagers to some particular problems. However, there were 116 respondents (38.7%) who said that they faced no problems during their fieldwork.

Major Suggestions

The suggestions are recorded on the basis of primary data through questionnaire, observation, and focused group discussions with student respondents, educator respondents and agency supervisors.

Regarding Fieldwork Curriculum and Social Work Method

- University should frame the specific practical syllabus for fieldwork training based on their proposed specializations, nature and structure of the agency, community or slum community and clear-cut objectives keeping in the mind different fields of social work.

- Before sending students to the agency/community, they must be given proper orientation for the field according to the needs and challenges in each of the field.
- Proper planning or preplanning and prioritization have to be chalked out according to the needs and resources of the agencies before sending students to the fieldwork.
- University should form a practical base and special committee or group, consisting of educators, agency supervisors, practitioners or the experts from other universities to frame the valid and practical syllabus considering the present problems of the society.
- The framed syllabus has to be interlinked with social work theory taught in the classroom also, so that students could understand better and practice as per their understanding and aspirations in the fieldwork.
- It is seen that most of the schools are not practicing community organization method properly and they are also not properly trained. So placement in the community should be encouraged more as the main problems in the society is based on community and in this regard specific syllabus could be framed by the respective schools.
- It was also found that social action method is completely missing and neglected in the fieldwork training, and it is known that in Indian setting it is the most needed method to follow and to solve those multifarious problems in the society.
- The libraries in the schools should be developed for their own and required books on fieldwork should be available.
- All the schools should start field action projects (though some schools already have) and students could be placed for fieldwork.
- The schools of social work should have their own social agencies (as Delhi School of Social Work has in Burari village in Delhi) for fieldwork placement of the students, generating employment and developing the community structure also.
- Utility of the fieldwork, done by the students in the agency and in the community is less according to the agency supervisor. So the students have to work in such a way that the total work could be useful for the agency's policy and programmes and also to the community.
- The direct practice or service component should be the determining factor for the selection of students in the field and only such

fields should be selected from existing ones, which offer more opportunities (for direct practice).

- Placement of the students could be considered based on the interest of the students.
- It is suggested that only required number of students are placed in the agency, not more than that.
- Method-based training should be provided and implemented.
- In the agency, students should be given only social work based practice work for their learning and training, so that they interestingly could practice their theories, methods and techniques and explore their understanding as well.
- It is suggested that block placements could be completed before ending their final semester, so that it should be seriously undertaken and it should be based on course curriculum.
- Seminars and conferences on fieldwork should be organized regularly by the schools.
- Extension lectures should be made regular in all the schools so that students get exposure of the various fields and new emerging issues from time to time.
- Regular agency-school meeting or workshop should be organized so that the understanding and perspectives about the fieldwork curriculum is adaptable to both the institutions, and the students get more focused and oriented with the issues.
- Every institution should have an adequate building for classrooms, library facilities, reading rooms, faculty rooms, extension services, administrative offices, community centres, internet facilities, etc.
- In every institution, there should be a Research Cell to provide consultancy services in social work research and help in doing research work, which in turn would enrich the department as well.
- A Development Cell could be established in the department to assist the agency/NGOs/VOs or outside administrative work.
- Department could utilize the institutions/organizations for fieldwork and research which could enrich the input and output of the department in the longer run.
- Educators should be encouraged to initiate or associate with new and innovative field projects extending the fieldwork base among students of social work providing definite practice assignments and jobs to trainers in fieldwork and other related agencies/NGOs.
- The fieldwork practice curriculum needs to be reviewed from time to time to acquaint with the new changing scenario.

- The educators and students should be well equipped with knowledge and proper understanding of emerging issues/problems and their ill-effects on society at large. They also need to explore those issues/problems using social work techniques/methods.
- Few schools select their ex-students for teaching or call guest lecturers from other backgrounds without having any professional competence. This also brings down the quality of teaching and guidance in fieldwork.
- The department should bring positive and justifiable change in the fieldwork practice as well as theoretical emancipation due to the complexity and variety of social changes in the society. The department, as well as the students, should also focus more on new approaches like action-oriented or rights-based approach.
- The government should not give permission to open new social work schools if proper infrastructure related to fieldwork is not up to the mark, and the responsibility of evaluation and review should be given to professional associations like ASSWI (Association of Schools of Social Work in India), NAPSWI (National Association of Professional Social Workers in India) or a committee facilitated by UGC.
- There should be a uniformity of pattern in fieldwork, and fieldwork could be a separate subject to teach in the schools.

Regarding Fieldwork Supervision

Fieldwork curriculum could be more effective and realistic if there is proper and effective supervision and guidance by the department supervisors or agency supervisors. It also provides proper sequences to the students relating to different components and problem-related issues. The suggestions made are:

- All the schools of social work should have a different fieldwork wing headed by fieldwork director or coordinator so that concurrent fieldwork, field visit, rural camp, study tour, fieldwork training workshop could be managed properly, though very few schools have it.
- UGC should create a separate post for the director or coordinator of fieldwork in all the schools.
- Supervisory methods should be strengthened for increasing the effectiveness and efficiency of the students to solve the problems.
- The educators with the help of the department should organize fieldwork seminars and conferences regularly to make field supervision more effective.

- The school supervisors should pay their visits to the agency or community regularly so that students could resolve their problems and other obstacles in the field only.
- All the schools should have proper facility of their own like vehicles, etc., to supervise and do extension work from time to time systematically.
- The students should be placed only in the agency where the trained professionals (having the background of social work) are working.
- There should be cordial and good relationship and understanding between the department and the agency supervisor, and from time to time they could come for extension lectures in the department.
- Recording should be properly made by the students and submitted in the schools and in the agency also so that the corrections can be made and suggestions are made possible accordingly.
- Workload of the teachers/educators is more than that prescribed by the university or the UGC. Around 15 students are placed for the fieldwork under a teacher; hence teachers felt that it should be reduced in number. This aspect has to be taken care of to make the environment cordial both for educators and agency supervisors.

Regarding Fieldwork Evaluation

- There should be a separate evaluation committee in the department consisting of experienced faculty members.
- Agency supervisors should be involved in the evaluation procedure/process (though some of the schools do this).
- Largely, it is found that diaries are not considered for the evaluation of the performances of the students in the fieldwork but only few questions decide the outcome of the fieldwork. Proper diaries should be maintained by the students which should be submitted to the fieldwork unit or to the department supervisor.
- According to some respondents, it is said that in the department favoritism is there in the evaluation process. So, teachers should not be biased towards any student and should maintain the social work ethics and dignity.
- All the agencies should send the evaluation report of the students to the department so that transparency is maintained.
- In the evaluation process, there could be a small written test based on fieldwork practice before viva voce by the department.

- It is suggested that evaluation should be periodical, i.e., periodical assessment should be done that may be every month or fortnightly (but most of the schools do their assessment after the end of the semester or year) in front of the students so that they could understand and assess their positions and could develop themselves in that way.
- The schools of social work should possess the evaluation sheets or charts covering different items in it. These sheets should be completely different according to the method-wise training in the first year and specialization-wise in the second year (or according to the situation in a semester system).
- Students should undertake projects or activities in coordination with the previous projects and they should be linked, i.e., if previous batches of students did some projects/works then after completing their semester the new batches of students should start from that part onwards only. Also, there should not be much gap between completing (end of the semester as well as fieldwork) and inducting of new batches of students for the fieldwork.
- There is a need to offer short-term in-service training for untrained personnel employed in job positions in social work or welfare agencies, for para-professionals or auxiliary personnel and also orientation course for co-professionals.

Recommendations for the Development of Fieldwork in India

From the Educator Respondent's Perspective

- Each student will have to establish that the methods or process applied in the field practicum has yielded some tangible and clear/transparent results.
- Substantial inputs and efforts are necessary to develop professionalism in the students of social work and for this curriculum there should be a component on personal and professional growth.
- More experiential learning opportunities should be provided and Skill Laboratory Method is essential. Hence, whatever fieldwork assignments are given, these have to be supported and refined by providing the above mentioned teaching-learning inputs.
- Good students should be encouraged to accept this social work as a profession and build up their career either as a social activists or for more reformative approach and to become more creative.

- Supervision should be made by the faculty regularly both in the agency and community.
- Proper and regular coordination between agency and school supervisor and department need to be maintained.
- Revision of fieldwork syllabus is needed if any.
- Encouraging students to give focus on doing project during fieldwork programme if any.
- Introducing the payment of a specified 'fee' to the agency (supervisor and management), so that it may arouse/increase the interest of both student trainee as well as agency supervisor towards their involvement and participation. In other words, it will make them more focused and accountable.
- Conducting workshops to discuss and identify new areas for fieldwork and research, etc.
- To gather data and publish them in the form of article with the consent from the agency only.
- Regular individual conferences and group conferences, report checking and proper inputs should be given to students from time to time.
- The supervisors should understand student's point of view and focus on his/her learning; no matter whether it be good or bad experiences.
- Students should be provided lots of ideas but do not impose the same on them.
- Hold group meetings with all of the supervisors and encourage them to share in groups.
- Teachers should relate fieldwork examples during class teachings and vice versa.
- Teachers should be given Orientation/Refresher courses on fieldwork.
- There should be uniformity related to fieldwork curriculum and fieldwork system, etc., in all the institutions all over India.
- There should be more practice-based sessions in the department in all the schools of social work.
- In all the schools, there should be well developed and specified curriculum of fieldwork.
- Supervision, camp, department visit should be made compulsory and suggest a common syllabus in fieldwork.
- Fieldwork with result-oriented practice of social work profession should be encouraged.

- Education tour should be included in all the schools for dual purpose of exposure to different settings and improve the fieldwork based on that.
- Fieldwork should be based on the need of the people incorporating the issues that are emerging due to globalization, liberalization, etc.
- We should also think and act about eradication of poverty, which is the main cause of all the social problems and marginalization of the marginalized.
- The department should adopt villages/community/slum community nearby the department and take different projects involving students in it through fieldwork.

From the Student Respondents' Perspective

- Students should be more empowered to cope up with their problems themselves in the field.
- A weekly/fortnightly meeting between department/institution and villagers should be organized to acquaint with the problems from time to time, so that the villagers would be more energetic and helpful to cooperate with students when dealing with the problems.
- New application of balance theory related to fieldwork should be strengthened.
- Area of work should be properly specified so that students would be well aware about the maintenance of time and work capacity.
- Timing should be changed according to the availability of client, group or community people.
- Resources should be properly mobilized and proper guidance should be provided by the supervisors for that matter.
- Before going to dealing with the problems, it should be properly studied in detail by the students with the help of the agency, department or external agency.
- Manage time between theory and practice and utilize it.
- Too many students in a community or agency should be avoided.
- Plan properly according to the availability of resources and then deal with the issue or problem.
- Need a follow up after completing one semester to the start of next semester.
- Proper and timely individual conferences, group conferences and rural camp should be organized frequently by the department.

- Cooperative approach in dealing with problems has to be initiated and programmes should be goal-oriented rather than development-oriented with the help of the community participation.
- Before starting the fieldwork, proper orientation in fieldwork by the department is needed to give an overall idea and understanding to the students.
- Subject should be taught based on the fieldwork placement, as before going to do community work or group work there is need to teach community organization or group work subjects first.
- Introducing a concept of Workers Conference (WC) in the department, like individual conference and group conference.
- Discarding the unethical norms by the supervisors of meeting with resource persons in the community or in the agency.
- The work of the students should be rectified by the teachers in the individual conferences, instead of scolding them in the community or in the agency.
- MSW students should be placed in the new villages to inculcate their learned ideas/techniques/skills.
- Inculcating high values and morals dealing with the problems or issues.
- The student should have the ability to think logically, practically and at the ground level.
- Appreciate the religious practices and sentiments of the community when dealing with the problems.
- The world is always open for a 'true leader' which depends upon workers genuineness, endeavour, credibility and acceptability in a community/society where gradually 'I' sentiment will melt to give way to 'We'.
- Student should have confidence and positive outlook to handle any situation.
- Accept challenges, control temper and patience.
- There should be frequent department-community-agency meetings.
- Placement of the students should be nearby the department location so that the students could give more focus on their work rather than wasting time to visit the community or the agency.
- Basic knowledge about the fieldwork should be provided to the students.
- Awareness and motivation should be provided about the importance and need of social work and its fieldwork to other professionals.

- Special bus or communication facilities for fieldwork should be provided to the students by the department.
- The evaluation of fieldwork should not be based on only viva voce but also a special examination should be conducted.
- The agency and its mechanism should be improved to help students for dealing with social issues from time to time.

Recommendations for Future Research

The total overview of the study and its findings shows that fieldwork practice has many areas which could be the area of social work research for future to strengthen its other dimensions. The areas which could be touched upon are:

- Fieldwork and emerging social problems in India
- Fieldwork – need for new mechanism for practice
- Comparative study of fieldwork in agency and in community
- Supervision and fieldwork – need for emphatic understanding
- Problems of fieldwork in India – need a practical measures
- Fieldwork and utilization of core social work methods

Bibliography

Books

Bhanti, Raj (1995), *Field Work in Social Work Perspective,* Himanshu Publications, Udaipur.

Boswell, G. (1997), "The Role of the Practice Teacher", in M. Davies (ed.), *The Blackwell Companion to Social Work*, Blackwell, Cambridge, MA.

Bradford, W. Sheafor, Charles, R. Horejsi and Gloria, A. Horejsi, *Techniques and Guidelines for Social Work Practice*, 4th Edition, pp. 50–52.

Desai, Murli (2002), *Ideologies and Social Work: Historical and Contemporary Analysis,* pp. 140–41.

Gore, M.S. (1981), "The Scope of Social Work Practice", in T.K. Nair (ed.), *Social Work Education and Social Work Practice*, ASSWI, Madras.

Harriet, M. Bartlett (1970), *The Common Base of Social Work Practice: Integrating Social Work Methods.*

Hessle, S. (ed.) "International Standard Setting of Higher Social Work Education", *Stockholm Studies of Social Work,* Stockholm University.

Jacob, K.K. (1994), *Social Work Education in India: Retrospect and Prospect,* Himanshu Publications, New Delhi, pp. 206–09.

Johnson, L.C. (1995), *Social Work Practice: A Generalist Approach,* Allyn and Bacon, Newton, M.A.

Lawani, B.T. and Pathan, K.G. (eds.) (1990), *Field Work Training in Social Work Education.*

Lawani, B.T. and Subedar, I.S. (2006), *Social Work Perspectives*, pp. 53–54.

Lorenz, W. (2001), *Social Work in Europe: Portrait of a Diverse Professional Group.*

Lum, D. (2000), *Social Work Practice and People of Colour: A Process Stage Approach*, Brooks/Cole, Belmont, CA.

Morales, A. and Sheafor, B. (1986), *Social Work: A Profession of Many Faces,* Allyn and Bacon, Boston.

Payne, M. (2001), *Social Work Education: International Standards.*

Ranade, S.N. (ed.) *Encyclopedia of Social Work in India,* Ministry of Welfare, Government of India, Vol. 3, pp. 134–42.

Schon, D. (1983), *The Reflective Practitioner,* Basic Books, New York.

Singh, R.R. (ed.) (1985), *Field Work in Social Work Education: A Perspective for Human Service Profession,* Concept Publishing Company, New Delhi.

Singh, Surendra and Srivastava, S.P. (eds.) (2003), *Social Work Education in India: Challenges and Opportunities.*

Srinivas, M.N. (1979), *The Field Worker and the Field,* Oxford University Press, Delhi.

Taylor, Charles (1983), *Social Theory as Practice,* Oxford University Press, Delhi.

University Grants Commission (1978), *Review of Social Work Education in India: Retrospect and Prospect,* UGC, New Delhi.

Walter, Friedlander (1964), *Introduction of Social Work,* 2nd Edition, pp. 541–42.

Williamson, Margaret (1950), *Supervision: Principles and Methods,* Woman's Press, New York.

World Development Indicators (2001), The World Bank.

Journals

Banerjee, G.R. (1975), 'Professional Self and Supervision in Social Work', *The Indian Journal of Social Work,* Vol. 35 (4), pp. 309–16.

Barbaro, Fred (1979), 'The Field Instruction Component in the Administration Concentration: Some Problems and Suggested Remedies', *Journal of Education for Social Work,* Vol. 15 (1), pp. 5–11.

Barker, R. (1991), 'Should Training for Private Practice be a Central Component of Social Work Education?' *Journal of Social Work Education,* Vol. 27 (2), pp. 108–11.

Barlett, Harriet M.M. (1970), 'Common Base of Social Work Practice', *National Association of Social Workers,* New York.

Brauns, H.J. and Kramer, D. (1986), 'Social Work Education in Twenty-one European Countries: A Comparative Description', *International Social Work Journal,* Vol. 29 (3), pp. 203–06.

Cooper, B. (2001), 'Constructivism in Social Work: Towards a Participative Practice Viability', *British Journal of Social Work,* Vol. 31, pp. 721–38.

Desai, A. (1987), 'Development of Social Work Education', *Encyclopedia of Social Work in India,* Ministry of Welfare, New Delhi.

Desai, M. and Narayan, L. (1988), "Challenges for Social Work Profession towards People-Centered Development", *The Indian Journal of Social Work,* Vol. 59 (1), January.

Desai, Murli (2000), 'Curriculum Planning for History of Philosophies of Social Work', *The Indian Journal of Social Work*, Vol. 61 (2), pp. 221–39.

Devi Prasad and Vijaylakshmi, B. (1997), 'Field Instruction in Social Work Education in India: Some Issues', *The Indian Journal of Social Work*, Vol. 58 (i), pp. 65–75.

Dominelli, L.D. (1996), 'Deprofessionalizing Social Work: Anti-Oppressive Practice Competencies and Post-Modernism', *British Journal of Social Work*, Vol. (26), pp. 153–75.

Gangrade, K.D. (1975), 'School of Social Work: Field Work Agency Liaison', *The Indian Journal of Social Work*, Vol. 35 (4), pp. 350–57.

Gangrade, K.D. (1975), 'Student Recording in Field Work Supervision', *The Indian Journal of Social Work,* Vol. 35 (4), pp. 353–57.

Kapoor, J.M. (1961), 'The Role of Fieldwork in Modern Social Work Education', *The Indian Journal of Social Work*, Vol. XXII (2), September, pp. 113–20.

Kulkarni, P.D. (2000), 'Teaching of Social Sciences in Schools for Social Work', *The Indian Journal of Social Work*, Vol. 61 (2), pp. 189–95.

Lam, Ching Man and Hung Wong and Leung, Terry Tse Fong (2007), 'An Unfinished Reflexive Journey: Social Work Student's Reflection on Their Placement Experiences', *British Journal of Social Work*, Vol. 37, pp. 91–105.

Manis, F. (1971), 'Education for Social Workers: Field Work in Developing Nations', *International Social Work*, Vol. 14, pp. 17–20.

Manshardt, C. (1985), 'Education for Social Work', *The Indian Journal of Social Work*, Vol. 45 (1), pp. 1–5.

Mathew, Grace (1975), 'Educational and Helping Aspects of Field Work Supervision', *The Indian Journal of Social Work*, Vol. 35 (4), pp. 325–31.

Maurya, Moti Ram (1962), 'Field Work Training in Social Work', *The Indian Journal of Social Work*, Vol. XXIII (1), pp. 9–14.

Mehta, V.D. (1975), 'Integrated Methods Approach: A Challenging Possibility in Field Work Instructions', *The Indian Journal of Social Work*, Vol. 35 (4), pp. 335–44.

Midgley, J. (1990), 'International Social Work: Learning from the Third World', *International Social Work*, Vol. 35 (3), pp. 295–301.

Moorthy, M. Vasudeva (1953), 'Scientific Approach to Field Work', *The Indian Journal of Social Work*, pp. 144–59.

Nagpal, Hans (1988), 'The Profession of Social Work in Contemporary India', *Indian Journal of Social Research*, Vol. 29 (4).

Nair, T.K. (1981), 'Social Work Education and Social Work Practice in India', *ASSWI*, Madras (now Chennai).

Noble, C. (2001), 'Researching Field Practice in Social Work Education, Integration of Theory and Practice Through the Use of Narratives', *Journal of Social Work*, Vol. 1 (3), pp. 2–16.

Patford, J. (2000), 'Can I do Social Work and Do I Want To? Students' Perceptions of Significant Learning Incidents during Practica', *Australian Social Work*, Vol. 53 (2), pp. 21–28.

Pathak, S.H. (1975), 'Supervision in Social Work: Historical Development and Current Trends', *The Indian Journal of Social Work*, Vol. 35 (4), pp. 317–23.

Pathak, Shankar (1973), 'Social Development Aspect's 1985 of Social Education', *ASSWT*.

Prasad, Rajeshwar (2000), 'Social Work as a Profession', *National Journal of Professional Social Work*, Vol. 1 (NIMHANS), Bangalore.

Ramachandran, P. (1988), 'Perspective for Social Work Training – 2000 AD', *The Indian Journal of Social Work*, Vol. 49 (1), pp. 11–20.

Ryan, M. and Martyn, R. (1996), 'Writing about Social Work Education: A Content Analysis of Australian Journal Article 1983–93', *Australian Social Work*.

Siddiqui, H.Y. (1987), 'Towards a Competency-Based Education for Social Work', *The Indian Journal of Social Work*, Vol. 48 (1), pp. 23–32.

Singh, R.R. (2005), 'Configuring Field Practice and Field Education in Social Work', *Rajagiri Journal of Social Development*, Vol. 1, Golden Jubilee Issue.

Spencer, A. and McDonald, C. (1998), 'Omission and Commissions: An Analysis of Professional Field Education Literature', *Australian Social Work*, Vol. 51 (4), pp. 9–18.

TISS Social Work Educators' Forum (1997), 'Declaration of Ethics for Professional Social Workers', *The Indian Journal of Social Work*, Vol. 58 (2), pp. 335–41.

Papers/Articles

Barbara, *A New Portrait of Social Work*, p. 25.

Midgley, J. (1991), "Professional Imperialism: Social Work in Third World", Heinemann, London.

Nadkarni, Vimla, TISS (Unpublished Paper, Bombay).

Nair, T.K. (1978), "Field Instruction in Schools of Social Work: A Survey", *Association of Schools of Social Work in India.*, Madras.

Paul, Kurian (1990), "Rational Energy Strategies", *Economic and Political Weekly*, Vol. XXV (2), January 6, p. 35.

Rosemary, Reynolds (1961), "The Relationship of Field Placement to Classroom Teaching", *Teaching of Students and Staff Supervision*, p. 54.

Reports

Charles, Guzzetta (1984), MSW Education, The Present State, Hunter College of the City University of New York School of Social Work, New York.

Howard, Jacob K. (1994), "The Future of Social Work in Changing Economy: Preparing for the Year 2000', *27th IASSW*, Amsterdam, p. 9.

Institutional Accreditation, "Manual for Self-Study of Social Work Institutions", NAAC, UGC on Curricular Aspects of Fieldwork Practicum.

Report of the Curriculum Development Centre in Social Work Education, New Delhi, 1990.

Sajid, S.M. (1999), "Field Work Manual", Department of Social Work, Jamia Millia Islamia, New Delhi.

Second Review Committee (1978), "A Review of Social Work Education in India: Retrospect and Prospect", UGC, New Delhi, February, p. 298.

Tata Institute of Social Sciences (1988), *Social Work Education in India: A Report*, Mimeographed, p. 28.

Tata Institute of Social Sciences (2000), "Annual Report 1999–2000", Mumbai.

The Second Review Committee Report by UGC Review of Social Education in India.

Index